Praise for *When Evil Lived in Laurel*

"Reads like a Greg Iles novel. . . . [R]ich with details."
—Debbie Elliott, NPR, "Best Books of the Year"

"*When Evil Lived in Laurel* is set during the civil rights movement of the 1960s, but its concerns could not be more central to our current moment: voting rights, white supremacist terror, and the ground-level mechanisms of white radicalization. With meticulous research and all the tools of a novelist, Curtis Wilkie chronicles the Klan-ordered murder of activist Vernon Dahmer, and Tom Landrum's infiltration of the White Knights. Read this book if you want to understand how racist words and ideas turn into violent, murderous action."   —Patrick Phillips, author of *Blood at the Root: A Racial Cleansing in America*

"Curtis Wilkie's riveting account of the murder of Vernon Dahmer by the KKK is a window into the depths of racism and white supremacy. But it is also a beautifully written tale of courage and morality featuring a man with deep local roots who knew right from wrong. *When Evil Lived in Laurel* can help us understand the civil rights era in the South and also our country today."
—Walter Isaacson, Leonard Lauder Professor of American History and Values, Tulane University

"*When Evil Lived in Laurel* is an extremely useful book, in addition to being impossible to put down. It's *about* evil; terrible men doing terrible things to their fellow humans. But it's also about convention and cowardice and hypocrisy and ignorance and public lies—and also about quiet heroism—all matters of vital concern to us in America at this very moment."   —Richard Ford

"Though the frightful history of the struggle for civil rights in Mississippi is a familiar one, Curtis Wilkie's account of the 1966 murder of Vernon Dahmer is astonishing. Drawing on voluminous, remarkable FBI documents, court records, congressional hearings, and interviews, Wilkie paints a compelling picture of the dogged pursuit of justice by law enforcement officials, heretofore untold acts of courage by ordinary citizens, and the involvement of the White Knights of the Ku Klux Klan—alternately pernicious and inept. *When Evil Lived in Laurel* may well be the finest book on the civil rights era."   —Richard Howorth, Square Books

WHEN EVIL LIVED IN LAUREL

Four sons of Vernon Dahmer (from left) U.S. Army Sgt. George W. Dahmer, U.S. Air Force Staff Sgt. Martinez A. Dahmer, U.S. Air Force Master Sgt. Vernon F. Dahmer Jr., and U.S. Army Specialist 4th Class Alvin H. Dahmer, called from military service to attend his funeral, inspecting the ruins of his home. (PHOTOGRAPH BY CHRIS McNAIR)

CURTIS WILKIE

WHEN
EVIL
LIVED
IN
LAUREL

The "White Knights" and the
Murder of Vernon Dahmer

W. W. NORTON & COMPANY
Independent Publishers Since 1923

For information about permission to reproduce selections from this book,
write to Permissions, W. W. Norton & Company, Inc., 500 Fifth Avenue,
New York, NY 10110

For information about special discounts for bulk purchases, please contact
W. W. Norton Special Sales at specialsales@wwnorton.com or 800-233-4830

Manufacturing by Lakeside Book Company
Book design by Brooke Koven
Production manager: Julia Druskin

Library of Congress Cataloging-in-Publication Data

Names: Wilkie, Curtis, author.
Title: When evil lived in Laurel : the "White Knights" and the murder of
Vernon Dahmer / Curtis Wilkie.
Description: First edition. | New York : W. W. Norton & Company, [2021] |
Includes bibliographical references and index.
Identifiers: LCCN 2021001786 | ISBN 9781324005759 (hardcover) |
ISBN 9781324005766 (epub)
Subjects: LCSH: Dahmer, Vernon Ferdinand, 1908–1966. |
Landrum, Tom, 1932– | Bowers, Samuel Holloway, 1924–2006. |
Ku Klux Klan (1915–). White Knights of the Ku Klux Klan—History. |
United States. Federal Bureau of Investigation—Officials and employees. |
African Americans—Crimes against—Mississippi—History. |
African American civil rights workers—Mississippi—History. |
Laurel (Miss.)—Race relations.
Classification: LCC E185.93.M6 W55 2021 | DDC 305.8009762/55—dc23
LC record available at https://lccn.loc.gov/2021001786

ISBN 978-1-324-03592-3 pbk.

W. W. Norton & Company, Inc., 500 Fifth Avenue, New York, N.Y. 10110
www.wwnorton.com

W. W. Norton & Company Ltd., 15 Carlisle Street, London W1D 3BS

1 2 3 4 5 6 7 8 9 0

For Mimi

The only thing necessary for the triumph of evil is for good men to do nothing.

—*attributed to* EDMUND BURKE

Author's Note

The quotations in this book come from several different sources. In many cases, verbatim quotes come directly from Tom Landrum's reports and other documents, such as FBI interviews, transcripts of testimony in trials, depositions, and records of congressional hearings. Some direct quotes were found in newspapers and periodicals published during the time when the White Knights were active, while others were taken from books. Specific attributions are in the endnotes.

Many of Landrum's conversations were reconstructed by me based on interviews with him and his wife, Anne.

In other cases, I re-created dialogue. In every instance, I relied on available information about specific activities and personal encounters to keep these quotes in the spirit of the actual exchanges among these men.

I realize some of the language may be offensive. The Klansmen were generally rough characters; most of them used racial epithets and profanity freely. There is no good way to sugarcoat their behavior. In the interest of reality I preserved their crude and ugly words.

WHEN EVIL LIVED
IN LAUREL

Prologue

MAY 8, 1951. Tom Landrum would remember the night and its grim details for the rest of his life. While the humid evening held the prospect of another searing summer, a carnival atmosphere gripped his hometown of Laurel, Mississippi. More than a thousand people had gathered near the Jones County courthouse to await the execution of Willie McGee, a thirty-five-year-old Black man whose case had become a worldwide cause célèbre. McGee had been charged with raping a white woman six years earlier. The truck driver insisted the affair had been consensual, but he was convicted and sentenced to death in 1945 shortly after the woman filed a complaint. The verdict was overturned by a higher court; so was a second decision, following a trial where another all-white jury took only eleven minutes to find him guilty. After a third conviction, the U.S. Supreme Court refused to intervene, even as an international clamor grew over this latest example of Mississippi justice. If a Black man was accused of violating a white woman, it called for the supreme penalty. Even if there was doubt about his guilt.

Scores of other Black defendants had been sent to death row on dubious charges in Mississippi and attracted little notice. Unlike those cases, McGee's impending doom attracted countless sympathizers, including Albert Einstein, the Mississippi novelist William Faulkner, and the acclaimed singer-actor Paul Robeson.

Demonstrators took to the streets on McGee's behalf from London to the lawn of the White House. At the Lincoln Memorial, protestors wearing "Free Willie McGee" T-shirts chained themselves to pillars near the stone image of the Great Emancipator.

Yet the out-of-state activity had little impact in Mississippi, in part because McGee had been represented during his appeal by firebrand New York attorney Bella Abzug, a dedicated leftist whose arguments questioned Mississippi values. Since his defense was financed by the Civil Rights Congress, Mississippians were quick to link the group to the Communist Party and the far left. Support for McGee by thousands of union members outside the South did little good in a region historically hostile to organized labor.

The outcry by those foreign to Jones County only solidified belief in Mississippi that McGee should be put to death—legally, yet without more delay. Earlier, National Guard units had to be deployed to prevent his lynching between trials. Now, to ensure that McGee's death would be carried out properly, preparations had been made to bring the state's portable electric chair—a device known as Old Sparky—to Laurel and install it in the same courtroom where McGee had been convicted. To ensure adequate voltage, a cable attached to an outside generator was strung through a courthouse window and connected to the electric chair.

With the climax of the long drama at hand, excitement coursed through the town. As the midnight hour for McGee's death approached, a local radio station carried live reports for those who had not come to the courthouse. An announcer commented that an execution was not necessarily a joyful occasion, but he added, "When it becomes necessary, it must be done." On the streets surrounding the scene, knots of white people waited, some in lawn chairs as if for a picnic. More youthful spectators climbed into trees to get unobstructed views of the courthouse. When a state highway patrolman announced that the time had come for McGee to die, the news provoked cheers. Inside the courtroom, one hundred privileged witnesses had been allowed to see the execution; hundreds of others surrounded the grounds of the courthouse. They knew the procedure had begun when the generator groaned loudly; some imagined that lights dimmed, as happened in such scenes in the movies. The crowd clapped enthusiastically and shouted. They cheered again, a few minutes later, when McGee's lifeless body, covered with a white sheet, was loaded onto the hearse of a funeral home serving Black residents of Laurel.

TOM LANDRUM, a high school senior dressed in working-class denims, watched on the streets of Laurel that night, drawn with his schoolmates to the spectacle. An offspring of one of Jones County's largest and best-known families, the boy followed the proceedings from a vantage point outside a downtown theater. Some of his friends were among those clinging to high branches of trees. At first Tom was caught up in the excitement over an event that was winning worldwide attention. But when the exercise ended, he recognized the enormity of the activity. It resulted in the death of a man, scorned by the community and condemned to a final, proverbial last supper. The boy was suddenly gripped by the poignancy of the moment; he felt sickened and personally diminished. He said to himself: I should never have come. And he vowed: I will never do something like this again.

CHAPTER 1

MORE THAN A DECADE LATER, racial antagonism still burned in Jones County, a south Mississippi setting with a complex history. Though the region had earned curious celebrity during the Civil War for a revolt against the Confederacy by a short-lived "Free State of Jones," few of those liberal spirits survived. The county's white population was hard-core conservative, reflecting the fundamentalist religious beliefs that prevailed there. Laurel, one of two county seats, was not established until twenty years after the national conflict over slavery had ended and thus could claim none of the nobility attributed to the Old South. No antebellum mansions or stately cypress and oaks dripping with silver threads of Spanish moss graced its streets, as in New Orleans, which lay 150 miles to the south. Instead, Laurel grew up as a small, rough-natured city named for a toxic native bush but nurtured by a timber industry fed by dense surrounding pine forests. Because Jones County often displayed its violent passions in public, few were surprised when in 1964 it became the headquarters for a new and virulent organization known as the White Knights of the Mississippi Ku Klux Klan. The ranks of the local group were mostly made up of resentful men who worked the small farms, oil fields, or logging camps or held jobs on the line at Masonite, a monstrous factory that loomed over the landscape like a brutal force, converting waste wood into fiberboard.

The White Knights quickly achieved national notoriety after being accused of orchestrating the murder of three civil rights workers in another rural county sixty miles away, during the same Freedom Summer that produced the century's first great Civil Rights Act and sent hundreds of student volunteers into the South to challenge Jim Crow. To respond to the growing movement, there were calls within the Jones County councils of the Klan to create havoc in their own area: To burn the car of a young Black man said to have impudently followed a vehicle containing two white schoolteachers. To blow up a dam in order to empty a lake where Blacks had the audacity to swim. To destroy a panel truck being used by civil rights workers. To capture a troublesome man known as the "Black Stallion" so he could be flogged. To burn crosses in the yards of any local white leaders who might express concern, in order to warn them not to stray from the staunchly segregationist politics of the day. The recommendations even called for night riders to paint a Catholic church's outdoor statue of the Virgin Mary the color black to protest the denomination's stand on integration.

Their fiercest curses were directed at a man in neighboring Forrest County whom the Klansmen called the "Dahmer Nigger," dignifying him with neither a first name nor an honorific such as Mister. The man was known to be engaged in voter registration in defiance of Mississippi rules as well as the Klan. Because the "Dahmer Nigger" owned a small farm and a grocery store, he was not beholden to a white employer. Freed of economic constraints, Dahmer had been able to engage in civil rights work and was well known for it because he had been encouraging Blacks to vote for years, before any mention of a Voting Rights Act. With the prospect that federal officials would begin monitoring the registration process, he was now urging adults to take advantage of widening freedoms. It seemed that the "Dahmer Nigger" could not be intimidated. He ignored threatening crank telephone calls, and he had not been deterred by vandals who knocked out windows in his store and torched a shed full of hay on his land. The Klan believed something drastic needed to be done about the "Dahmer Nigger," and there was talk of eliminating him.

Targeting Dahmer would be another deadly tactic in the guerrilla war being waged by Klan units in pockets of Mississippi in their efforts to turn back new court orders and federal legislation designed to strike down discrimination. The times called for desperate measures. Old methods to thwart dictates from Washington no longer worked. Mississippi authorities—who once used local courts to impose segregationist laws—found themselves failing when jurisdiction moved to federal courts. The old guard had been unable to prevent a Black student from enrolling in the state's flagship university, a racially pure white institution known as Ole Miss, in 1962. The doctrine of segregated schools, a policy that had endured as long as Mississippi had been a state, had fallen for the first time, and more change was approaching.

Despite the power and seniority of the state's two U.S. senators, Jim Eastland and John Stennis, each a venerable committee chairman in the vanguard of conservative southern Democrats who had been blocking progressive legislation in Congress for decades, a major bill opening restaurants, hotels, theaters, and other public facilities to Blacks won passage in 1964. Now, in the summer of 1965, a companion Voting Rights Act, which would enfranchise hundreds of thousands of Blacks in the South, was on the verge of becoming law. Suddenly, Mississippi was bustling with activity by local Blacks and sympathetic outsiders, emboldened by their success.

Once-dependable devices of obstruction no longer worked for the old guard, the staunchest advocates of white supremacy in the state. As a result, the most extreme elements of their constituency felt they had nowhere to turn but to become vigilantes.

The Ku Klux Klan first emerged in the South a century earlier during another time of desperation, following defeat and military occupation after the Civil War. The Klan was never a monolithic organization. Different—and sometimes rival—Klan groups enjoyed popularity across the region, parading publicly in hoods and robes by day and conducting terrorism by night. To some southerners, it represented a romantic means to build a new, white-dominated society out of the ashes of the Lost Cause. For several generations, schoolchildren were taught that the post–Civil War South had been set upon by carpetbaggers, "Yankee" opportunists who came south to exploit the situation; and scalawags, local people who collaborated with the Reconstruction. In the middle of the twentieth century, any Mississippi schoolchild who achieved an eighth-grade education had been exposed to a state history textbook that told of the glories of the Klan. *Mississippi through Four Centuries* described the Klan as the "most important" group in the South during this period. "A Negro who had been giving trouble in a community might awake some night to find a ghost-clad figure standing by his bed," according to the textbook. "If these attempts to frighten them did not change the Negroes, the Klansmen would resort to whippings and in extreme cases to killing. The organization helped the South at a difficult time."

To appeal to the many practitioners of Protestant fundamentalism living in the South, the Klan had a religious element. Klan leaders used the cross as a symbol and cited biblical verse as justification for segregation. They liked to be known as "redeemers," true believers determined to restore the values of the Old South and to purge the region of Reconstruction.

The Klan thrived for a time following the Civil War, but their campaign of terror became unnecessary after southern politicians regained enough power before the end of the nineteenth century to ensure continued segregation, either with their own local laws or by bottling up civil rights bills in Congress. Yet the secret resistance movement never really died. After the *Brown v. Board of Education* decision by the Supreme Court in 1954, outlawing racial segregation in public schools, followed by a wave of new federal court orders and legislation out of Washington, white supremacists realized that extraordinary measures had to be taken.

It led to the resurrection of dormant clandestine organizations and to the birth of the White Knights, a corps of men committed, in extreme cases, to murder and terror to preserve segregation. Their leader was Sam Bowers of Laurel, a grandson of a Mississippi congressman. Though he dealt with jukeboxes and pinball machines for a living, many of Bowers's followers thought him a genius because he had completed a couple of semesters at Tulane and Southern Cal. By cobbling together two separate faiths worshipped in the region— stern Protestant beliefs and a xenophobic conviction that force was necessary to prevent an invasion of foreign ideas—Bowers became an exponent of a philosophy he called "Christian militancy." After seizing control of the new group from a rival Klansman and being anointed imperial wizard, Bowers established branches of the White Knights in towns scattered around the state. The group arose as a new and secret power, challenging other Ku Klux Klan organizations that had existed for years but now appeared to be lagging in their diligence to defend the old ways.

The White Knights' stronghold was Jones County, in the heart of the "Piney Woods" area in the southeastern part of the state. But the tentacles of Bowers's group extended well to the west, to Natchez and the Mississippi River, and northward to Meridian and Neshoba County, where the White Knights were responsible for one of the civil rights era's most horrific incidents.

The birth of the White Knights coincided with the outset of Freedom Summer, a time when passage of a landmark Civil Rights Act appeared inevitable and several hundred students who were enrolled in colleges from New England to California descended on Mississippi to take part in the freedom movement. The Klan counterattacked. To discourage the idealistic young people, the White Knights burned a Black church being used for a voter-registration workshop in rural Neshoba County, then set a trap to eliminate one of their primary targets, a young Jewish volunteer for the Congress of Racial Equality named Michael Schwerner, who had been working in nearby Meridian. Schwerner's dedication, his alien Judaism, even his goatee—these offended the White Knights. Accompanied by two other young men, James Chaney, a Black Mississippian, and Andrew Goodman, a Jewish student at Queens College in New York who had just arrived to take part in Freedom Summer, Schwerner ventured to Neshoba County to inspect the ruins of the church. Local law enforcement officers intercepted the trio, held them briefly on a bogus traffic violation, then turned them over to an assembly of Klansmen, who took the young men to a remote farm, executed them, and buried them in a man-made dam.

The three men vanished in June. Some of Mississippi's most prominent officials called their disappearance a hoax. But President Lyndon B. Johnson was outraged. He ordered navy personnel already stationed in the state to conduct a search for the missing men. Assuming they were dead, the servicemen combed swamps and bayous for bodies. Johnson also arranged for the dispatch of an additional 150 FBI agents to Mississippi to pursue leads that local sheriffs and police were unwilling to explore. In early August, after the FBI had paid thousands of dollars to informants, the investment produced a return. A Klan insider told the FBI where the men were buried, and the bodies of Schwerner, Chaney, and Goodman, caked with the moist red clay of Neshoba County, were excavated from their makeshift grave.

The investigation eventually led to eighteen men, a motley group including the sheriff and deputy sheriff of Neshoba County, a fiery part-time Baptist minister, and other adherents of the White Knights. The imperial wizard, Sam Bowers, was not on hand when the men were killed, but he was believed to have authorized the action.

State officials were unwilling to prosecute the group believed to be responsible for the murders, so federal authorities eventually arrested the men on allegations that they had been engaged in a conspiracy to deprive the victims of their civil rights. The charges were dismissed by a Mississippian serving as a U.S. commissioner, then reinstated by a federal grand jury only to be dismissed again for all but two of the defendants by a federal judge from Mississippi. The defendants remained free as federal prosecutors mulled over further strategies. During the long proceedings, the public learned for the first time some of the details of Bowers's organization. It earned him a nefarious reputation, but also won him respect among those bitter Mississippians prepared to battle to the end.

≈

TOM LANDRUM, the youthful witness to the 1951 events at the Jones County courthouse, had experienced something of an epiphany the night Willie McGee was put to death. He was conscience stricken. Not only should he have avoided the affair, he knew he should have listened to an admonition by his father, who had told him years earlier of a terrible incident he himself witnessed as a young man. According to Tom's father, he had been working on a logging job in the woods of Jones County when a passing pickup truck skidded to a stop near the crew felling timber. The driver's face was flushed. "Come on! Hop in!" he shouted. "They're lynching somebody over in Ellisville," another town in Jones County. Tom's father joined the men jammed together in the flatbed of the truck. "When we got over there," he related to his son, "they had tied this Negro between two trees and were shooting him with rifles. It was the most horrible thing I ever saw." He told Tom, "Don't you ever get involved in something like that."

Tom's racial sensitivities were strengthened in his childhood by other experiences. When he and his father visited a local hamburger stand they never encountered problems, but young Tom saw Black children his age denied entrance. The youngsters were forced to order their food through a dingy opening cut into the building for the purpose of serving Black customers outside rather than have them darken the all-white atmosphere inside the café. To Tom the situation reeked of indignity and injustice. He heard stories in school of night riders burning down homes in order to frighten Black farmworkers who were thought to represent a challenge to the system, and he wondered what type of man would resort to terror against people who lived simply and worshipped God respectfully. Black parents who lived in Tom's country neighborhood made an impression on the boy by dressing in hand-me-down suits and self-stitched white dresses each Sunday in order to shepherd their large families to all-day church services.

As a boy, Tom had walked behind a mule-drawn plow himself and picked cotton by hand on a small two-acre plot his father cultivated as a sharecropper for more prosperous members of the widespread Landrum family. Tom knew how it felt to be dirt poor, to attend services regularly at his own Baptist church, and to be belittled by wealthier members of local society.

Despite his early poverty, Tom had a sense of pride because the Landrum name enjoyed a certain status in Jones County, where the first of his ancestors had settled the land as yeoman farmers years before Mississippi achieved statehood in 1817. Like so many southern families, the Landrums had emigrated from Scotland, passing through Virginia on their way to carving farms from a region of primeval forest in the territory that would become Mississippi. Though some of the Scottish immigrants pushed on toward the powerful river to create plantations on richer soil in the land known as the Delta, becoming property owners in a cotton economy, the Landrums chose to establish homesteads in the tougher Piney Woods countryside in what would become the southeastern part of the state.

Two Landrum brothers, born in the area around the turn of the nineteenth century, sired a total of fifteen sons, and their numbers multiplied in the decades leading to the Civil War. Family Bibles were used to try to keep track of the kin, but there were so many descendants that records were blurred. Landrum liked to say that his family background included "more Tom Landrums than you can shake a stick at."

The Landrums represented the quintessential Jones County family rent by internecine conflict during the Civil War, when a local renegade militia took up arms against the Confederacy, objecting to the conscription of poor white men while the sons of the planter class escaped military service. There were few slaves in Jones County and little vested interest in going to war to preserve the system. Nevertheless, the Confederate army was easily stocked at the beginning of the war in 1861 by young men eager to enlist.

However, as the war ground on, it took its toll and enthusiasm ebbed. Shiloh, the first great military engagement, caused twenty-four thousand casualties and made vulnerable a critical railroad hub in Corinth, Mississippi. A week after that loss, the Confederate Congress passed a Conscription Act that threatened to sweep up most healthy white men between the ages of eighteen and thirty-five. A subsequent law that exempted plantation owners with more than twenty slaves from military service led to a rebellion and the creation of a "Free State of Jones," a jurisdiction to be defended by a small pro-Union force. A former Confederate soldier named Newton Knight amassed enough men to form a company and conduct guerrilla warfare against the Confederacy in the area. Some dissenters sided with Knight; others chose to take up arms with Union forces. Four Landrum men eventually enlisted in a Union regiment, including a Thomas S. Landrum, who had originally served in the Confederate army before turning over three mules to the Union army when he joined them in 1864.

Local historian Ed Payne wrote in a monograph: "The Landrum family offers insights into the way in which the Civil War entangled those Southerners who did not share in the region's passion for secession. Once the war began, however, neutrality was not an option. Landrum men would enlist as Confederate and Union soldiers, and two served in both armies—while one died trying. They became, like the nation as a whole, a house divided by war."

Historians concluded that "a lawless element exercised considerable power and control" in Jones County. The place, which had been clawed out of murky swamps and thick woods, already had a reputation for being peculiar, so no stigma was attached to allegiance to the Union. But Union sympathy was a rare sentiment anywhere else in Mississippi in the 1860s, and that little bit of background seemed especially ironic a century later when Jones County grew into a hotbed for the Klan.

~

BY THE TIME Tom Landrum was born in 1932, members of his extended family lived on farms scattered throughout the county. Some were prosperous; others, less so. Tom's father fell into the latter category. During the Great Depression, Tom's parents abandoned Jones County for a while, seeking a better life on the Mississippi Gulf Coast, but returned in time for Tom to attract notice as a high school football player. He excelled in a sport worshipped in the South, but he rejected the offer of a college scholarship in order to marry Anne Geddie, a girl who sent him into a swoon the first time he saw her on a school bus. He joined the air force at the start of the Korean War. Tom shared duties with Black enlisted men— his first experience with integration—and had no problem with it. He and Anne lived in Pensacola while he was stationed at nearby Eglin Air Force Base. Hitchhiking between his home and the base, Tom did not fail to notice that the motorists most inclined to pick him up were Black people. That recognition, coupled with his childhood labors at sharecropping, fed his sympathy for the underdogs in southern society at the time.

After completing his military commitment Tom enrolled at Jones County Junior College, part of a network of two-year Mississippi schools that perennially featured outstanding football teams. (After Landrum transferred to play at the University of Louisville, the JCJC Bobcats traveled to Pasadena, California, in 1955 to play an integrated squad from Compton Community College in the Junior Rose Bowl. Somehow the Jones County team faced none of the resistance from the political establishment that for another decade prevented other all-white Mississippi schools from engaging in competition with Black players, and the Bobcats became the first white athletes from the state to compete against an integrated opponent.) Landrum grew into an imposing physical figure, standing over six feet tall and weighing more than two hundred pounds in an age when most of his contemporaries were smaller. His performance at the gritty position of tackle won him a football scholarship to Louisville, but after a season there he left to go home and obtain a diploma from Mississippi College, a Baptist institution near Jackson. With his bachelor's degree he worked as a high school teacher and coach before taking the job of Youth Court counselor back home in Laurel.

Landrum considered Laurel "home," though he and his own growing family lived on a rural road a few miles outside the city limits. The Landrums believed in the basic goodness of Jones County and its God-fearing people. It was, they were convinced, a good place to live. With a population of nearly twenty-five thousand, Laurel served as a marketplace for those who resided in surrounding hamlets and went there to shop on Saturdays. Yet like virtually all southern towns, it was divided into neighborhoods by race. The chief business district lay in a white section dominated by the courthouse, where Landrum worked. The downtown streets were lined with the cheerful storefronts of pharmacies and shops selling clothing, hardware, shoes, variety items, and cheap knickknacks. On one block, squeezed between commercial buildings, were the offices of the local newspaper, the *Leader-Call*, which printed reports of the unsavory activities of the White Knights despite the town's general tendency toward boosterism.

Blacks made their homes in the poorer side of town. Two of Laurel's native sons and daughters had recently achieved national fame: Leontyne Price, a soprano with starring roles at the Metropolitan Opera in New York, and Ralph Boston, who captured a gold medal in the long-jump competition at the 1960 Olympics in Rome. Both were products of Laurel's Black community. Despite their accolades, the city was still known as the site of the Willie McGee execution and was haunted by a lynching in 1942, when a white mob invaded the jail, yanked a Black man from his cell, and put him to death.

And now Laurel served as host for the White Knights of the Mississippi Ku Klux Klan.

≈

LANDRUM WAS NEITHER an outspoken man nor ready to challenge publicly the system that governed Mississippi and Jones County. But as he grew older he began to resent the overt racism. Like a quiet and outnumbered minority of other white Mississippians, he felt a nagging concern over the horror of the Neshoba County murders and the refusal of the state's political leaders to accept any laws that might weaken segregation. By the time Tom Landrum was a young man working in county government, he saw that most of the white citizens had been inhibited by Mississippi's strong inclination to resist change. He, too, was reluctant to speak against the system. By maintaining this silence, he knew he was abetting an unfavorable international image of white Mississippians as no better than a bunch of ignorant louts and bigots.

There seemed little incentive to speak out. The white churches were timorous, the newspapers in the state were mostly supportive of segregation, and politicians who might have been willing to make peace with the federal government had been defeated in the past two statewide elections. Inside white Mississippi, no civic clubs or social organizations dared to question segregation. If one were to raise opposition to the status quo, Tom saw, it would have to be done privately.

≈

IN THE FEVERED CLIMATE of the 1960s, Sam Bowers found it easy to recruit volunteers to join his group. There were no laws against Klan membership and his followers believed that the White Knights represented the South's last, best bulwark against racial integration. Some were attracted to Bowers's group by a commitment to the cause of white supremacy. Others were lured by the camaraderie. The White Knights served as a sort of men's club offering an excuse to get out of the house at night. To some members, the protocol seemed not a lot different from that of the Masons, with an emphasis on robes and secret ceremony that excluded Catholics and Jews. Those eager to legitimize the Klan compared the group to the American Legion, the superpatriotic veterans' clubs that kept watch to ensure that no communists set foot in their neighborhoods.

The White Knights had a diverse membership. Some were lonely men who held unrewarding jobs and looked to the White Knights for excitement. Sprinkled into this element were a handful of well-to-do businessmen or ambitious young men on the make. Still others were lured by the ministry of rogue preachers who gave the Klan their blessing. A few of them, like Bowers, felt the mission of the White Knights represented a divinely ordained undertaking.

But for Leonard Caves, the circuit clerk of Jones County, the Klan offered a political opportunity. Caves had been elected in 1963, to hold one of the most important jobs in county government. His office supervised voter registration and the operation of the local circuit court, which had responsibility for conducting criminal trials and important civil lawsuits. An enthusiastic segregationist, Caves was prepared to salt the court's list of potential jurors with the names of Klansmen to ensure protection for any White Knight facing trial. As voting registrar, Caves was also able to administer harshly the literacy tests that applicants needed to pass in order to qualify as voters. The circuit clerk arbitrarily flunked prospective Black voters. It was a common practice in Mississippi.

Caves presided as something of a lord at the Jones County courthouse, where Tom Landrum, now thirty-three years old, worked as a county employee, counseling teenage boys who had run afoul of the law for violations such as shoplifting or petty vandalism. Landrum's office was located in an annex attached to the old, pillared building where Willie McGee had died. The courthouse was a hive of activity where political gossip and rumors flourished, and much of the scuttlebutt gravitated around the office of the Jones County circuit clerk. It was a place where Landrum heard soliloquies of crude segregationist philosophies.

Landrum was a frequent visitor in Caves's office. The two men were about the same age and had known each other for years, a friendship built on their experiences teaching and coaching at schools in Jones County when they were just out of college. They engaged in small talk about the weather or sports or in speculation about political comings and goings. Caves seemed consumed by politics, and Landrum was amused by his behavior as a candidate. Caves would carefully dress in a starched white shirt and necktie, adorned with a dark suit, before setting out for door-to-door campaigning. Turning on the heat in his car in the midst of the Mississippi summer, he would sweat profusely to achieve the desired effect. Before leaving the car for house calls he would loosen his tie to give the appearance of a hardworking man, burdened but nonetheless willing to extend himself to reach out to voters.

Caves had no apologies for his zeal, and he frequently lectured Landrum on the art of politics. "Tom," he said, "I know you're interested in politics yourself, and there are things you need to do to succeed." One recommendation was to embrace the Klan.

Even as federal power seemed to be closing in on Mississippi, the Klan in Jones County had been adding to its rolls. Hundreds had joined and Caves appreciated the organization's strength. "There's a lot of votes out there," he told Landrum. "A lot of good men, respectable men," he said of the membership of the White Knights. "If you want to make it in politics, it's important to befriend these people." They could deliver more than their own votes, Caves said. The numbers increased when they were able to convince family members and friends to rally behind candidates quietly endorsed by the Klan. The organization could make the difference in close local elections where no more than a few thousand people voted. According to Caves, the Klan's support had helped elect the current mayor of Laurel, Henry Bucklew, because the Klansmen liked what they heard from him when he was a candidate. Caves wanted to ensure that he, too, had locked up Klan votes when he ran for reelection.

He hinted to Landrum that he had gone beyond the role of political supplicant and actually belonged to the White Knights himself. More than once, he encouraged his friend to join the group, not necessarily to wage war on local Blacks but to forge personal associations that would be politically helpful in Jones County. Landrum was not persuaded and gently declined Caves's overtures. He did not tell Caves of his unhappiness over the violence in Jones County or that he abhorred the Klan.

≈

IN THE MIDDLE OF JULY 1965, another man made a very different approach to Landrum. Bob Lee, an FBI agent assigned to the bureau's Laurel office several years earlier, was a regular visitor to the courthouse. As a native southerner—his formal name was Robert E. Lee and he had served as a highway patrolman in South Carolina before joining the FBI—Lee's presence was acceptable to the county officials in Jones County. By this time, he was considered something of a local guy himself and not part of the greatly resented FBI task force of outside agents sent to the state the year before. He moved easily among the courthouse personalities.

Lee often dropped by Landrum's office when in the building. He liked to keep track of youthful troublemakers. After completing college and coaching for a few years, Landrum had talked with Lee about the possibility of becoming an FBI agent himself. He dropped the thought after being told that a law degree was probably necessary, even though Landrum's formal education was richer than that of most Mississippians.

Though no longer hopeful of becoming an FBI agent, Landrum developed a friendship with Lee. In his position with the Youth Court, he often talked with Lee about cases that might require formal referral to the FBI. Occasionally they touched on current events in Jones County involving racial violence. From their conversations, Lee recognized Landrum as a sensible fellow who had genuine concerns about his youthful charges. It also seemed clear to the FBI man that Landrum was disturbed by the influence of the Klan in Jones County. He heard Landrum openly deplore an outbreak of arson in Black neighborhoods that he attributed to the Klan.

The day after several Black families' homes were shot into by night riders, Lee felt comfortable about mentioning a sensitive subject. Pulling his chair to sit closer to Landrum in the small courthouse office, Lee told him of his difficulty not only in combating the violence but in finding good men to take on an assignment that would help.

"Tom, you know we need to penetrate the White Knights," Lee said. "They're running amok around the state, causing all sorts of trouble. They're a bunch of bullies, picking on poor colored people. They think nothing about burning down a house or a church. Look what they're doing here in Jones County. They're a bunch of sorry bastards. They've killed innocent folks. They're ruining the reputation of Mississippi, Tom, and they're destroying our own little community here.

"My job is to try to learn as much as I can about Sam Bowers's operation. Now you know the FBI's not here to protect the folks involved in civil rights work. That pisses off some of their workers. They think we should serve as their bodyguards. They don't understand that our job is to collect as much information as we can about the Klan. We're here to investigate, not to protect anybody. But we are especially interested in breaking up the White Knights. Our job is to investigate them, come up with good information, and turn it over to prosecutors to put them out of business."

Landrum nodded. He seemed interested, so the FBI agent continued. "Tom, what we're looking for is people we can trust to work with us. We've got some paid informants already, men who are in the Klan, and they tell us things. But we can't always trust them. Some of 'em are in it just for the money, and in some cases, they're likely to give us bum information or stuff that's totally bullshit.

"What we need is somebody we can trust," Lee said. "I know you know a lot of people around Jones County. Do you know anybody who might be willing to help us?" He paused. "Would you be willing to work with us?" Lee's use of the word "trust" resonated with Landrum. As Lee made his appeal for Landrum to aid the FBI by joining the White Knights, the idea began to sound like a civic duty. It also offered a touch of adventure, for Landrum was still a young man. But he knew he had responsibilities that might prevent him from volunteering—a wife and five children and a home a few miles from Laurel that required regular maintenance to shelter his growing family.

"I don't know," Landrum replied, searching for a proper response. "It's something I have to think about." He was not prepared to rush into an arrangement with the FBI. He needed to talk with his wife and other members of his family. But he was intrigued. Instead of dismissing Lee's call for help, Landrum told him, "Let me get back to you."

WHEN HE LEFT his office that afternoon, Landrum was already thinking, Somebody needs to do something. Bob Lee's request called for an enormous personal decision, and it was not one Landrum could make alone. He would never dare take any initiative without consulting with his wife, Anne. She had matured from the winsome girl on the school bus to the mother of their five children, and she deserved to be heard on anything that could change their lives. Besides, he recognized her good judgment and often deferred to her.

After their children were asleep that night, Tom told his wife about Lee's visit. The assignment held potential for disaster. Spies were executed, even in civilized countries. Landrum would surely be confronted with dire consequences if he were discovered to be a traitor in a band of lawless men. But as the couple talked, they also considered the possibility that had been presented to Tom to make an impact, to reduce the violence and restore some peace to Jones County. Anne felt instinctively that he should do it.

Before reaching a conclusion, however, they both knew there was one other person who should be brought into the discussion— Anne's mother, Gertrude Geddie, a no-nonsense woman whom Tom looked on as a second mother. A few days later, the Landrums assembled their children and packed for a trip to meet the older woman the family called "Gert" for a weeklong expedition to the

Florida Panhandle. The trip had the appearance of a vacation on the Gulf Coast, camping out at facilities at Fort Pickens, not far from where Tom had served in the air force. But it was also a retreat for them to thrash through the arguments—pro and con—regarding the call from the FBI.

They played in the weak surf, sunbathed, and took pleasure in late afternoon visits to a sno-cone stand. In the evenings they withdrew to their rental quarters, washed the sand from their children, and settled down for a late dinner while the children slept.

As the discussion about the Klan began among the adults, Gert set the tone. "First," she said, "we have to pray." Like many Mississippians, the family members were Southern Baptists and were uninhibited about practicing their religion. They prayed for guidance. They knew that by joining the White Knights, Tom might be publicly identified as a consort of men committing unspeakable acts. Yet by doing so, he might be in a position to provide the FBI with valuable information—even though there might never be any official recognition of the risk he took. If he were found out, he could be killed. Terrible things could be visited on his family members. Those fears were mitigated by something like a spiritual calling, a belief in seizing the rare opportunity to do good.

Landrum was inclined to take up the offer. He harbored contempt for the Klan and derisively referred to them as "kluckers." The family weighed the perils and the rewards, and then Gert told her son-in-law, "You have to do it."

The Landrums returned home, and Tom called Bob Lee.

≈

THE NEXT EVENING, Landrum met secretly with Lee and another agent, Don Schaefler, one of the FBI newcomers sent to the state. On the pretense of car trouble, Landrum borrowed a friend's unrecognizable Dodge to drive to Lee's house, where he and the two FBI men hammered out an understanding. Landrum's code name would be "Jackie." Lee was to be called "Mr. Young," and Schaefler "Adam."

Landrum was expected to give frequent written reports to the FBI, detailing the activities of the White Knights. He was given a special telephone number for the Laurel FBI office but instructed not to call unless an emergency arose.

Landrum was told that the only ones other than his own family who would know about his commitment were Lee; Schaefler; Roy K. Moore, the FBI special agent in Jackson in charge of Mississippi operations; and J. Edgar Hoover, the FBI director in Washington.

Though it had been rumored during the Neshoba County investigation that the FBI was making significant payments to informants, Lee did not offer Landrum money and Landrum did not ask to be paid. The FBI agreed to reimburse him for modest expenses and to use a government scale to determine payments for mileage when he used his car.

Landrum had one special request. He asked for a letter from Hoover, the nationally renowned crime-fighter who had led the FBI since its inception in 1935, something that would document the legitimacy of his work for the FBI. Landrum wanted it for posterity, to be able to show to his children when they were grown, or to be able someday to reassure law enforcement officials or friends that he had joined the Klan for a positive purpose. Lee agreed to the letter, but his Washington headquarters was unwilling to issue it. Lee was told that the bureau feared Landrum might write an unauthorized book about his experiences. J. Edgar Hoover was very possessive of his image. The director wanted no wildcat books, no stories that did anything other than burnish his reputation and that of his empire.

≈

LANDRUM'S NEXT STEP was to tell Leonard Caves, the circuit clerk, that he had decided to join the White Knights. Caves was gleeful. He had corralled another recruit from among the courthouse personnel. Caves's bailiffs, who handled the selection of juries, were already in league with him. So were several highway patrolmen and local police officers as well as a few elected constables, who had law enforcement powers. Caves was such a vigorous advocate that he had even tempted his own brother into the fraternity of the Klan.

He told Landrum he would pass his name on to the White Knights. Landrum would be investigated for fitness for the Klan, a process that might take a couple of weeks. Membership would come at a price. He would be expected to pay a ten-dollar initiation fee.

A week later, Landrum learned from Bob Lee—who heard the news through other FBI sources already embedded in the Klan— that he had been accepted. Another week passed before Caves called to say that the White Knights had formally cleared him for membership.

"Meet me at my house at seven o'clock and bring your dues," Caves said. To impress the initiate, Caves promised, "We'll be joined by Charlie Blackwell," a recent graduate of the University of Mississippi law school who was already a member of the state legislature and had higher political goals.

When Landrum joined a few prospective members at Caves's home on a rainy night in August, he understood they were going to be sworn in. To cover their movements, a nervous Caves drove the men to a rendezvous in the parking lot of a bowling alley, where they were transferred to a small caravan carrying other initiates. As they drove into the dark countryside, Landrum grew uneasy.

After a few miles, they reached their destination, a wooded area behind an out-of-the-way Methodist church. Landrum wondered whether the Klansmen might already have been tipped off about him. In his most troubling moments—triggered by men in black hoods and robes who carried shotguns and stopped the cars—Landrum wondered if he might have ridden to his own execution. The Klan guards were a ghostly sight, their eyes so deeply recessed behind the holes in their hoods that they had a menacing, vacant appearance. Working with their hands, they patted down the clothing of each visitor to ensure that none of them wore concealed electronic devices.

Landrum was disconcerted when one of the hooded men frisking him murmured, "Excuse me, Coach." He recognized the voice of

Charles Noble, a young man he had once coached while employed by the local school system.

Moisture left over from a mid-summer thunderstorm dripped from the trees. Leaving the checkpoint, Landrum stepped carefully along a muddy trail leading into a copse of pines where several other men, dressed in white hoods and robes, waited among a larger group. Not everyone was hooded and Landrum saw that he could identify a few of the men present. Some he had coached or taught. He was also appalled to see one of his own family members in the group of fifteen men waiting to be sworn in to the White Knights.

On a sudden impulse, as a way to save his family member from a poor decision, Landrum whispered to one of the guards that his relative was married to a Catholic. While Blacks led the Klan's list of untouchables, Landrum felt sure that Catholics and Jews were objectionable, too. As he would learn a few minutes later, during a reading of the White Knights' bylaws, Section 6 of Article 10 declared that no member "shall ever attempt to recruit an alien for membership who is a negro, jew or papist; nor shall any alien who is cohabiting with or married to, by common law or pagan ways, a negro, jew or papist ever be allowed membership in the Klan."

Landrum's alert caused sudden consternation among the Klansmen when they learned the mate of a Catholic had shown up in their midst. After a huddle, the guards escorted Landrum's family member out of the meeting. The discovery caused confusion. With rain beginning to pelt the meeting place, the group heard a dreary recitation of the bylaws, but the swearing-in ceremony was put off until later. In his first missive to the FBI, Landrum wrote, "There is a lot of hog wash in the constitution and I plan to get a copy if I can."

He also thought to himself: What have I gotten myself into?

CHAPTER 2

THE NEXT DAY—Landrum noted the date ruefully: Friday the thirteenth of August—he was picked up by a part-time preacher named Cecil Sessum and taken to complete the swearing-in ceremony. Landrum knew Sessum slightly. He was a couple of years younger and Landrum had thought of him as a fine family man before learning of his Klan affiliation. Sessum actually looked more Lions Club than Klan. His frame appeared too meager to qualify as a fearsome Klansman. (Landrum outweighed him by nearly one hundred pounds.) A large pair of horn-rimmed glasses dominated Sessum's face. He seemed almost scholarly, and he preferred starched white shirts to the gritty denim and khaki worn by the local laborers drawn to the Klan. Actually, Sessum was bona fide white-collar. He worked for his uncle, Victor Walters, who owned a wholesale distributing business and had recruited his nephew and sworn him in to the Klan.

Sessum dabbled in religion on the side. He was affiliated with the Sharon Missionary Baptist Church in Laurel; divinity school degrees were not required for the autonomous Baptist churches or the homegrown Pentecostal congregations in Jones County. Sessum occasionally showed up in their pulpits, larding his sermons that warned of eternal damnation with messages of how God intended for the races to be separated. Was it not part of God's plan, he asked his audience, that wildlife in His kingdom was segregated? Cardinals flew only with redbirds. Sparrows flocked with their own. And blackbirds were the only species that swarmed in the sky by the hundreds, all by themselves.

Sessum followed a gospel laid down by some of the fundamentalist giants in the South, such as the Reverend Bob Jones Sr., whose ministry had been supported over the years by contributions from the Ku Klux Klan before he settled down at a university he named for himself in Greenville, South Carolina. Jones found justification for racial separation in the scriptures. In a famous Easter Sunday radio address in 1960—weeks after the first sit-ins by Black students in North Carolina—Jones spoke of "a Satanic agitation striking back at God's established order." And in that "order," God had established racial separation. "Racially, we have separation in the Bible," Jones assured his listeners.

Sessum believed in the evangelist's words with the fervor of a convert. Though more outwardly gentle than most of the White Knights, Sessum was passionate on the subject of race and enthusiastic about his devotion to the Klan, for their white supremacist doctrine was overlaid with quasi-religious symbolism. Driving Landrum to the meeting, he bubbled with pride about the White Knights.

"You're doing the right thing, Tom," he said. "We're the kind of group that's needed in Jones County. You'll like the men you'll be working with. They're God-fearing men, good salt-of-the-earth people who're filling a gap caused by a bunch of weak-kneed politicians that threw in the towel to the integrationists and communists. We know that race-mingling will lead to the destruction of our civilization, and we're going to fight to preserve our way of life."

They pulled up in front of John's Restaurant, a fixture in downtown Laurel. Located at a busy intersection near a railroad overpass, the building featured a low-slung, red-brick exterior and looked to be limited to one floor. But closer inspection revealed a wood-framed second floor jutting from the roof like a camel's back. The café had an inexpensive menu that featured cheap steaks, hamburgers, and blue-plate specials overflowing with vegetables. Many of the dishes were fried. There were seats at the counter near the kitchen, as in an old-fashioned diner, and Formica tables took up the rest of the floor space. It catered to the working class, who were satisfied that they could get an honest meal there for a fair price. The clientele was dominated by truck drivers, Masonite employees, and men who worked in the Jones County oil fields that had sprouted derricks across the land in recent years, towering pumping devices that popped up almost as quickly as overnight mushrooms.

John's Restaurant had another purpose. It served as a sanctuary for the White Knights. Its proprietor was Deavours Nix, a hard-bitten forty-year-old son of Jones County who was considered by local Klansmen to be the right-hand man of their leader, Sam Bowers. Nix had the track record of a desperado. He had failed to finish the ninth grade at a rural high school and enlisted in the navy as a teenager. His six years of service were distinguished by little more than a handful of courts-martial. Though he later enrolled in a GI Bill school to complete his high school education, Nix failed again and went to work for a while as a roughneck for an oil-field drilling contractor. In 1962 he opened a joint called Nub's Steak House in Laurel. It flopped, too, and Nix moved to California in search of an elusive occupation that might stabilize his fortunes. He worked as a salesman for a year or so with a company called Southern California Heat Treat, and when that job played out he returned to Jones County. He claimed he came home "to help the boys" in their struggle against the "niggers" and the "Yankees" and the "Reds" he felt were threatening the South. He took charge of the operation of John's Restaurant, but he actually lived on the income he received from payments by various insurance companies. He had a history of filing claims for injuries suffered in dubious accidents.

Tom Landrum knew Nix slightly. He was a fellow who fit the White Knights profile far better than Sessum. He had an impressive rap sheet that showed he'd been arrested three times for assault in the past three years—once for pummeling a suspected integrationist into submission. When the new Klan initiate was presented to Nix inside the restaurant, Landrum had one thought: the man could play the part of a mobster in a movie. Nix looked capable of killing someone on a minute's notice. His dark hair was slicked straight back and lacquered by a rank-smelling pomade, and his complexion seemed as dark as the Choctaws who once roamed the region.

They went upstairs to Nix's office, where he would administer the White Knights oath in a decidedly informal ceremony. Sessum served as the only witness. Nix seemed slightly put off by Landrum's presence, and vented his foul mood in a diatribe about the inferiority of Blacks. He spoke favorably of his own divinely ordained mission "to keep the niggers in their place." Nix was proud of his standing in the White Knights. At a statewide meeting of Klan members in June he had been elected grand director of the Klan Bureau of Investigation. He likened it in importance to the position of J. Edgar Hoover, the director of the FBI. Nix wanted to ensure that Landrum knew he was being sworn in by a man of authority.

Landrum was repelled by Nix's boasts, but stayed silent.

"Tom," Nix told the new Klansman, "you're going to find my dedication to the White Knights is stronger than horseradish. I seen from the time I was growing up the worthlessness of niggers. Not just here in Jones County, but out in California, too. A couple of years ago, I felt the calling to come back here, that I was needed at home. The White Knights needed a man of my leadership qualities, not some timid-assed fellow who's gonna let the niggers run over us. I ain't afraid to take matters in my own hands when I see niggers trying to push us around. I ain't afraid to get arrested, and I ain't afraid to burn down a nigger house or beat the shit out of a nigger or one of them nigger-loving Jews come down to try to integrate us. The White Knights demand a strong commitment from our membership, and we gotta be ready for action."

Landrum nodded. Nix asked if he knew Sam Bowers. "Not really," Landrum said, "but I sure know who he is."

"You're gonna find Sam is a natural-born leader of men. You'll meet him soon enough, and you're gonna like him. He's smart and got a good education and a powerful philosophy. He's smarter than me, but we a lot alike, him and me. We're not gonna put up with any of the bullshit from the niggers and we're prepared to take whatever steps necessary to preserve the purity of our race."

Nix continued to eye Landrum suspiciously, but congratulated him on his decision to join the White Knights. The following day, Nix was arrested again and charged with another assault.

≈

LANDRUM HAD A low opinion of Nix before this encounter, and the performance did nothing to sway his earlier judgment. When he got home he completed dictating to his wife the first of his secret missives to the FBI. After providing a brief report on the meeting with Sessum and Nix, Landrum could not resist an editorial observation: "I have known Nix for several years and in my book he is one of the lowest characters I have ever known. Is bad to drink and runs with other women."

Anne scribbled down Landrum's remarks as he talked. Afterward, always watchful that no one looked over her shoulder, she used the typewriter in his courthouse office, where she was also employed, to make the message legible, even if pockmarked by occasional error. She apologized to her husband for her lack of stenographic skills. "My typing is horrible, too," she professed. Tom hugged her to show his appreciation for her partnership in the venture and her stealth in ensuring that no visitor to their office saw what she typed. They both knew that the danger extended to members of their family.

Landrum realized that without her support—and the reinforcement from her mother—he might not have agreed to the appeal from the FBI. He revered his mother-in-law more than his own mother. From the beginning of his union with Anne, Gert had exuded the warmth that he had missed in his own home while growing up. He respected her belief in the value of education and her faith in God. She had always pressed classic books on Anne and her siblings. And Tom had heard—more than once—the family story of how Gert had once taken her children to church for a midweek prayer meeting and found no one else there. "We were delighted and thought we could go home," Anne recalled. "She said, 'No, we are at church and we are going to have a prayer meeting.'" So they held their own little service. Gert's Christian certitude at the family get-together in Florida helped convince Tom to take up the FBI assignment. And now Gert also had a regular role in the undertaking.

Without informing the FBI, Anne was careful to make a carbon copy of each report she typed. The Landrums didn't dare leave the copies at their home, so duplicates were mailed for safekeeping to Gert, who lived in Jackson, the state capital. To keep a record of Tom's reports, Gert filed the copies in a lockbox in her bank.

When he agreed to go undercover for the FBI, Landrum made arrangements with Bob Lee to quietly hand over material to various agents meeting him in nearby Hattiesburg, in the library of Mississippi Southern College. The library was thought to be the last place a Klansman might show up.

～

ONCE LANDRUM PAID his ten-dollar initiation fee and became a member of the White Knights he was assigned to the Jones County East Group, a unit of about twenty men. Sessum and Nix assured him that he would be surprised to learn who belonged to the Klan. At his next meeting, Landrum recognized Tommy Thornton—who drove a milk truck by day—and realized Thornton was another of the men who had helped frisk him at his first Klan gathering in the woods. He learned that some were proud of their funny-sounding titles. The organization had a penchant for mythical job descriptions such as "grand dragon" and "exalted cyclops." Bowers reigned as the "imperial wizard" and had structured the White Knights' own form of state and local government. Lawrence Byrd, who ran a radio and TV repair shop, was designated the Klan's "senator" from Jones County. A lesser county official served as a "giant." The Jones County giant was "Red" Caldwell, named for his auburn hair and perpetually flushed face. Landrum knew Caldwell as a blowhard who wore a Stetson hat, smoked cigars, and enjoyed talking of his success as the owner of Dixie Auto Sales. Landrum thought of him as an ordinary used-car salesman, but Caldwell described himself as a business leader who owned a "yacht" moored on the Mississippi Gulf Coast. Landrum was amused that Caldwell pronounced it "yak."

≈

LANDRUM SAW THAT HE, an erstwhile teacher, had much to be taught as a member of the White Knights of the Mississippi Ku Klux Klan.

Although the Klan movement claimed its strongest constituency in the Deep South, organizations exuding hate and violence were scattered into dozens of different racist and anti-Semitic groups around the country. Bigoted groups had actually thrived outside of Dixie earlier in the twentieth century, winning political power from Pennsylvania to Oregon. The Klan itself was glorified in the most famous epic of the silent-film era, *Birth of a Nation*. But there was never much national cohesion. Diffused by the vast size of the continent, Klan-like units functioned under an assortment of names, ranging from Aryan Knights to Soldiers of the Cross. In many instances the groups vied with one another over the years to become the strongest voice for racial purity. Individual organizations were afflicted with internal strife; warring factions spun off into competing groups. Even in a citadel of segregation such as Mississippi, the Klan was fractured, as Landrum would discover.

But first, Landrum would see just how pervasive the White Knights had become in his own Jones County. He encountered several of his former students and realized he had taught the daughters of one prominent member, Spec Stewart, when he worked in the Jones County school system. Landrum had thought of him as an outstanding citizen in the Glade community outside Laurel. Stewart belonged to the local Lions Club and took part in many of his neighborhood activities. He was employed as an electrician by the Masonite corporation, where he worked alongside another of Landrum's friends, Gerald Martin. To Landrum's dismay, he found that Martin—who held an elected position as a county constable— had enlisted in the Klan, too. So had many other Masonite workers, as well as local white-collar businessmen.

The FBI had asked Landrum for two things in each report—an account of the latest meeting he attended and a list of those present. As he considered his description of his early, uneventful Klan gathering, he pondered his job of informant. He paused before identifying his friends in his dispatch. In school, he remembered, the least popular playmates were the tattletales, the weak-hearted boys who hoped to win favor from their teachers by whispering accusations of mischief. And from movies, Landrum knew that criminal snitches were known as untrustworthy "rats." Yet in the World War II films from the same period, the heroes were often Allied espionage agents risking their lives to defend freedom to speed the defeat of the Nazis. Landrum preferred to think of himself as a spy. It simplified his decision to convey names to the FBI. But he included mitigating material that made them look better. He wrote of Stewart's reservations about aspects of Klan behavior and Martin's complaints that the organization was being taken over by "rumheads." Landrum was interested in Martin's viewpoint because he thought the constable drank too heavily himself.

Before he joined the White Knights, Landrum had assumed that most of the members came from poor backgrounds. He now realized that the group included popular church deacons, respectable businessmen, and civic leaders. He found that Masonite Corporation, the pillar of commerce for Laurel and one of the largest industries in the state, was infested with Klansmen earning respectable salaries. The firm was conceived in the 1920s by the inventive mind of William H. Mason, who once served as an apprentice for Thomas A. Edison and married into a family that owned considerable timberland and sawmills in Jones County. Since Mason needed wood chips and sawdust for his experiments, he moved to Laurel, where he found a way to convert the worthless material into fiberboard. Though he was unable to render a paper product, Mason developed a process that pressed the waste into synthetic lumber, a hard particleboard he called Masonite. Because of its cheap price and relative strength, Masonite attracted heavy demand from construction companies. The inventor's dream eventually materialized into a giant factory where nearly three thousand employees labored under a tin-roof canopy a half mile long, implanting a gritty industrial component into the local economy's rural base.

But Landrum's original perception of the White Knights' membership held up. Many of the Klansmen felt wounded by society. Poorly educated, ignorant of modern skills, and consigned to unrewarding jobs, they seethed over their own situations. Some had served blue-collar apprenticeships as roughnecks on treacherous offshore oil stations in the nearby Gulf or labored on the drilling rigs that dotted Jones County. Others held grim places on the line at minor factories or scrabbled for irregular income as shade-tree mechanics, lumber mill operatives, gas station grease monkeys, door-to-door salesmen of shoddy goods, or farmers striving to wrestle a prosperous crop from the punishing soil in a region too far from the Mississippi River to have been blessed by its rich alluvial deposits.

Resentment boiled up in them like bile from an unsettled stomach, and it somehow hardened into a hatred of the Black man. The alchemy proved powerful in Mississippi, with its history of slavery and suppression. It involved a woolly belief in "the southern way of life," where whites enjoyed dominance and gentle darkies existed to serve them. Even as many of these Klansmen struggled themselves, it was essential to their pride to keep their place above the bottom. The idea of white supremacy was nourished not only at clandestine meetings but also publicly, either from the pulpit, by self-appointed preachers espousing racial doctrines rarely taught at divinity schools, or through myths perpetuated by a long line of political leaders specializing in demagoguery.

As Landrum became better acquainted with his White Knights associates he saw that amid the scores of blue-collar members, public office was represented by not only Leonard Caves, the Jones County circuit clerk, but Charles Blackwell, a young man elected to the state house of representatives only three years after he was old enough to vote.

Caves demonstrated the importance of having Klan members in elective offices. He bragged of his ability to plant at least one White Knight on any prospective jury; in a private conversation with Landrum at the courthouse, Caves told of the latest attempt to subvert the local criminal justice system. Efforts had been made to entice a judge in Laurel to join their group, but the plan had been thwarted when Bob Lee, the FBI agent, learned of the scheme and warned the judge not to get involved. It was obvious to the White Knights that the agent had become well versed about their organization, and that knowledge led to suspicion and rumors about which members might be acting as informants in their midst.

Caves said Lee had come to him recently to inquire about voting records in Jones County. Claiming that he denied the FBI agent access to the files, Caves declared, "I don't care who knows I'm in the Klan." Despite that private boast, Landrum knew that Caves wanted to keep his membership secret.

In some circles in Jones County, belonging to the White Knights was an acceptable way to battle encroachment by the federal government. And the presence of local law enforcement officers in the Klan group—from state highway patrol troopers to policemen and county constables—was thought to counter the work of the FBI.

"I can see this is a group of men who profess to be Christians and claim to be organized to keep the white race pure," Landrum wrote the FBI following one meeting. "A lot of these men are sincere." But he added, "In this organization there are men who will go to any length to achieve personal goals."

⁓

LANDRUM GOT A better sense of the White Knights' modus operandi and commitment to violence at a joint gathering of a couple of the smaller Klan units—which were called "klaverns"—in a remote pasture in late August 1965. It was easy to find out-of-the-way places to meet in Jones County, on uncultivated farmland overgrown with weeds or in clearings in the pine forests. In foul weather, the Klansmen gathered inside, in the privacy of outbuildings owned by members. For meetings, the men sat on portable chairs or wooden benches that had once served as church pews before being sold as junk. Some preferred to stand. After Landrum was welcomed into the fold he was told to feel free, though a newcomer, to speak up if any of the "projects" on their agenda troubled him. He chose to listen to the rambling discussion among the two dozen men present. There were complaints that the Jones County units had become lazy and needed to step up their activity. In some cases, action was advocated in neighboring counties where local segregationists affiliated with rival Klan organizations had dropped their vigilance.

One example lay just to the south, in Forrest County, where the voter-registration efforts of Vernon Dahmer—the "Dahmer Nigger," as he was called—were going on with little interference. The Voting Rights Act—the second leg in President Johnson's civil rights offensive—had become law just three weeks earlier, and Dahmer was said to be working all-out to register as many Blacks as possible. Although the county was named for Nathan Bedford Forrest, the Confederate general who helped found the post–Civil War Klan, some of the Klan's modern supporters in Forrest County had fallen down on the job.

Landrum heard Lawrence Byrd, the senator for the Jones County White Knights, say the problem could be traced to the "sorry-assed" Klan units in Forrest County, which were linked with another organization, the United Klans of America, based in Alabama. "Some of you may say we been lazy," Byrd complained, his voice rising, "but them United boys are downright hopeless. Nobody in his right mind should think of joining up with them, and I'm gonna go down there and tell them to stay the hell out of Jones County. I don't trust the bastards. The FBI is trying to buy people, so I'd be careful who you talk with. Especially anybody connected with United."

Following Byrd's tirade, there were murmurs of approval for a raid into Forrest County that might serve two purposes. It would inhibit the "Dahmer Nigger's" work, and it would demonstrate the superiority of the White Knights over the United Klans group. Sam Bowers was known to have long favored this approach. But he was not on hand that evening, and there were other matters to consider.

One involved the young man they called the Black Stallion, who required punishment for his effrontery toward white women. He was said to have driven behind a pair of schoolteachers for miles, leering behind his windshield as they traveled over back roads. Terrified by the specter of rape, the women reported that the Black motorist had tried three times to force them to pull over. A law enforcement inquiry was handled by Landrum's friend Constable Martin, who informed the Klan that the suspect was twenty-year-old Larry Parker, who lived in neighboring Jasper County. Parker had been subsequently arrested, hauled before a justice-of-the-peace court, and fined fifty-nine dollars—roughly a week's salary—for speeding and carrying a pistol.

The White Knights felt the case called for additional punishment. Several argued that Parker's impudence warranted a severe beating, but extreme action required authorization from the full Jones County council. So the group had to content themselves with terror tactics. They decided to burn his car; maybe his home, too. Someone had another thought: Burn a cross at Bailey's Lumber Company, where Parker worked. If his employer failed to heed the message to dismiss Parker, then the White Knights should burn down the company's sawmill.

A few nights later, Landrum reported that he heard details about a strike delivered by a delegation of White Knights, who laughed as they described their adventure to fellow Klansmen. According to their tale, the men set out for Parker's house in a car bearing a bogus Alabama license plate supplied by a friendly owner of a Laurel automobile dealership. They found a Ford Falcon, painted turquoise and matching the description of Parker's car provided by the constable, parked in the yard, but the house appeared to be empty.

"Come out, you black bastard," one of the men yelled, but the shout produced no movement.

"Screw it," another in the raiding party said. "We'll blow his fucking car to kingdom come." With that, the men trained their shotguns on the Falcon, blasting it with buckshot.

For good measure, the men stopped on their way back to Jones County at a small frame house where a Black woman named Julia Green lived. She had been rumored to be collecting money for the NAACP. She did not seem to be at home, either, so the visitors emptied a plastic gallon jug filled with gasoline across her front door and set fire to the house. The raiders believed their excursion into Jasper County would prove important because it showed the willingness of the Jones County group to help neighbors in a county without its own strong Klan unit.

"While we're torching things," another Klansman suggested at the meeting, "we should burn up that panel truck being used by the COFO people." Landrum learned this referred to volunteers involved with the Council of Federated Organizations, an umbrella group for four major civil rights associations that had sponsored Freedom Summer in Mississippi the year before.

"Red" Caldwell, the county giant, brought up another possibility for burning—the office of a Black physician named Murph. "His floor is made of good heart pine," Caldwell noted with a laugh. "It'll burn real nice."

The recommendations seemed to grow more reckless as the meeting went on. The home, barn, and tractor of an unnamed "uppity" Black man living in the countryside had been burned the week before. In retaliation, the victim and a group of his neighbors had formed a protective ring around the property and were reported to be stopping all cars driven by white men. Caldwell and others suggested a plan in which several White Knights, armed with shotguns, would hide in the back of a pickup; if the Black guards tried to stop the truck, the Klansmen would rise up and start shooting.

Caldwell brimmed with other proposals. "A bunch of niggers been swimming outa Lake Bogue Homa. We need to take some action. What we need is to get about fifty pounds of dynamite and plant it around the gate. Maybe blow a hole in the dam. That'll put a stop to these black nigger bastards."

Not all of the Klan's targets were Black. One scheme called for vigilante action against a white couple said to be involved in an illicit affair. For the White Knights—who had their share of philanderers—to begin imposing moral values sounded silly to Landrum. But others seemed drawn by the sadomasochistic eroticism of the proposal. A raiding party would track the couple to their trysting place, snatch them from their parked car, strip them of whatever clothing they might still be wearing, administer a beating with Black Annie, a whip, then burn their car, leaving them naked and stranded.

The project would never be undertaken. Other ideas would be abandoned as foolhardy. For all the bravado, Landrum detected anxiety among the Klansmen concerning the FBI. There were grumblings about informants and rumors that the White Knights had already been infiltrated by the federal investigators. He heard suggestions of summary punishment—either emasculation or hanging—for anyone caught cooperating with the FBI.

In his dispatch to the FBI the next day, Landrum wrote that the White Knights "are always on guard and think they can outsmart the FBI. Their long range goal is to get a member of the KKK elected President of the United States."

≈

THE NOTION OF a Klansman president sounded preposterous to Landrum, but it had resonance with Klan leaders like Sam Bowers. If the White Knights could hold Jones County in their grip, was it not possible to gain control of Mississippi? Many of the state's leaders were already sympathetic to their cause, if not members themselves. And if the movement spread to other southern states, what was to stop the Klan's march?

The imperial wizard was a student of history, and he believed the Klan could be returned to the grandeur it had enjoyed earlier

in the century, when the Invisible Empire claimed to have six mil-
lion followers nationwide. He was aware that the organization had
numbers and political influence back then. Klansmen had marched
openly, thousands strong, down Pennsylvania Avenue in Washington. There had been a glorious moment in 1924 when the Klan
preyed on the national Democratic convention in New York, where
the Catholic Al Smith seemed close to obtaining his party's presidential nomination in a city teeming with Jews. While the convention staggered through days of deadlock, twenty thousand hooded
Klansmen gathered on July 4 for a picnic on a New Jersey field across
the Hudson River from Manhattan. They were joined by hundreds
of Democratic conventioneers, who also opposed the idea of a Catholic standard-bearer. While a huge wooden cross flamed, the Klansmen tortured effigies of Smith. Five days later, Smith was denied the
nomination; it was given to John W. Davis, a thirty-second-degree
Mason from West Virginia.

With God's blessing, Bowers reasoned, the Invisible Empire
would return to greatness. And in its vanguard would be the glorious White Knights of the Mississippi Ku Klux Klan.

CHAPTER 3

I N THE WEEKS following his induction into the White Knights, Landrum went to sporadic, sparsely attended meetings of his Klan group, usually filled with gossip about Jones County residents—both Black and white—perceived as enemies of the Klan. He heard boasts of actions that could be taken against anyone who might challenge their authority. Fire, he learned, was the weapon of choice, an instrument of destruction that had been perfected by the Klan as a method of spreading terror for post–Civil War raiders in the latter years of the nineteenth century. They sought to restore Confederate values by frightening freed slaves with flaming crosses or by burning out their humble homes in the countryside. Fire now served as an essential tool for the modern Klan. For all of the imperial wizard's talk of Christian militancy, his followers subscribed to the pagan belief that fire was a purifying agent.

The exalted cyclops of Landrum's group, Speed Lightsey, holding forth at a meeting in his barn, noted approvingly that fire had already consumed a quarter-million dollars' worth of property in Jones County, sending an ominous message. One coordinated series of mysterious conflagrations in Laurel had consumed nearly thirty houses. One night the Klan torched a collection of buildings recently vacated by Black residents in order to divert the fire department from their real target—a structure that served as headquarters for the civil rights organization known as COFO, which they also burned down. "It's one way to keep the nigger under fear," he said. Since Lightsey operated a service station in the rural community of Shady Grove, he was looked on as a reliable source of fuel. Landrum had known Lightsey for years, thinking him to be a well-educated man who had a large farm and owned a couple of gas stations on the side.

Lightning might be blamed for fire in a dry season, but it was obvious that the outbreak of fires in Jones County was caused by arson, and the Klan's threats extended to unfriendly whites. After several burn-outs in the Sandersville community, the White Knights heard that a local man said publicly that responsibility could be traced to the Klan. The group preferred gasoline, the man claimed, because "they know kerosene doesn't burn fast enough." When the remark got back to the gang at Speed Lightsey's barn, it caused anger and provoked suggestions of punishment—either a Code Two (cross-burning) or Code Three (serious beating). The man's wife was also said to be "too talkative." But any strong discipline was supposed to be approved at the organization's county level. In the end the man was simply warned to "keep his nose out of Klan activities."

Landrum, already uneasy attending the meetings, grew even more uncomfortable after hearing a suggestion to burn the home of his friend Charles Pickering, the county attorney whose antipathy toward the Klan was well known.

LANDRUM DUTIFULLY FILED reports to the FBI about these discussions as well as recommendations he overheard. To follow up on a recent fire that had leaped from one small frame house to another in Laurel, there were calls to torch entire blocks in Black residential neighborhoods in the city as a tactic of intimidation. But the targets were usually small frame homes in sparsely populated areas. A few relatively harmless cross-burnings were also carried out.

Some members felt the scattered activity failed to deliver a strong message. One young and enthusiastic member proposed "hanging a nigger in every county throughout the state" to show they meant business. Landrum, who had just been elected secretary for his klavern, finally felt he had the credibility to speak up. Violence of this sort, he warned, would be counterproductive and would bring down the wrath of the federal government on Mississippi.

To Landrum, the meetings seemed pointless. Then one night his group was visited by the leader, and the agenda took on more purpose. Sam Bowers was known as a man of action who had risen in less than two years from obscurity as an inconsequential businessman in Jones County to take charge of a shadowy organization spreading terror across the state. Bowers was a suspect in the murders in Neshoba County; the FBI believed he was the mastermind behind the plot. As his infamy spread, he actually appeared to enjoy the notoriety.

Landrum had never seen Bowers before. On first impression, Bowers was a puzzling figure. Compared to the other Klansmen, his speaking manner was articulate, his grammar polished. But there was something odd about him. Not only did he seem to be proud to be implicated in the Neshoba County affair, he bragged of being subpoenaed to appear before a congressional committee investigating several Ku Klux Klan organizations operating in the United States. Bowers told Landrum's klavern of a coming trip to Washington when he hoped to be accompanied by Klan warriors who might fill an entire car on the Crescent, a passenger train that ran daily from New Orleans and passed through Laurel on its way to the nation's capital. A big turnout would demonstrate the White Knights' power and solidarity. Bowers promised that the committee would get no information from him, and he predicted that none of the other southern Klan leaders summoned to Washington would cooperate with the congressmen. To underscore Bowers's vow of silence, one of his followers shouted before the brief meeting ended, "Anybody doing any talking in Washington will not live to get back to Jones County."

Bowers reappeared a week later at a larger meeting in Lightsey's barn, where he spent nearly an hour encouraging the group to have more confidence in a task he described as divine. He spoke again of the necessity for a "Christian militancy" to combat a moral laxity in society. He talked of the value of having White Knights serving as "chaplains" to open each meeting with a prayer. Bowers also cited scriptural references to buttress his assurances that the work of the White Knights was a righteous enterprise. Landrum was astonished to hear Bowers tell the group of his strong Christian beliefs while engaged in a campaign involving terror and murder. He wondered about the true character of the imperial wizard.

≈

BOWERS TALKED LITTLE of his personal religious experiences, but he once confided to a theologian that he had been saved by a sudden intervention by God during a dark moment in his life in the 1950s. The experience occurred, he said, while he was driving a pickup truck, thinking of suicide. "The living God made himself real to me even when I did not deserve it," he claimed, though he was reluctant to compare it to the apostle Paul's conversion on the road to Damascus. "God used his blackjack on Paul a lot more vigorously than he did on me." But his conversion led him to study "the majesty of language" in the King James version of the Bible and he became convinced that he had been called by the Lord to take up the work of preserving the purity of his blood and his land.

In private conversations with individuals he thought of as intellectuals, he revealed many of his inner thoughts. He felt ordained to cleanse the countryside of "heretics," such as civil rights activists, "liberal media whores," and "pagan academics." Rigidly anti-Semitic, he declared Jesus a "Galilean" rather than a Jew. After ascending to his leadership position in the White Knights, he imposed his own religious strictures on their ranks. He knew his members were not strangers to profanity, but he discouraged curse words in formal meetings. In one Klan recruiting bulletin he wrote that the national government was "under the actual control of atheists who are Bolsheviks by nature." His Klansmen, on the other hand, were described as "Christians who are anxious to preserve not only their souls for all eternity, but who are MILITANTLY DETERMINED, God willing, to save their lives and the life of this nation" by ensuring the racial purity of their descendants. According to the pamphlet, Jews were unacceptable "because they reject Christ" and were subjects of an international banking cartel; Catholics were considered hopeless because "they bow to a Roman dictator."

For a leader who commanded a following of thousands of Mississippi Klansmen committed to fighting the civil rights movement, Bowers did not appear particularly messianic. The forty-two-year-old man had a slight frame, lacked a strong speaking voice, and looked more milquetoast than menacing. He wore his hair long enough to allow a careful part, but an unruly lock repeatedly fell across his forehead, giving him the appearance of a hapless character from the comics pages of daily newspapers.

Yet within two years Bowers had built the White Knights into a deadly operation. He believed his work was not only inspired by God but blessed by his ancestors. Bowers's pedigree was stronger than that of most Klansmen. He had a touch of college and could claim class from a family background imbued with southern gentility and political influence. Still, he had an affinity for the uneducated, working-class men usually associated with the Klan. He expressed admiration for "these simple, disadvantaged, low-economic people who were standing up on their hind legs and defying the Federal government." Once, in a long, philosophical discussion of his role as a leader, Bowers said, "I am not ashamed to be an uncultured, uncouth, ignorant redneck." But he also sought the company of better-educated men—lawyers and preachers—whom he lured into his organization.

When he talked about himself, it was apparent Bowers had cultivated an unconventional persona from an early age, drawing on his great-grandfather's role as a vengeful Confederate cavalry officer turned postwar night rider. He also cited shamelessly his grandfather's reputation as an unreconstructed four-term congressman, as well as his father's checkered employment record of bouncing from job to job, a malcontent who despised bureaucrats. Like his forefathers, Bowers bore allegiance to the fallen Confederacy; more emphatically, he took inspiration from the "underground guerrilla tactics and conspiracies" carried out by the remnants of the rebel army in the years after Appomattox. Bowers delved even further back into history, tracing his nonconformist spirit to earlier Scottish ancestors, a family tree that he said included revolutionaries as well as kings' chancellors. "I draw from both revolutionary and establishment people," he claimed. "I think that is rather unique."

Reasons for Bowers's reactionary beliefs and bloodlust could be found in his own rendering of his family history. The imperial wizard was especially proud of his great-grandfather E. J. Bowers, whom he characterized as a "war criminal" because of his take-no-prisoners approach while serving as an officer in the army of the Confederate States of America. After he found one of his scouts hanged, the body left dangling from a tree, he "lynched every Yankee soldier he got his hands on," the great-grandson noted approvingly. Later, Bowers noted, the officer became a "conspirator," part of an "underground guerrilla movement who threw the Yankee Reconstruction carpet-baggers and scallywags out of here." The guerrillas wore no robes and did not follow quasi-religious rituals. They called themselves the "Confederate Officers Corps" rather than the Ku Klux Klan. But according to Bowers, they engaged in night riding "to recover Southern civilization," using Klan tactics of kidnapping, whipping, burning, and lynching. As a result, he said, these men from a vanquished army were able to achieve "a near miraculous social revolution overnight."

One hundred years later, Sam Bowers would say, "If any stability is ever brought back into our public life, it is going to be done by the same kind of people." The Klan leader did not shrink from the word "fascism"; he embraced it. Not the "horrible" communist kind of fascism, he said, but a "religious fascism" that could lead to the highest type of government. His theories would evolve into the "Christian militancy" that became a tenet of the White Knights.

Sam Bowers believed this strange tradition of conspiracy and fascism passed naturally from E. J. Bowers, CSA, to that man's son, E. J. Bowers Jr., a man born the year the Civil War ended in 1865 and destined to be elected to Congress in 1903 as the representative of a south Mississippi district that included the Gulf Coast region. "Had he not been part of what I consider to be an underground, ideal fascist conspiracy operating for the benefit of the former Confederacy" he would not have succeeded, Bowers said of his grandfather.

The imperial wizard had fond memories of the old congressman and the recognition he brought to the Bowers family. From his days as a schoolboy in Jackson, Sam remembered how prominent men "would point me out as being E.J. Bowers' grandson, as if I was the grandson of the pope." The politician was said to have parlayed his service on President Theodore Roosevelt's Panama Canal Commission to win federal appropriations to control yellow fever, a move resulting in money for Mississippi. Congressman Bowers, who believed in the innate ignorance of Blacks, was considered part of an "apostolic succession" of hard-core segregationists who held the district's congressional seat from his era to the present, when Representative William Colmer used his legerdemain as chairman of the House Rules Committee to stall civil rights bills. (Ironically, Bowers had been defeated in 1910 by a future governor, Paul Johnson Sr., whose own son, Paul Johnson Jr., was elected governor of Mississippi in 1963. Though the younger Johnson attracted thousands of segregationist votes, he was now thought by the Klan to be too accommodating to Blacks.)

The strength of the Bowers legacy began to wilt with Sam's own father, Samuel H. Bowers Sr. A cotton broker when his son was born in New Orleans in 1924, he abruptly moved his family to Florida in pursuit of cashing in on a land boom when Sam was an infant. After his dream faded, Sam Sr. wound up in Jackson, where he took advantage of the former congressman's connections to get a job as a policeman for the Illinois Central Railroad. Rather than thinking of his father as a failure, Sam praised him for being a rebel, "highly individualistic and opinionated," and unwilling to be "fit into the bureaucratic mold."

While boasting of the unorthodox characters among his paternal ancestors, Bowers was also proud of a possible connection on his mother's side in the World War II years, one that most Americans would have hidden. Intrigued by genealogy, he traced her family back to Germany. Bowers claimed his own facial characteristics were more German than Celtic. Doubling down on his German connection, he said he was not embarrassed to speculate about a family link to Rudolf Hess, a bizarre figure in Nazi lore. Hess had been Hitler's deputy führer before taking off on a mysterious flight to Scotland in 1941. After being captured, Hess claimed he had wanted to broker a peace with the United Kingdom. Instead, he was held in British custody until the end of the war, when he was returned to Germany to stand trial as a war criminal. After conviction, he lived in Spandau Prison until he hanged himself at ninety-three.

By the time young Bowers became a student at Jackson's Central High—the city's only white high school—his father and grandfather had slid into "genteel poverty." His parents were separated and he lived with his mother in a respectable neighborhood in the state capital. He had a brother and a sister but seldom mentioned them. The teenage Sam Bowers had fallen under the influence of a classmate named Bill Thompson, a troublesome maverick who practiced "guerrilla tactics" of his own. Thompson organized a secret band of renegade students—Sam was one of them—who would break into the school building at night and tear up the homerooms of teachers they felt were "persecuting" them. The teenage vandalism was a precursor to the activities Bowers encouraged among the White Knights a generation later.

Looking back, Bowers happily admitted his youthful indiscretions. "I refused to acknowledge authority," the Klan leader said. "I don't regret I'm not an insurance company lawyer, which is what I would have been if I had conformed."

The last bit of conformity forced on him came from the military during World War II. Shortly after Pearl Harbor Bowers enlisted in the navy, before finishing high school. He served more than three years but never rose above the rank of first-class petty officer as a boiler-room mechanic. Originally assigned to ships confined to the San Francisco harbor, he finally sailed aboard a vessel ferrying matériel to marines in the Pacific during the closing stages of World War II. He saw no combat action.

His navy records indicated only one minor indiscretion. After being recorded as "absent without leave" for six hours, a court-martial docked his pay nineteen dollars a month for several pay periods. He was honorably discharged.

As a young civilian, he used his navy experience to qualify for enough credits to earn a diploma from Fortier High School in New Orleans, and he spent a semester as a student at nearby Tulane University under the GI Bill, then wandered to Los Angeles, where he enrolled at the University of Southern California. After receiving a grade of D in physics and withdrawing from a course in math, Bowers dropped out. He returned to New Orleans with no real vocation in mind. His father called from Mississippi. He told Sam he had met a man who was going broke and wanted to sell his pinball business in Laurel. In those days, many small-town cafés and truck stops had the devices tucked into their corners as a source of revenue. Customers would spend a nickel competing to see who could best maneuver rolling steel balls beneath a glass shield; the game required a gift at flipping levers to control the direction of the balls.

"I had become fascinated by these things," Bowers said. "I was mechanically attracted to the wiring complexities of these machines." He settled in Laurel and invested in the modest enterprise, despite his complaint that "you deal with the real seamy side of life . . . real low-class" in the pinball and jukebox business. Even though he bragged of his refusal to conform, Bowers at the same time appreciated his links to southern aristocracy.

It was an attitude shared by Byron De La Beckwith, the free-lance Klansman who had murdered the civil rights leader Medgar Evers in Jackson in 1963. After his arrest, Beckwith called attention to his family's once-privileged status in the Mississippi Delta city of Greenwood. No matter that the old Beckwith homestead was in shambles; he still felt part of the elite class. "Country Club Missis-sippi," Beckwith sneered, "is tired of this crap the Jews, niggers, and Orientals are stirring up."

≈

THOUGH BOWERS HAD returned to the Deep South with what he called "loose and liberal West Coast attitudes," he changed as he adjusted to life in Laurel. "I gradually came to like the backward-ness and ruralness" of Jones County, he later told an interviewer. He moved into living quarters in the back of his business, which he gave the eponymous name of Sambo Amusement Company, which occu-pied a grungy building with a front door of corrugated metal and windows that were boarded and sealed, in a predominantly Black neighborhood. The place looked more appropriate for a junkyard dog than a man, yet it served as home for his fairly primitive lifestyle. A few years later, Bowers was joined by a friend from his Southern Cal days, Robert Larson, who became a partner in Sambo Amusement and moved into the building, which was reportedly filthy inside. Their living arrangement caused at least one visitor to speculate that Bowers was "queer," but it seems unlikely that members of the White Knights, who exuded machismo, would have accepted a homosexual as their leader. Bowers remained single and childless. Reflecting on his monastic state, he would say, "I grew up with some of the nicest girls in Jackson, Mississippi. I had a fairly decent name in that soci-ety. I could have married one of those girls. I could have gotten a fairly decent job in Jackson. I could have raised a decent family and keep my mouth shut and done an honest day's work and been a good husband and all that. But I just wasn't fitted for that kind of thing."

In Laurel, the Masonite plant was his closest neighbor, and he eventually chose as his friends a cadre of working-class men. Though they were largely uneducated, he felt they were equipped with hon-est wisdom in their racial views and their hatred of a misguided fed-eral government in Washington.

He found biblical foundation for his views. He joined the

congregation of a Baptist church a couple of miles outside Laurel and began teaching a men's Sunday-school class, where he honed his philosophy of "Christian militancy."

≈

BOWERS ESPOUSED THE doctrine of segregation that was prevalent in the area, and he came to believe that a violent approach was necessary to preserve white civilization and culture. Meanwhile, the South boiled over the dictates from Washington that threatened tradition. Following the 1954 desegregation decision, billboards appeared on Mississippi highways demanding the impeachment of the chief justice, Earl Warren. Only half facetiously, Bowers endorsed the idea of lynching members of the court. "I suppose that if that bunch around Masonite could have gotten hold of any of those Supreme Court judges they would have given them the benefit of some rope elevation," he said. "I think that I would have probably joined more enthusiastically in hanging a white Supreme Court judge than I would be a nigger rapist. . . . I am really more of an enemy of white Washington than I am the black race."

In 1959, a real lynching took place in Pearl River County, about fifty miles south of Laurel. With the apparent complicity of law enforcement officers, a mob stormed the jail, jerked a Black man named Mack Charles Parker from his cell where he was awaiting trial for rape, and executed him before the state could perform the task. Bowers approved of the action. He described the rape victim as a defenseless white woman and Parker as "a savage male beast who happened to be black."

Three years later, the state of Mississippi exploded after a court order demanded that the state university in Oxford permit a Black man, James Meredith, to enroll as a student. The rebellion was led by Governor Ross Barnett, a garrulous country lawyer who had ridden to office with the support of a statewide Citizens' Council organization that had been formed to fight integration. By rejecting the court order, Barnett provoked a constitutional confrontation between the state and the federal government. The showdown came on a Sunday night in September in Oxford, when hundreds of white supremacists, energized by the mentality of a lynch mob, took over the campus and battled federal marshals and U.S. troops sent to enforce the order. When the bloody riot was over, two were dead, hundreds wounded or arrested, and thousands of soldiers were in place in Oxford to impose what was effectively a form of martial law over the area. To Mississippi segregationists, the occupation became a symbol of a neo-Reconstruction being visited on Mississippi. Bowers didn't blame Barnett; he considered the governor a patriotic hero.

As Bowers saw it, the situation in Mississippi had evolved into war with Washington. It was time to take up arms against the federal government. He wanted to become a "patriotic warrior" himself, helping to mobilize "a group of politically incompetent rednecks down in Mississippi standing up against imperial police authority." He was also willing to serve as a spiritual leader of that effort.

A new effort was needed, he felt, because political opposition to federal court decisions had failed to block integration at Ole Miss, and the dominant segregationist group in the state, the Citizens' Councils, had proved ineffective in slowing the momentum of the civil rights movement. By the beginning of 1964 Congress was moving toward sweeping legislation that would extend basic rights to Black citizens. On top of that, there were rumors of an invasion of northern students that summer dedicated to changing southern society. The developments called for immediate action by white supremacists willing to take the fight to the last ditch.

In February 1964, a new organization was formed at a rally in Brookhaven with remnants of the Mississippi chapter of a Louisiana-based group, the Anti-Communist Christian Association, which also called itself the Original Knights of the Ku Klux Klan. At its birth, the White Knights of the Mississippi Ku Klux Klan promised to adopt stronger measures to confront the integrationists.

The first leader of the group, Douglas Byrd, was under suspicion for mismanaging funds for the Original Knights and became an easy mark for Bowers. He overthrew Byrd after a brief power struggle. Gaining control, Bowers traveled up and down the state, helping to establish White Knights outposts in many counties. Drumming up support among Klansmen in Lauderdale County, where Meridian represented an urban center with a number of prominent Jewish residents, Bowers told the group that "Zionists were a greater threat" than the Blacks. Nevertheless, he said, Blacks posed their own threat to the southern way of life and had to be dealt with. His remarks helped spawn a situation where the White Knights in Meridian were known as "Jew-Haters" while their associates in neighboring Neshoba County won a reputation as "Nigger-Haters." Their differing priorities actually led to a fistfight before they came together for a bloody operation.

Two weeks before the three young civil rights workers disappeared in June, Bowers spoke at a state meeting of the White Knights in Raleigh, a small town near Laurel, where he delivered a curious message. Noting that activists were about to arrive in Mississippi, Bowers advised his followers to "catch them" outside the protection of federal law. That way, he said, under Mississippi law, "you have the right to kill them." To give an example of the successful practice of violence, he falsely claimed that rioters had succeeded in killing six federal marshals during the disturbance at Ole Miss. The "information" had been suppressed, he said, by Attorney General Robert Kennedy because the marshals had been sent to the campus illegally.

It was in the first days of Freedom Summer that Michael Schwerner and Andrew Goodman, two Jews, and James Chaney, a Black man, were slain by Bowers's men. Before the end of June, FBI agents were swarming in the region and the investigation was leading to the White Knights. Bowers said he had "inside information" that a spy existed among the "Jew-Haters" in Meridian. Implicit in his talk was the prospect of death for anyone cooperating with the FBI. A web of suspicion settled over the Klan units that had been involved in the Neshoba operation. Bowers returned to Meridian in November and suggested that one of the prime movers in the murders, a backwoods preacher named Edgar Killen, might have been getting money from the FBI. "I don't believe he's talking," Bowers said. But to be sure, Killen was not invited to an important meeting of ranking figures in the White Knights in Meridian the next day.

Killen and seventeen others were rounded up by the FBI three weeks later and arrested on federal charges of conspiring to deprive the three slain civil rights activists of their constitutional rights. Two others were accused of withholding knowledge of a felony. Federal authorities took action because the state of Mississippi had shown little interest in participating in the investigation or in filing more serious charges of murder against the suspects.

The Klan's fears that they had been infiltrated were justified, but they suspected the wrong man. It was not Killen but another self-declared minister, who reveled in wearing a clerical collar and had grown up not far from Neshoba County. Twenty-six-year-old Delmar Dennis had been given the title of Klan "chaplain," and like an old-fashioned circuit-riding preacher he traveled to White Knights events in numerous counties to ask for God's blessings. But he was also reporting to J. Edgar Hoover's agents.

$$\approx$$

ALTHOUGH BOWERS ESCAPED the early wave of arrests by the FBI, his activities were being closely followed. Bob Lee, the FBI agent in Laurel who would later recruit Landrum for his undercover role, was given the assignment to stalk Bowers. The FBI first interviewed Bowers in May 1964—only months after he was crowned as the imperial wizard—following an explosion that rocked the offices of the *Laurel Leader-Call*, the local newspaper. He denied that he was a Klan member and said he knew nothing about the bombing. Larson, his roommate, corroborated his alibi that they had been out collecting money from vending machines late that night.

Bowers spurned another attempt by Lee to interview him, in January 1965, as the FBI was closing in on suspects in the Neshoba murders. He insisted he had no connection with the White Knights. He speculated that "some Tory had conceived the idea." Investigators knew otherwise from their informers in his midst. Lee was well known in Laurel, and his conversations with Bowers took on the aspect of a cat-and-mouse game. Their first extended talk took place in February, triggered by a strange letter from Bowers to J. Edgar Hoover in Washington. In it, Bowers complained that FBI agents had forced their way into his home in an attempt to implicate him in the Neshoba killings. At the same time, Bowers expressed admiration for Hoover for carrying out his crusade against communism. Throughout his long career, Hoover curried a flattering image for himself, not only as a courageous G-man fighting organized crime but as a relentless foe of communism in America. During the early stages of the Cold War, after World War II—formative years for Bowers—Hoover cooperated with radio shows that praised him fulsomely. In the 1950s—long before television came to the Deep South—listeners followed weekly exploits of *I Was a Communist for the FBI*, a spin-off of a popular book, on a national radio network. Hoover himself wrote a bestseller in 1958, *Masters of Deceit: The Story of Communism in America and How to Fight It*. Bowers's letter seemed to indicate that Hoover, the director of the very agency laboring to track down members of the Ku Klux Klan, was a hero to the imperial wizard of the White Knights.

A copy of the letter was bucked from FBI headquarters in Washington back to Laurel and into the hands of Lee, who was ordered to follow up. When Lee knocked at the front of Sambo Amusement, Bowers peeked out cautiously. But once Lee showed him the copy of the letter, Bowers began to talk. He again praised the FBI director for his anti-communist work and eventually opened the door wider to make the conversation easier. The FBI agent took advantage of the opportunity to bring up the role in Mississippi of the White Knights, who considered communists to be as grave an enemy as integrationists. Lee noted that after the arrests in the Neshoba case apprehension appeared on the rise in the klaverns. "I hear people are drifting away from your group," he told Bowers.

Bowers squatted in the doorway, looking anxiously up and down the remote street. He ignored Lee's remark. They talked a bit more. Bowers never acknowledged any connection to the Klan. But he knew Bob Lee was compiling a dossier on him.

The pair had another conversation a month later. This time Bowers lectured Lee, telling him that communists had infiltrated the federal government at all levels. He accused the FBI of becoming "tools" of the subversive movement. When Lee asked Bowers about problems with his own organization, Bowers said, "Oh, things are going all right."

A few weeks later, Lee received some interesting correspondence from Bowers, who had enclosed two pieces of mail sent to the Klansman from white supremacist groups—one was from the American Nazi Party—as well as a copy of a letter from Bowers to the postmaster asking him to "abstain" from delivering such objectionable literature. In a personal, typewritten letter to Lee, Bowers declared, "I am a loyal citizen of the Republic" dedicated to "the preservation of our Christian nation." He closed by telling Lee, "I sincerely appreciate the work which your organization has done in the past in tracking down the deadly communists who are destroying our country." He signed it "Yours sincerely, Sam H. Bowers."

Yet when Lee approached him again, Bowers was uncommunicative. In his memo for the growing FBI file, Lee reported that Bowers "terminated the interview" abruptly and gave him a business card:

SAM H. BOWERS JR.
Political Investigator
Christian American Whig
820 South Fourth St.
Laurel, Miss.

Bowers was resolute. Another restless summer was at hand. The klaverns Bowers had established in the area around Neshoba County had been sapped by the arrests and seemed to be rife with informants. It was clear the FBI wanted to ensnare him, while the civil rights movement marched forward to new goals. To strike back, Bowers decided to call on his power base in his home, Jones County, and to move against the "Dahmer Nigger," who seemed to be operating with impunity next door in Forrest County.

CHAPTER 4

TOM LANDRUM KNEW of the Black activist as simply the "Dahmer Nigger," the term that he heard Klansmen spit out with contempt. Outside his own corner of Mississippi, Vernon Dahmer was not widely recognized. Even among civil rights leaders, Dahmer's name had yet to be established in the pantheon of American heroes. Though his work in his home community was largely unsung beyond Forrest County, his tenacious efforts to register Blacks as voters and his defiance of threats by angry segregationists were finally beginning to earn him a strong reputation locally and were turning him into a target for the Klan.

Dahmer enjoyed more independence than most Blacks in the South. As a successful farmer and businessman he was free from the economic pressures often used against others, who faced the prospect of losing their jobs if they dared challenge the system. He lived a few miles outside of Hattiesburg, a small city slightly larger than Laurel, on the same farm where he had been born in 1908. His family's roots in Mississippi could be traced to the latter part of the eighteenth century—actually running deeper than those of most of his white adversaries. The Dahmer place was located in Kelly Settlement, a community named for one of his ancestors. Though his formal education had ended in the tenth grade, Dahmer prospered on the land he owned, expanding its size over the years from the forty acres he inherited to more than two hundred. With the number of acres planted in cotton regulated by the federal government, Dahmer had one of the largest allotments in Forrest County. He was among the first in the area to invest in a mechanical cotton picker, and he shared it with at least one other, white, farmer. Over the years, he added a small store adjacent to his home that sold groceries, some clothing, and miscellaneous toiletries. He also built a sawmill to take advantage of the thriving timber industry in the Piney Woods. Dahmer was not only a lifetime resident of the area; he was respected by most of his neighbors—white and Black.

Despite his relative comfort Dahmer was not content. He began to take a role in local affairs in 1946 when he and B. F. Bourn, a fellow farmer at Kelly Settlement who operated a grocery store in a Black neighborhood in Hattiesburg, founded the Forrest County chapter of the National Association for the Advancement of Colored People (NAACP). They discovered a growing interest in the organization, especially among Black servicemen who had returned from the war to find the same old discrimination at home. Four years later, Dahmer joined fourteen others in filing a lawsuit against the circuit clerk, Luther Cox, for his refusal to allow Blacks to register to vote. As a young man, Dahmer had once been qualified to vote, but when authorities ordered a re-registration to purge the rolls in 1949, Cox rejected his attempts to sign up again. Relying on a state law that permitted voting registrars to test applicants with an interpretation of a selected provision of the Mississippi Constitution, Cox repeatedly denied Dahmer. He said Dahmer and dozens of other Blacks were unable to explain the meaning of one sentence: "No person shall be deprived of life, liberty or property except by due process of the law." Cox reassured local whites that he could keep the voting rolls pure by asking other questions of Black applicants, such as "How many bubbles are in a bar of soap?" The lawsuit against the county official got nowhere during this period when it was considered unthinkable for Blacks to take legal action like this.

Instead of accepting his fate, Dahmer continued to push for the right to vote. He encouraged others to beat a path to the courthouse, a foreboding brick structure with a long flight of steps and four enormous white pillars guarding the entrance. Though they were all turned down, Dahmer built a record of their rejections that could be used someday. He invented a mantra for his effort: "If you can't vote, you don't count." In a few years his work gained momentum when even more Mississippi Blacks—beaten down by a history of slavery, discrimination, and oppression—grew impatient for change. They were inspired by the Supreme Court's decision in 1954 outlawing segregation in public schools, and energies were further aroused the next year by the murder of Emmett Till in the Mississippi Delta and the bus boycott inspired by Rosa Parks in Montgomery, Alabama. Finally, there were more than mere murmurs of discontent. The modern civil rights movement was underway, and Dahmer became its leader in Hattiesburg.

≈

DAHMER NEEDED few incentives to challenge the system, but he was galvanized by the cruel punishment meted out to his friend and neighbor Clyde Kennard after Kennard, a decorated Korean War veteran two decades younger than Dahmer, attempted to break the color barrier at Mississippi Southern College (now the University of Southern Mississippi), the largest four-year school in the lower half of the state. After serving as a paratrooper and studying at the University of Chicago, Kennard had come back to start a small poultry enterprise near Dahmer's land. Kennard made several efforts to enroll at the all-white college in Hattiesburg, beginning as early as 1956. Each time he was rejected. When he applied again in 1959, his persistence resulted in a series of retaliations. A farming cooperative attempted to foreclose on Kennard's poultry operation and an insurance company canceled liability coverage on his car. The Mississippi Sovereignty Commission, a state agency recently created to preserve segregation, investigated Kennard and found that, among other things, he had associated with a Jewish "self-confessed communist."

Local segregationists considered some drastic schemes to put Kennard in his place, including a proposal to rig dynamite to the starter of his car, but they decided against violent means. There were easier ways to take care of Kennard, in the courts of Mississippi.

On the same day Kennard attempted to enroll at Mississippi Southern in 1959, he was arrested after local lawmen claimed he had been driving recklessly. The officers reported that a search of his car yielded several bottles of whiskey. Since Mississippi still officially observed Prohibition, Kennard was accused of bootlegging. He insisted he had been framed. No one in authority listened to him, and he was fined $600 after an appearance in a bush-league Mississippi court.

A year later Kennard was arrested again. This time he was sent to prison to serve a seven-year sentence after being convicted by an all-white jury of stealing five small bags of chicken feed. (The key witness against him later recanted his testimony.) While imprisoned at the state penitentiary at Parchman, a sprawling twenty-one-thousand-acre work farm in the Mississippi Delta, a medical diagnosis found Kennard suffering from colon cancer. He was allowed to undergo surgery at the University of Mississippi Medical Center in 1961 but then sent back to Parchman to work as a laborer. Two years later he was released to die. The comedian Dick Gregory, a tireless civil rights activist, paid for Kennard's flight to Chicago to be treated there for the last five months of his life.

After his neighbor was sent away, Dahmer and his sons helped support Kennard by collecting eggs from the hens on Kennard's farm and taking them to a grocery store for sale. As the longtime president of the county NAACP, Dahmer was upset by the injustices visited on his friend and worked to inject new life into an organization dominated by elderly members. It was invigorating for him to be associated with two of the better-known civil rights leaders of the organization, Medgar Evers, the ubiquitous NAACP field secretary who traveled to hot spots around the state, and Aaron Henry, the group's state president.

After attending a civil rights rally on the same night that President John F. Kennedy first championed the movement in a major speech, in June 1963, Evers had reason to feel elated. Clutching a handful of NAACP T-shirts as he emerged from his car in the driveway of his home in Jackson, he was shot in the back and killed by a sniper. Evers became one of the first well-known martyrs of the era, but his assassination failed to daunt the movement in Mississippi. In fact, Dahmer was energized by fury.

In Hattiesburg, the county seat of Forrest County, which lies immediately below Jones County, Dahmer began working in concert with a new coalition of civil rights groups, the Council of Federated Organizations. The council represented four organizations that had previously been driven by differing philosophies and competed for contributions and membership: the NAACP, Martin Luther King's Southern Christian Leadership Conference (SCLC), the youthful Student Nonviolent Coordinating Committee (SNCC), and the Congress of Racial Equality (CORE). In a rare instance of cooperation, the various organizations had come together to form a single group to oversee activity in the state.

≈

ON TOP OF HIS civil rights activities there was an unusual characteristic about Dahmer that posed a special irritant to the Klan. His complexion appeared almost ashen, so light that he could have posed as a white man and not been discovered. One member of the White Knights confessed to his mates that he once completed a business deal with Dahmer by unwittingly shaking hands, "thinking he was a white man." In racist circles it was taboo to shake hands with a Black man because the act could be perceived as putting him on equal footing.

Some of the White Knights called him the "white nigger," resenting him for having flesh as pale as their own sun-weathered skin. Dahmer became accustomed to getting threatening telephone calls at home. Occasionally the callers would refer to his complexion.

"You may think you're a white man," they would tell him. "But we know you're nothing but a no-good black nigger."

Dahmer was a burly yet handsome man. He kept his hair closely cropped and groomed a thin mustache as debonair as that of the movie star Errol Flynn. Yet he made no effort to pass for white. He exhibited his pride in being a Black man through his leadership role with the NAACP. It was not widely known, but Dahmer happened to look like a white man because he was descended from three generations of a family whose racial distinctions were as tangled as the doomed Sutpen family in William Faulkner's novel *Absalom, Absalom!*

Dahmer was a product of what Natasha Trethewey, a Mississippi-born poet laureate of the United States, would call the "muck of ancestry" affecting Black populations in the South. Dahmer's great-grandfather was an Irishman named Osborn Kelly who moved from Georgia to Mississippi territory in 1790 and established a frontier home in a tract of land between the Bowie and Leaf Rivers that eventually became known as Kelly Settlement. After building a homestead, Kelly acquired a slave girl named Sara, who eventually bore twelve children said to have been sired by either Kelly or other white men. All of the children, who grew up in slavery, took Kelly as their family name. The youngest was a boy, Warren Kelly, who married a young slave woman named Henrietta. She, too, was the product of an interracial relationship, between her mother and a white Mississippi man named McComb. Eleven children came from this union, including a daughter, Ellen Kelly, who married a local man named George Dahmer. George's father—Vernon's grandfather—was Charlie Dahmer, the son of a German settler and a half-white slave woman. The marriage of George Dahmer and Ellen Kelly, whose ebony African roots had been diluted by more than a century of interracial coupling, produced a son, Vernon, in 1908 who could have enrolled in an all-white school without being questioned.

Vernon's own marriages were more traditional. He first fathered three children with a youthful bride, before they divorced. He had three more children with a second wife, who died from cancer before she was forty. He then married a schoolteacher named Ellie Jewell.

They were the parents of two children, Dennis and Bettie, who lived with them in the neat brick home next to the family's store.

Vernon and Ellie Dahmer seemed to have no problems in the farming community, where whites lived alongside Blacks on Monroe Road. Ellie was known to be industrious and once had the reputation of being able to pick one hundred pounds of cotton in the afternoon after coming home from school. Although her job as a teacher in the segregated public school system in a neighboring county was jeopardized by her husband's civil rights activity, Ellie Dahmer did not seem to worry about it. She was discreet and was careful to keep her occupation separate from his work, which involved not only his interest in voter registration but his vocation as a farmer-businessman and a lay leader in his church.

Like his father, Vernon served as a pillar of the Shady Grove Baptist Church. He was a Sunday-school superintendent who insisted that his children attend church services. As a member of the congregation's "Sick Committee," he sometimes visited as many as ten ailing Baptists during a weekend.

Dahmer's lifelong relationship with the church grew strained once he became committed to his voter-registration campaign. In his haste to hold an organizational meeting he told his NAACP allies that it could be scheduled at Shady Grove. But when he sought formal permission from the congregation during Sunday services, an influential minister from a large Black church in Hattiesburg intervened, arguing that churches should have no affiliation with politics. Many Black churches in the South served as battle stations for the movement, offering sites for rallies and sanctuary for activists whose lives were endangered. Rev. Ralph Willard, however, had a long record of cooperating with local law enforcement officers to discourage unrest among his parishioners. After he spoke out against Dahmer, Shady Grove Baptist Church was unwilling to take any risks. The congregation voted not only to deny Dahmer the use of their facilities, they expelled him for a time from their membership rolls.

IN SPITE OF the heartbreak he suffered from the experience with his church, Dahmer persisted in his campaign to register new voters. Cox, his original nemesis, died in 1958 but was replaced in an election the next year by a new circuit clerk who proved to be even more obdurate, a man named Theron Lynd, whom Dahmer and the civil rights division of the U.S. Justice Department would eventually challenge in court.

Meanwhile, the freedom struggle moved to different fronts— lawsuits to desegregate schools, boycotts of businesses that discriminated against Blacks, and the development of an alternative political apparatus as a rival to the old guard, segregationist Democratic Party that ruled the state. Suddenly, there were new faces to confront the system in Hattiesburg. Among them was Victoria Gray, a local woman in her thirties who became a field secretary for SNCC, the Student Nonviolent Coordinating Committee, an organization composed of youthful and daring men and women who tackled dangerous projects. SNCC's tactics were bolder than those of the NAACP, which had historically been controlled by older men. Gray succeeded in persuading her own church to allow SNCC workers to set up workshops for citizenship classes and to offer literacy lessons for those ineligible to vote because they could neither read nor write. Gray also became a major voice for the Mississippi Freedom Democratic Party at the Democratic National Convention in Atlantic City in 1964 and later was a candidate on a Freedom Democrats slate for the U.S. Senate seat held by John Stennis.

Recognizing the tensions between the NAACP and SNCC, Dahmer sought to breach the generational differences by supporting an alliance with Gray's upstart group and volunteering to host on his farm two rambunctious SNCC operatives, Hollis Watkins and Curtis Hayes, who had been unable to find anyone in Hattiesburg willing to offer them housing. As a condition, Dahmer expected the young men to work at his farm and sawmill as well as to canvass the countryside for prospective voters. Dahmer drove a demanding schedule for himself, his family, and his visitors. They were all up before dawn for chores, and the SNCC workers were also subjected in the evening to a daily postmortem concerning their canvassing accomplishments.

Hayes eventually left the farm for more urban assignments in Jackson. But Watkins, who had grown up in another rural and volatile south Mississippi environment, was comfortable with his situation and stayed on with Dahmer for several more months. He called Dahmer "a real down to earth father."

While he was in Forrest County, Watkins took part in a mission to record an incident at Lynd's circuit clerk office for a CBS camera crew. Wearing a body wire for sound and carrying an attaché case rigged with a hidden camera, Watkins approached Lynd in an attempt to capture his behavior on film. Lynd was suddenly joined by someone from the sheriff's office, who began to interrogate the unwelcome visitor, even as Watkins tried to manipulate his camera. The CBS crew, located three blocks away, recorded some of the conversation, in which the law enforcement officer asked Watkins if he knew how to handle a bush ax. "Oh my God," Watkins thought, "they're getting ready to send me to the county farm." He was able to get away from the office before the body wire and camera could be discovered.

His footage was not used, but Lynd was featured on the CBS Reports show that aired in September 1962, called "Mississippi and the 15th Amendment." When the program was shown during a training camp in Oxford, Ohio, for civil rights volunteers preparing to work in Mississippi during Freedom Summer in 1964, the youthful audience laughed at the sight of the portly Lynd, whose body was blimp-like. But a more seasoned instructor knew of the danger the students would soon be facing in Mississippi and told them, "This is no laughing matter."

Dahmer, whose four oldest sons had enlisted in the military, felt an affinity with the young men that some of his older NAACP allies lacked. He enjoyed hearing Watkins's report of his narrow escape at the courthouse and admired his courage in taking on the assignment for CBS.

When another youthful activist, Lawrence Guyot, came to

Hattiesburg from the Gulf Coast to direct a program for CORE, Dahmer offered counsel. He warned Guyot of the opposition he would encounter, and he asked, "Are you strong enough to do this? Do you know what these folks around here are capable of doing?" Guyot assured Dahmer he would be up to the task.

Dahmer's diligence attracted the attention of civil rights forces that were massing for a major offensive in Mississippi in 1964. As a result of his groundwork, Hattiesburg was selected as the site for the movement's first major project of the year.

At a COFO meeting in January, attended by such legendary figures as the mystical Bob Moses of SNCC, who had been bloodied while directing civil rights campaigns in southwest Mississippi, and Guyot, who became chairman of the fledgling Mississippi Freedom Democrats, the Hattiesburg Project was on the top of the 1964 agenda. It served as a precursor for a greater Summer Project, which called for hundreds of sympathetic students from across the country to flood the state. The Hattiesburg Project was to be launched with a Freedom Day when students would boycott school, adults would swarm the courthouse to try to register as voters, and COFO personnel would stage a demonstration on the streets of the city.

Some of the older people who attended the meetings and lived in Hattiesburg objected to the plans. They had fears that brazen acts on behalf of civil rights would lead to sterner crackdowns by authorities and drive extremists to terrorize their neighborhoods. Following the murder of Medgar Evers, it seemed possible that they might die in a racial Armageddon.

But Dahmer remained steadfast in his support of the COFO representatives and the strategy they mapped out for the summer, even as it triggered violence at flashpoints around the state. Volunteers from colleges mostly located on the East and West Coasts had prepared for the resistance they would meet in Mississippi at training sessions before they arrived, and they quickly encountered it. Two weeks after the three men affiliated with COFO's Summer Project went missing in Neshoba County, Dahmer decided to try to boost spirits among the visitors in Forrest County.

The Civil Rights Act had just become law, so he hosted a Fourth of July celebration on his farm for more than two hundred workers in the movement, ranging from battle-hardened young veterans from Mississippi who had already spent time in jail to untried volunteers from California colleges, the Ivy League, and smaller liberal arts schools. Hattiesburg harbored one of the largest contingents of out-of-state students; about ninety of them—many of them white and unfamiliar with Mississippi—had been assigned to Forrest County. For an afternoon and evening, Dahmer's gathering blossomed into a festival. The group played games and sang hymns of freedom. Newcomers learned the words of James Weldon Johnson's "Lift Every Voice and Sing," which had become a civil rights anthem, and they were introduced to the joys of the Mississippi summer staple, watermelon. The day ended with a hayride and a fish fry. Dahmer patrolled his property making sure that his visitors felt welcome. It was another gesture by the elder statesman of the movement to reach out to the younger generation, to make the struggle he had waged for years their own.

Dahmer knew he needed to prepare for the battles ahead. The next week, the Freedom Schools in Hattiesburg, which had expected no more than one hundred teenagers, overflowed with six times that number. There were dozens of young elementary-school children in attendance as well as eighty-year-olds, all anxious to take part in the exercise.

The Freedom Schools, the demonstrations that served as public quests for rights, the songs of commitment were all fine, Dahmer thought. But voting rights had always been his priority, and he intended to follow the treacherous path he believed would lead to enfranchisement for the Black people of Forrest County.

CHAPTER 5

TOM LANDRUM GOT A mysterious phone call at home in late October 1965. A man said he had a child in trouble and asked if he could come talk about it. The request itself was not that unusual. Working with the Youth Court, Landrum often met with parents worried about children who had been caught breaking the law. But the caller did not identify himself or the youngster. Landrum was alone, and the request made him a bit nervous. Nevertheless, he invited the concerned father to come see him right away and gave directions to his house. It was the evening before Halloween, but because the day for trick-or-treating fell on a Sunday that year, the annual parade of children going door-to-door was taking place on a Saturday night. Anne had all five of the Landrum children away, ferrying them in the family car to friendly homes scattered for several miles through the countryside. There was little Halloween traffic around the Landrum home, off a county-maintained road about five miles from Laurel.

A few minutes later, a man arrived, but it was not a troubled father. Instead, Landrum recognized, his visitor was Lawrence Byrd, a ranking member of the White Knights in Jones County. By day, he ran a radio and TV repair shop in Laurel. From his own experiences as a customer, Landrum had seen Byrd behave pleasantly with white people around but occasionally bristle with anger and become short in his manner when dealing with Blacks. To Landrum, his visitor was a good example of so many men he knew in Jones County; Byrd was cordial among other whites but turned hostile without provocation when dealing with Blacks.

Declining Landrum's offer of a cup of coffee, Byrd quickly got to the purpose of his visit. He gave Landrum an assignment for the next day: he was to drive for nearly an hour before dawn to a service station near the town of Magee, where he would meet other Klansmen before proceeding to a distant rendezvous. He handed Landrum a small piece of paper with a code—0132—written in orange along with instructions for the second part of his journey:

From Magee, Mississippi, go Highway 28 West 20 miles to Strong River, cross the bridge go 300 yards west turn North on gravel road go past power line 300 ft. car will be backed up on a log road at this point.

Before departing quickly, Byrd warned Landrum not to lose the paper. He would be expected to turn it over to Klan guards when he reached his destination. Landrum fingered the sheet with its orange code and wondered if it were the Klan equivalent of a dark message he remembered from his childhood when he had seen the movie *Treasure Island*. In a scene from the adventure tale, pirates warned a man that he was marked for death by sending him a piece of paper embellished with an ominous black spot.

When Anne came home, Tom told her of his meeting with Byrd. She shared his apprehension and advised him not to go. His cooperation with the FBI might have been discovered, she said, and it could lead to a beating—or possibly death. But to reject the assignment, he countered, would be a tacit admission that he was not loyal to the Klan and would lead to suspicion that he was one of the informers in their midst. That seemed a more dangerous course. He concluded he must go on the assignment.

He slept fitfully that night, climbed from bed early, and dressed in a suit as if for church, for it was Sunday. When he pulled away from his house, Anne felt gripped by panic for the first time since they had undertaken their undercover work. She wondered if she would see her husband again. Overwhelmed by desperation, she broke the FBI's admonitions about secrecy and drove to a pay telephone booth where she could place an undetected call to the number Tom had been given in case of emergency. She thought the agent she reached was dismissive of her fears; the call did little to comfort her. Anne was confronted with a whole day to worry. To ease the hours, she tried to concentrate on the positive aspects of her husband's affiliation with the White Knights. She reasoned that they had made a family decision about the FBI's appeal, and the risk had been mutually agreed on. This was no time to grow faint, Anne thought, and concluded that Tom had been right to go. It would validate his standing with the White Knights and at the same time underscore his commitment to the FBI.

～

LANDRUM ARRIVED AT the service station in Magee at 6 a.m. to find Cecil Sessum and two other men waiting for him. He recognized Robert Rivers, the exalted cyclops of the Klan unit in the Shady Grove community of Jones County. The fourth man turned out to be a friend of Sessum's, an exalted cyclops from nearby Perry County. The quartet ate breakfast at a diner, then followed the directions from the note given to Landrum. As they drove, Landrum learned they were headed to a statewide meeting of the White Knights. Rivers said he was "hitching a ride" because he had loaned his Volkswagen to Sam Bowers. He sounded pleased over the fact that the imperial wizard had asked to use his car. The Perry County traveler grunted that his name was Tucker; he ran a sporting-goods shop and repaired television sets on the side. Otherwise, the men did little talking.

At their destination on the logging road, they made contact with other Klansmen and received another set of directions to follow several gravel roads and state highways that would wind them toward an old log building in Copiah County. Reaching the next stop, they were greeted by a Klan guardsman, who asked for Landrum's paper with the orange code, then directed them to a parking place off a narrow road. The security arrangements resembled those for a military base. Landrum saw several men with automatic rifles walking through woods buzzing with activity. By this time it was clear that the day's events involved a major Klan rally and not an occasion to ferret out traitors. He calculated their location must be somewhere near Crystal Springs, just south of Jackson.

Before the foursome took a footpath into the forest, where they were told they would be searched, Sessum recommended that they empty their pockets and leave all of their personal belongings in the car. At the next checkpoint they were frisked to ensure that no one carried a recording device or an unauthorized weapon. The path emptied into an open pasture where several hundred men were milling about in ordinary clothing, without robes or hoods. Landrum saw two or three men he knew from different towns around the state; Jones County seemed to be well represented. At mid-morning, Bowers and his trusted lieutenant, Deavours Nix, joined the gathering. The meeting began with a prayer.

For the first time, Landrum witnessed resistance to Bowers's leadership and dissension among the White Knights. When Nix introduced a motion to raise the initiation fees for the Klan from ten to twenty dollars there were shouts of disapproval and the measure was voted down. Tension was also evident between Bowers and another officer named Billy Buckley, the second-in-command of the statewide organization. Two months earlier, at a "Klonvocation" outside Byram, another town near Jackson, Buckley had vied with Bowers for leadership of the White Knights, Landrum learned. Buckley advocated a coalition with the United Klans organization. Bowers disapproved of the move, dismissing the rival group and exhorting his followers with a speech about the purity of the White Knights. Buckley's motion to consider merging with the United Klans never got as far as a vote. His effort to challenge the imperial wizard a failure, Buckley announced that he intended to resign as grand giant for the state and spend his time working with the *Southern Review*, a Klan-backed publication (not to be confused with the distinguished literary magazine with a similar name founded by the poet and novelist Robert Penn Warren).

With Buckley muted and relegated to the background, Bowers began a pep talk to invigorate his followers. He assailed the federal government and complained that too many members of the White Knights tended to talk too much. By breaking their vows of silence, he said, they had become "sellouts to our enemy, the federal government."

He was interrupted by the throbbing noise of a helicopter, distant at first but moving closer. When the copter cleared the trees and swept into view above the pasture it created havoc among the Klansmen. Bowers tried to keep order, but men began shouting that they were being invaded by the FBI. Or the state highway patrol. Or both. With propellers beating like deafening drums, the aircraft swooped downward, hovering over the heads of the men. Inside the copter's plastic bubble, a man with a camera could be discerned.

"I wish I had my goddamned 45 Thompson," Buckley yelled. "I'd shoot those shitasses out of the sky."

When the helicopter veered from the pasture to hover over the makeshift parking lot across the woods, Landrum heard someone warn, "They're taking pictures of the cars. They're getting car tags."

"I wish I didn't have a Northwest sticker on my car," another Klansman moaned, referring to a decal promoting his son's school.

The chopper made another pass over the group of men, a maneuver that triggered a stampede from the folding chairs that had been set out in the clearing. Rumors, based on speculation that the meeting was about to be raided by a force of several hundred FBI agents and highway patrolmen, contributed to the confusion. Shouts went up, "The Feds are here," followed by more yelling. "More helicopters are on their way," someone shouted above the din, "and they got powerful listening devices."

Realizing that he had lost the attention of the group, Bowers gave the swiftly departing Klansmen his blessing. "Let's get out of here.

You all who are not known by the FBI, go out the back way. Head into the woods," he shouted, waving toward the pine forest.

Fearing that he might be arrested or publicly identified as a Klan member, Landrum scampered from the scene. He sought shelter in a creek meandering through the woods, thrashing through the shallow water in his best blue suit and a new pair of leather shoes. He was desperate to avoid the humiliation of a newspaper photograph of himself at a Klan meeting.

Emerging from the creek near the parking lot, Landrum was embraced by Sessum, who flung him into the back seat of the car and threw a quilt over him. Landrum was thought valuable to the White Knights, and Sessum did not want him discovered. He gave the Klan additional presence at the Jones County courthouse, and he came to their weekly meetings more regularly than Leonard Caves, the circuit clerk who sometimes acted as though he were better than most Klansmen.

Landrum was relieved to make it home safely without being identified that day. But he was bruised by the experience. He found himself tormented by the possibility that friends and people in Jones County whom he respected would hear about the escapade and link him with the worst elements of the Klan.

That evening he managed to describe the chaotic day in a long dispatch to the FBI. He included details of the security measures and passed on the names of those he knew at the meeting.

"This was one of the most disturbing Sundays which I have spent," he dictated to his wife as she transcribed his words. "I could just see my picture on television and in the newspaper headlines. I talked to Bob Lee and told him that I would never make another trip to a state meeting, and he told me had I contacted him before they would have told me what was going to happen, and that if I got a chance to be sure and go."

In conclusion, Landrum reported, "I ruined my suit and shoes."

The FBI failed to reimburse him for the loss but did give him credit for mileage and repaid two dollars he had spent for Klan pamphlets and four dollars for dues. As agents at the FBI's state headquarters in

Jackson compiled an account of the latest Klan Klonvocation, they used information from no fewer than four different Klansmen with code names who had attended the meeting and reported to various agents supervising their inside work. Landrum never knew it, but his code name used by the FBI was JN 143-R.

≈

LANDRUM WAS NOT the only participant at the state meeting who left with a property loss. Robert Rivers, whose car Bowers had borrowed, learned that the imperial wizard managed to burn up the engine while making his escape, disregarding a broken fan belt critical to cooling the Volkswagen engine. At a subsequent meeting of the Klan, Bowers called for an assessment of two dollars per member to pay for repairs, but his efforts failed to collect much money.

≈

AS HE SENSED himself sinking deeper into complicity with the White Knights, Landrum would eventually seek reassurance from one of the few local officials willing to stand up to the Klan. As Youth Court counselor, Landrum came into regular contact with Charles Pickering, a young county attorney who served as prosecutor for relatively minor offenses in Jones County and assisted the district attorney, W. O. "Chet" Dillard of Laurel, in handling more serious criminal cases. As part of his job description, Pickering worked with Landrum in sorting out cases involving underage youngsters who had been arrested. Both were more interested in rehabilitation efforts than long jail terms for the boys, and they soon developed respect for each other.

Landrum liked Pickering's even-tempered approach. He even hired the twenty-eight-year-old attorney to handle legal work for his family, drawing up a will and checking property lines. Like Landrum, Pickering was a member of an established Jones County family that had lived near Ellisville—the other county seat—for decades. After graduating from high school, he, too, had started at Jones County Junior College, before enrolling at the University of Mississippi, where he received a bachelor's degree followed by a law degree in 1961. A fresh member of the bar, Pickering joined a Laurel law firm headed by the state's lieutenant governor, Carroll Gartin. Soon, Pickering was appointed city prosecutor there. Within two years, he plunged into politics and won election as county attorney. At the same time, Gartin won a third term as lieutenant governor, emerging as a leading contender to become governor in the next election. Pickering was known as his protégé.

In those years, every officeholder in Mississippi was a Democrat, tied to a staunchly conservative wing of the party that had dominated the state since the Republican "party of Lincoln" had been routed at the end of Reconstruction. But in 1964, Pickering broke from the Democratic Party and declared himself a Republican, becoming a pioneer in the political realignment just beginning to take place in the South. Many of the defecting Democrats expressed bitterness and aggravation over the liberal tendencies of the national party, embodied in President Johnson's support of the Civil Rights Act of 1964 and his vows to extend voting rights to Blacks throughout the region. Pickering was a dedicated conservative and concerned over some of the moves by the White House and the Democratic Congress that affected Mississippi. But he was also troubled by the violence breaking out in his home county and the repressive terror represented by the Ku Klux Klan.

From the time he took office as county attorney, Pickering had been meeting quietly with Bob Lee, the resident FBI agent. In some instances, Lee helped Pickering develop criminal cases that could be dealt with in local courts. Pickering was especially interested in any intelligence that Lee could pass on regarding the White Knights. Lee gave him a list of no fewer than one hundred "acts of violence" perpetrated by the Klan in the area. One case particularly bothered Pickering—the thirty houses in a Black neighborhood in Laurel that had been burned down by the Klan during an offensive against COFO elements in the community. He was outraged.

⩳

AT FIRST, Pickering had a strained relationship with Chet Dillard, the district attorney. Though both men were relatively recent graduates of the University of Mississippi law school and won election to their offices in 1963, Dillard was seven years older and had grown up in a decidedly backwoods environment outside of Jones County. By comparison, Pickering had a more distinguished local background, coming from one of the county's older families. Dillard acknowledged that his own election had been helped by some Klan support, and he suspected that Bob Lee thought of him as a Klan sympathizer. As a result, he was annoyed that the FBI preferred to deal with Pickering. Dillard harbored a bit of a grudge against the younger county attorney.

However, once it became apparent that Dillard opposed the Klan, the two prosecutors joined forces. After Pickering drafted a forceful denunciation of Klan violence in Jones County, both Dillard and Laurel mayor Henry Bucklew, another public official who once cultivated Klan support at the ballot box, joined the Jones County sheriff and the Laurel police chief in a bold public statement castigating the group. Members of the White Knights who had voted for Dillard and Bucklew felt betrayed and privately promised there would be reprisals.

Dillard began to take precautions. He regularly put tape on the hood of his car in order to detect whether someone had planted a bomb inside the engine apparatus. Pickering had already learned that the White Knights had issued a Code Two for him—a prospective beating—so he, too, kept his guard up.

One night Pickering was at Dillard's house, working on a case against the Klan, when his wife called to inform him that an unidentified Klansman had telephoned the Pickering home with a message that he had information he wanted to share. She told her husband that she had suggested the Klansman call Dillard's residence, which he did minutes later. Dillard answered the phone, talked with the caller, and agreed to meet him later in the parking lot of a Laurel funeral home.

Thinking it might be a setup, Pickering volunteered to provide cover for Dillard. The county attorney borrowed a pistol from a law enforcement agent and positioned himself inside the funeral home chapel with a window view of the parking lot. He watched as the Klansman drove up and stepped from his car and into Dillard's. The pair drove off and the district attorney safely succeeded in getting the Klansman's information. Landrum was not the only one talking with authorities. Several other men had grown worried that their membership in the White Knights would lead to trouble, and they wanted to develop more respectable, private understandings with law enforcement.

—

DILLARD AND PICKERING began collecting the names of Jones County men believed to be members of the White Knights and promised to bring the full force of the law down on them.

Pickering noticed that his friend, Tom Landrum, was hanging out with some of those suspected of taking part in the campaign of terror. He had seen Landrum with Cecil Sessum and Lawrence Byrd, among others, and it worried him. Meanwhile, Landrum detected a new uneasiness in his friendship with Pickering during their conversations at the courthouse in the fall of 1965. The county attorney seemed more guarded in talking of the trouble in Jones County. Knowing of Pickering's determination to challenge the Klan, Landrum sensed an air of personal disapproval. Just as he had feared that his exposure as a Klansman at the aborted state meeting would jeopardize his reputation, Landrum grew disturbed that Pickering now thought he had sided with the lawless band.

In fact, Landrum had been quietly protective of Pickering. After hearing Pickering mentioned as an enemy of the White Knights at one of the first Klan meetings he attended, followed by a call to burn Pickering's home during another meeting in mid-September,

Landrum drove twenty miles to the other side of Jones County where Pickering lived to ensure that no Klan assault took place that night.

Landrum decided that he needed to share his secret with Pickering. He telephoned and asked if they could go fishing the next Saturday on a lake beside Pickering's country home. There was something he wanted to talk about, Landrum said. Once they were on a small boat and had cast their lines to try to hook some bream, Landrum spoke.

"Charles, I've got to get something off my chest. I trust you, and you've got to keep this in strictest confidence. I know you've seen me with some of the boys who're in the White Knights, and I figure you think I'm one of them. And that makes me uncomfortable."

Pickering waited for him to continue.

"Can I tell you something that you don't dare tell to anyone else?" Landrum asked.

"Of course."

"Well, I've been talking with Bob Lee, the same way you have, about our problems with the Klan, and he asked me to join the Klan as an undercover operator for him. I've been doing that for the last two months or so. It's a risk I feel like I have to take if I'm going to live in Jones County and be a man and stand up, one way or another, against the Klan. Like you're doing in your own way as a county attorney. I wanted you to know I'm doing it in my way, too. I don't want you to think I'm part of that gang that's up to no good. I want you to know that I'm working with the FBI, and giving Bob Lee regular reports. But, please God, don't share this information with anybody else or it could cost me my life."

"Tom, I'm relieved to hear you say this," Pickering said. "I was worried about you, and I'm so glad to learn this. Of course I'll keep this in confidence. I won't tell anybody, you can rest assured about that."

Landrum told Pickering about the threats he had overheard. Some of it amounted to nothing more than idle chatter, he said. But there had been calls for violence elsewhere that he knew had been carried out, and he warned Pickering to be vigilant.

Motivated by a sense of relief after he divulged his secret to his friend, Landrum felt there was one other person he must contact. It was Carroll Gartin, the lieutenant governor and Pickering's elder partner in the law firm. Gartin was a generation older than Landrum, and an influential citizen of Jones County. Landrum counted him as a friend, too. As a boy, Landrum had mowed Gartin's lawn. He valued knowing him and always appreciated the warm greeting he got from Gartin when they met. He had followed Gartin's rise in politics from the time he had first been elected lieutenant governor in 1951, the same year Willie McGee had been executed. Now he was positioned to be the next governor, so Landrum believed it was important that Gartin know the reason behind his association with the Klan.

Gartin was a segregationist. No politician in Mississippi could succeed without supporting white supremacy. But Gartin belonged to the school of politicians known as "moderates." They shied from the acrid language of the racist candidates who openly used such words as "niggers" and "coons" to describe Blacks, and they endorsed more "moderate" means of preserving segregation through state law rather than terror. For years, they had battled the more radical segregationists who were represented in politics by such figures as the late governor and senator Theodore G. Bilbo, who had promoted the idea of deporting all Blacks back to Africa, and the more recent governor, Ross Barnett, who led the state into combat with the federal government at Ole Miss.

In his tangled view of Mississippi politics, Sam Bowers considered Gartin a "collaborationist" because, as lieutenant governor, he had been involved in the negotiations between the state and federal governments during the Ole Miss crisis.

Landrum had heard other members of the White Knights inveigh against Gartin as bitterly as they did when Pickering's name was brought up at the Klan gatherings. Both men were declared by the Klansmen to be "dead in the political world." On August 31, Landrum reported to the FBI that Gartin had been "discussed at length" among those who wanted to hold him accountable for his denunciations of the Klan. There were plans to burn a cross on his lawn—the same lawn Landrum once cut—in order to intimidate him.

Landrum respected Gartin, and after he told the lieutenant governor of his role, he felt another wave of relief.

Now there were two others besides his family and the FBI who knew of the assignment he had undertaken. Maybe that would increase his danger. But Landrum felt he had done the right thing by assuring Pickering and Gartin that he had not gone over to the dark side.

CHAPTER 6

ANGER OVER THE strides of the civil rights movement was a constant theme at the White Knights meetings. The challenge to Jim Crow had quickly grown from a handful of Black college students staging sit-ins at all-white lunch counters in 1960 to a swarm of activists daring to integrate buses as Freedom Riders the next year. Appalling retaliatory violence by segregationists served only to alter public opinion outside the South, strengthen the numbers of civil rights forces, and lead to passage of congressional bills critical to the overturning of decades of official racial discrimination. With this legislation in hand, the movement turned to the methodical task of registering Black voters while a sympathetic Justice Department and a corps of civil rights lawyers brought scores of suits to federal courts to integrate public schools. The Klan seethed over the success of their opponents, but as 1965 drew to a close Landrum noticed that a new emotion—fear—was creeping through the ranks of the men. Fear that fellow Klansmen were now working as informants. Fear that the FBI and other aggressive law enforcement authorities had been able to set up a wide net of surveillance of their activities, a belief that gained credibility after the helicopter invaded Sam Bowers's statewide meeting. And, following the arrests in the Neshoba County case, fear that membership in the White Knights might lead to prison.

Landrum found himself gripped by another kind of fear, a troublesome concern that rarely left him: that his arrangement with the FBI would be discovered. From the time he agreed with Bob Lee in August to feed the bureau regular reports, Landrum understood that he had endangered himself. But his anxiety intensified after word drifted into Jones County that a White Knights group operating out of Natchez had murdered one of its own.

The victim was Earl Hodges, a forty-seven-year-old mechanic who joined a White Knights klavern in rural Franklin County shortly after it was formed in 1964. The group was led by exalted cyclops Clyde Seale, who was believed responsible—along with his sons James Ford Seale and Jack Seale and another man—for the execution of two young Black men they believed to be "militants" in May of that year. The teenagers were captured by the Klansmen while hitchhiking and accused of consorting with Black Muslims, smuggling guns, and plotting an insurrection. After being beaten into submission, the pair were weighted down with automobile engine blocks and dumped into a watery slough of the Mississippi River. Partial remains of their bodies bobbed to the surface in the summer, at the same time that authorities were searching for the missing men in Neshoba County. The deaths triggered a new investigation that led to a rift among members of the White Knights in southwest Mississippi and suspicions that someone was talking too much.

Hodges never held an important role in the Klan. He was an army veteran who enjoyed friendships at an American Legion post in Franklin County and the dance halls in nearby Natchez. Divorced and a heavy drinker, he gravitated to the Klan, which attracted other men adrift. His fatal mistake occurred when he questioned the wisdom of Clyde Seale during a meeting in 1965. The exalted cyclops had recommended a Code Three—a severe beating—for a local white man suspected of trying to buy a list of the names of Klansmen. Hodges believed the man was innocent. After he objected to Seale's proposal, others in the klavern grew skeptical and the idea was dropped.

Seale did not like to be crossed, and his antipathy grew when

Hodges began behaving erratically during the period when law enforcement officers were interrogating everyone who might have knowledge about the abduction of the two Black teenagers. Hodges often appeared drunk and tearfully penitent about his wayward conduct. After he emerged from a "drying-out" spell in a veteran's hospital following his latest drunken binge, he told friends he intended to change his ways. Because his brother-in-law was a Mississippi highway patrolman assigned to a task force investigating the Klan, some of Hodges's associates jumped to the conclusion that he might be revealing Klan secrets to his relative.

On the same August weekend that Landrum took his oath as a member of the White Knights in Jones County, Hodges was found beaten to death in the backyard of his father's house in a country community nearly one hundred miles west of Laurel. His body, bearing welts from face to foot, had been brutalized, and there was a hole in the crown of his head.

A highway patrol investigator reported to the FBI that Hodges was one of the men responsible for a split in Seale's klavern, and that Seale thought Hodges was likely to inform on his group. Seale and his sons were questioned by authorities, but no arrests were ever made.

It took a while for the news of Hodges's murder to spread to other Klan groups around the state. But when it did, it caused tremors.

≈

THE DILEMMA OF THE White Knights of the Natchez area became the focus of a discussion led by Lawrence Byrd, the Laurel TV repairman, in a meeting Landrum attended a few weeks after Hodges's death. "These are some critical times for our friends over in Natchez," Byrd told the gathering of two dozen men slumped in chairs and weather-beaten sofas in the home of one of the members. "There's big trouble over there. The Feds are swarming the area; they been there ever since them two nigger boys got killed last year. And now, since this latest killing, it seems like they're questioning everybody in Natchez and Franklin County. It's a hot situation. The FBI thinks they can buy people, and some people have talked for cheap. Look what happened to one of them who did. It's a lesson. You need to be careful who you talk to, or you might wind up in some barrow pit or left out in the woods."

Byrd liked to display his authority with the White Knights. His office as senator made him privy to decisions Bowers and other state leaders made, and he strove to be the first to pass the word to the rank-and-file in Jones County. "Our state leaders have been approached by some of the City Fathers of Natchez for help. They want to know what we can do to take the pressure off them," Byrd told the group. "I say that Jones County has never failed to help when called on. We need to figure out what we can do to take the heat off them. We need to cause trouble in other areas to draw off the FBI from Natchez. We can set some fires. I was in a tank division in World War II and I know something about diversions. We had a motto: Hold 'em in the nose and kick 'em in the balls."

Byrd's use of the odd military slogan failed to spark much interest among the men who listened quietly as the Klan official urged them to shift the site of their raids to another part of the state. So he raised his voice. "We need to send help to Natchez right now," he shouted. "Not to the middle of the town, but to the country outside town. That's where the trouble is really located. And this is the time for us to show our worth. We know they ain't gonna get no help from the United Klans next door in McComb. They done pissed in their boot. They ain't got the strength of a pussy-livered little boy no more."

The rival United Klans had been briefly dominant in the area around McComb, a small city in Pike County, halfway between Laurel and Natchez. During the summer of 1964, vigilantes affiliated with the United Klans had terrorized the countryside, burning down or blowing up more than a dozen Black churches that had offered their facilities for civil rights activities. Several homes were torched. The COFO headquarters in McComb was rocked by a bomb, injuring two civil rights workers. Residents of the area were awakened so many nights by the sounds of concussions that it seemed as though sticks of dynamite were being tossed about as casually as Fourth of July fireworks. The violence earned the region the unofficial and unwanted title of "Church Bombing Capital of the World." But it provoked a reaction that the Klan had not anticipated. When local authorities showed little enthusiasm for an investigation, a team of FBI agents swept into the area. Before the end of the year, they engineered the arrests of a score of Klansmen. Just as the Klan in Laurel had drawn many members from the working-class rolls of the Masonite plant, the Pike County group included many employees of the Illinois Central Railroad, which had a major work yard in McComb.

On top of the successful prosecution of the Klansmen, a strong petition by several hundred of the area's leading white citizens condemned the Klan. In a full-page advertisement in the *Enterprise-Journal* of McComb the group said, "We believe the time has come for responsible people to speak out for what is right and against what is wrong. . . . There is only one responsible stance we can take, and that is for equal treatment under the law for all citizens regardless of race, creed, position or wealth." It was one of the first public manifestations by whites in Mississippi that the activities of the Klan were unacceptable.

The arrests in Pike County, coupled with the disapproval of the tactics of terror, left the United Klans enervated in the area. In Lawrence Byrd's mind, it created an opportunity for the White Knights to move into the vacuum and to extend their scope across Mississippi.

≈

INSIDE THE OTHER circles of the White Knights in Jones County there was rising concern over confidentiality. "Someone is talking to the FBI," Leonard Caves complained during a conversation in his courthouse office with Landrum and another Klan member. "A couple of days after I reported to the group that Raymond Swartzfager had decided not to join us, Raymond came by my office and said Bob Lee had just thanked him for not joining the Klan. How did Bob Lee know? Hell, it seems obvious somebody is talking."

Caves was already frustrated that he had failed to recruit Swartzfager, a promising young lawyer in town. He seemed doubly upset that the FBI knew about it. The circuit clerk realized that he needed to be more cautious about everything he said at the White Knights meetings. A few weeks earlier he had talked freely about his ability to control the work of the courts in Jones County. "Soon it's gonna be time to fill the jury boxes," he had told the group. "I need to be given the names of all our members so I can guarantee that if any member ever gets tried for taking part in one of our projects we will be sure to have a Klan member sitting on the jury."

If that word got out, Caves now thought, he could be subject to prosecution himself.

Caves was not the only one worried about loose talk. A week later, Landrum had a heart-to-heart conversation with his friend Gerald Martin, the constable for Beat Three in Jones County who had begun to rethink his decision to get involved with the White Knights. Martin said he had been disturbed ever since Bob Lee told him that the FBI knew he belonged to the Klan. "That's a kick in the ass for somebody who's got a job in law enforcement to be identified as a member of the Klan," Martin said. "It could ruin my reputation. But there are other things that bother me. I don't like this idea of shooting up houses, burning things down. As you know, I've been laying low lately. I don't approve of all this business. I think there are other ways to keep the niggers out of schools."

Martin said the White Knights should be more selective in their membership. "They need to get rid of all the booze heads and be more careful about who they pick to become members. Hell, the other night I saw Billy Ray Smith, drunk as a billy goat, staggering into John's Restaurant. The FBI could get all the information they want simply by listening to some silly son of a bitch like him spouting off. They wouldn't even have to pay for it."

Within a week, Landrum heard another Klansman express reservations at a meeting of his klavern. "The FBI has been to my house, and that concerns me. I got a lot of concerns. Some of this stuff is doing us no good. I don't believe in shooting people, burning houses. Some of the houses that been burned have become a problem for our little communities around Ellisville. When you burn a house, the ones who suffer are the kids. I think a whipping or a cross-burning would do just as good to keep people in line. I think our best job would be to get our voters to the polls. The niggers are beginning to register, so we need to be sure we get our people out to vote."

The troubled Klansman also had concerns about spies in their midst. "If the FBI is coming to my house, that means somebody is talking. We think we know who the informer of our group is, and we're going to give him just enough rope for him to hang himself."

Landrum listened quietly to the commentary. Increasingly, the Klan seemed to be preoccupied with informers. It was discomforting to Landrum, but he continued to file reports with the FBI. Following a meeting in Speed Lightsey's barn with about twenty members on hand, Landrum drafted an account of remarks by Red Caldwell, the White Knights' giant:

Caldwell stated that the sheriff of Jones County Merrill Pickering had told him that he knew he was a member of the Klan and that during a meeting Lake Bogue Homa had been discussed. There was to be 50 lbs of dynamite placed in the lock on the dam and blow out the whole dam. Sheriff Pickering stated that he with others were ready for the Klan to blow up the Lake for they would have gotten caught. Sheriff Pickering also told Caldwell that the Klan had been infiltrated by the FBI and the Sheriff's Dept. And the Sheriff's Dept was going to raid the Klan's meeting places. Caldwell states that the time is near for the ones who are doing the talking to be caught. He stated that the County Officers have a very good idea who is talking and that they should get out of the Klan before they got caught.

Hearing Caldwell's comments confirmed something Landrum had been thinking: he was not the only informant in the Jones County gang. Landrum had never given the FBI a detailed report on plans to destroy the Bogue Homa dam.

At the same meeting, Gerald Martin delivered a lecture on security, describing how arrangements had broken down recently when the White Knights conducted a series of cross-burnings across Jones County as a show of strength. He said a local small-time rancher had heard the sound of hammering from a pasture near his house. Thinking someone was stealing cattle, he went to investigate and "walked right up" on some men preparing to light the cross. "If the security had been as it should have been the guards would have noticed the fellow first," Martin said.

Martin chuckled as he related the end of the story. The rancher called the sheriff's office but was unable to locate a deputy to come to the scene. So the rancher called Martin, the constable for the area. Martin was not at home because he was out helping build the crosses. Eventually, the rancher reached Martin, who promised to investigate. "Which I did," he said. "I went out to talk with him and heard how he had been able to walk up on the men. But he told me he never heard any names."

Landrum closed his account to the FBI by passing on another admonition from Martin: "He stressed that there is a leak of information in the Klan and that it will be taken care of before long. He said Bob Lee of the FBI could get all the information he wanted from beer joints and people who drink."

≈

DESPITE FREQUENT DESCRIPTIONS of derring-do by members of the White Knights at the weekly meetings, Landrum learned that Klansmen were susceptible to danger, too. Following a discussion about finding a physician in Jones County who might surreptitiously treat the wounds of members of the White Knights, Speed

Lightsey told him of an earlier exchange of gunfire when a raiding party attempted to burn the home of a troublesome Black named Brewell Curie.

"As soon as our men drove up, the niggers started to shoot at them from inside the house and outside, too," Lightsey said. "Our men returned the shots, and while all the shooting was going on, some of them went about the business of burning the house while others kept firing. They had inner tubes filled with a gas-and-oil mixture, and they threw them on the roof and under the house. In all the fighting, two of the men from Group Four were hit. Both of them got shot in the leg. We called Lawrence Byrd, and he carried the wounded men to a doctor, who fixed them up. The cars got shot up, too, but they got took to a mechanic, and by 7 a.m. him and his son fixed 'em up to where you couldn't tell they had been shot." The mechanic owned a body shop in Laurel.

≈

LANDRUM'S OWN FEARS were compounded after he was told of a meeting of White Knights officials in Jones County that had taken place a few days earlier at Byrd's TV repair shop. Deavours Nix, Bowers's lieutenant and one of the roughest Klansmen in the organization, had called for a trial of Landrum, only two months after he had sworn the Youth Court counselor into the group. From the beginning, Landrum had sensed that Nix disliked him. When Nix appeared at meetings he seemed friendly to others but had nothing to say to Landrum. He merely glared at him.

Nix's grievance against Landrum had grown out of his arrest a year before in neighboring Jasper County by Landrum's brother, a Mississippi highway patrolman. He had stopped Nix for a traffic violation and found that the White Knights' high-ranking state investigator was armed with a gun. Nix wound up in jail on charges of carrying a concealed weapon. Tom Landrum had been approached by an intermediary and asked to prevail on his brother to drop the charges, but Landrum refused. Nix's anger toward the Landrum family intensified. When the case went to trial, a fellow Klansman on the jury helped persuade other jurors of Nix's innocence. He was acquitted, but he never forgot the experience.

In a burst of pique, he asked the Jones County leadership to take action against Landrum on the grounds that he was an informant who told his brother about White Knights activities. He had a second indictment of Landrum: at Klan meetings he sometimes expressed too much sympathy for "niggers."

The charge that Landrum had been talking to his relative in the highway patrol was ominous because that was believed to have been one of the reasons Earl Hodges had been murdered. Hodges's adversary, Clyde Seale, the exalted cyclops of their klavern near Natchez, had been convinced that Hodges was passing on information to his brother-in-law, also a highway patrolman.

When he learned of Nix's accusations, after the White Knights decided to ignore the complaint, Landrum was relieved to hear that Nix got no support from other leading Jones County Klansmen. Lawrence Byrd, Speed Lightsey, Red Caldwell, and several others who held the title of exalted cyclops for their various klaverns rejected Nix's request to put Landrum on trial. Lightsey was outspoken. He told Nix, "There better not be any cross burned around his house, either." There seemed to be a feeling among the group that Nix had gotten "too big for his britches" and tried to parlay his good relationship with Sam Bowers into power in the organization.

━

As Landrum spent more time with the White Knights, he began to understand that it was not a cohesive group but a collection of men with their own separate concerns and prejudices. Sam Bowers preferred to project an image of the organization as a monolithic force, determined to preserve racial segregation by whatever means necessary. But Landrum saw that the group was rife with dissension and sick with worry about informants.

At one meeting at Lightsey's home, the group absorbed a silent but painful rebuke. Lightsey's wife walked into the room while they were conducting business. "She looked very disgusted at the men in her house," Landrum reported. Leonard Caves, acting as though he had been slapped, left immediately. The others wandered outside, spent a few minutes talking in the front yard, then drove away.

The next meeting was moved from Lightsey's home to his unheated barn. The temperature had dropped in late autumn and the setting was uncomfortably cold. Yet it seemed better to endure the chill than to aggravate Lightsey's wife again. In a gesture to promote better manners, the men voted to police themselves with petty fines. They were reminded to refer to one another by their Klan numbers rather than their names. Anyone who used an actual name or an identifiable nickname such as "Bud" or "Hoss" would be fined twenty-five cents. To enforce the pseudoreligious nature of the gatherings, a decision was also made to fine anyone who uttered a curse word twenty-five cents. Landrum thought it was ludicrous to try to clean up talk among a bunch of coarse men. Of the effort he wrote: "I have heard the most vile language used, and then the same person be called to lead in a word of prayer. It is a mockery of Christian belief."

～

FOR SEVERAL MONTHS Landrum resisted a recommendation to invest in a Klan robe and hood to be used for special occasions. Knowing that the FBI would reimburse him, he finally fitted himself for the garments after being asked to take part in a formal initiation of new members. The robe, composed of sleek, shiny material, seemed to be professionally made. Landrum wondered if the Klan had its own tailor, stitching in a shop dedicated to Klan products. He was surprised by the bulk of the hood, pierced with two round eyeholes. It felt more like a helmet than a hood.

The ceremony took place inside Lightsey's barn, deep in the countryside of Jones County. For the true believers of the White Knights, it represented a sacred moment, when the Klan's "Veil of Secrecy" would be imposed. A table, arranged as though for a communion service, had been covered with white cloth and placed in the center of the barn. It held an unloaded pistol flanked by a line of bullets, a Bible, a knife, and a small cross made of pipe cleaners soaked with lighter fluid. The miniature cross would be set ablaze at the end of the initiation pageant.

While members prepared for the rites inside the barn, the initiates waited in cars outside in the darkness, surrounded by men carrying double-barreled shotguns and wearing the dark robes and hoods assigned to those serving as guards. Inside the building, a few men robed in white waited to conduct the swearing-in. More than a dozen other Klansmen who had failed to purchase robes were reduced to the role of spectators, hiding behind hay bales. After a Klan official declared that "all is in readiness," the initiates were given a last chance to back out. In the short history of the White Knights that Landrum knew, only one man had done so, a fellow named "Hamburger" Harrison, remembered as a coward.

Following a flicker of flashlight signals, the initiates were marched into the barn. The ceremony began with a prayer. The ritual included a recitation of the rules of the White Knights. The organization unapologetically promoted white, Anglo-Saxon supremacy. The vows were similar to the language in the group's recruiting leaflet. The words, written by Sam Bowers, amounted to a declaration of war against the federal government and members of ethnic groups deemed impure.

"The White Knights is, of necessity, a SECRET organization. The administration of our National Government is now under the actual control of atheists who are Bolsheviks by nature. As dedicated agents of Satan, they are absolutely determined to destroy Christian Civilization and all Christians. We have nothing dishonorable to hide, but we must remain SECRET for the protection of our lives and families." The White Knights' creed rejected "Jews . . . Papists . . . Turks, Mongols, Tarters [sic], Orientals, Negroes" and all others "whose native background of culture is foreign to the Anglo-Saxon system."

Once the ceremony was complete, the Veil of Secrecy was lifted. The new Klansmen were congratulated by members emerging from behind the stacks of hay. They were also expected to pay their ten-dollar initiation fee before they could leave.

≈

LANDRUM MADE HIS own vow—to himself—that he would never don a Klan robe again. He was becoming despondent. Subjected to a relentless litany of surly complaints, racial hatred, profanity, and threats at the meetings, he was unsure that his undercover work was having any positive effect. He worried that he sometimes forgot significant facts or failed to include relevant information in his reports. He would have liked to have access to a tape-recording device but did not dare use one. Landrum revealed his stress in a December 11, 1965, message to the FBI in which he lamented that it was "very hard to try to remember all that happens in a Klan meeting." He may have missed some things, he wrote, but he had never hyped a story. "All that is written is the truth." He added a plaintive note: "I have not taken the time to tell the feelings I have when a group of men is talking about killing the person or persons who talk to the FBI."

As he continued, the clinical tone of Landrum's report turned into a cri de coeur:

> I know that if it ever became known what I was up to it could mean my death, the welfare of my children and my wife, Anne. I would like to say that my family is being very much neglected due to me taking part in this secret agent role with the FBI, but I still feel that there is a stopping point and there has got to be a governor in the group's actions. I know beyond any doubt that I have helped in keeping some trouble down and keeping it to a minimum.
>
> The bad thing is I have a lot to lose and also can never tell what I have done or ever explain the reason I have done so. I know that there will be a time when my family will hear that I am a Klansman, and all that I can ever say is that they do not know what they are talking about.

Anne, my wife, has had a rough job in taking on more responsibility of the family and that she has come through with true colors. I am very lucky to have a person to give me such support and love and understanding as she has and to realize the danger and the good to come from it. I am very much in love with my wife and family.

CHAPTER 7

I N MISSISSIPPI, the emphasis of the civil rights struggle had shifted from direct-action campaigns involving sit-ins and protest demonstrations to the task of voter registration. The landmark Civil Rights Act, which swept aside legal footing for racial discrimination in public accommodations in 1964, led to the enactment of a companion Voting Rights Act a year later—a week after Tom Landrum joined the White Knights.

The latest congressional action was spurred by an assault by a mounted sheriff's posse on a march by voting-rights supporters in Selma, Alabama, in March 1965. Scenes of the violence—reminiscent of raids by murderous Cossacks during Eastern European pogroms—were carried on national television, provoking widespread indignation and a determination by President Johnson to win passage of the bill. It was another instance where terror by extremist defenders of racist codes proved counterproductive. As many southern whites began to recoil from the violence, recognizing that it was no longer helpful in preserving segregation, the reputation of the Klan was further diminished. Still, the White Knights attracted zealots prepared to use any means to fight off change even though they appeared to be engaged in a losing battle.

Eight years after the 1954 *Brown v. Board of Education* decision, the University of Mississippi had been integrated, and two years later the Civil Rights Act finally gave Blacks the right to eat in cafés, stay overnight in hotels, and attend theaters that had previously been segregated. Nonviolent defenders of the Lost Cause turned to new tactics. They felt racial integration could be circumvented bloodlessly by establishing all-white private academies and turning public establishments into clubs.

Extending voting rights to Blacks, however, posed a different and more significant threat for the segregationists, because it could not be easily overcome by an end run around federal law. It raised the specter of Black voting power, which could undo the political structure of the region. With Blacks accounting for nearly half of the population of Mississippi, the legislation could cause a cultural earthquake. Blacks would become a pivotal force at the polls, and in the rich land of the Delta, where their number dominated the population, they were poised to take over the government of cities and counties. For these reasons, critical battle lines were being drawn.

The federal legislation of 1965 was designed to eliminate barriers thrown up by segregationists to prevent Blacks from registering to vote by employing capricious literacy tests, poll taxes, requirements for property ownership, and arbitrary judgments by voting registrars on the moral character of applicants. The Voting Rights Act would diminish the power of circuit clerks like Leonard Caves in Jones County, his counterpart next door in Forrest County, Theron Lynd, and John Wood of nearby Walthall County, who once became so annoyed with a Black applicant that he pistol-whipped him on the way out of his office.

The law provided stronger teeth for the U.S. Justice Department, whose civil rights division had already been actively investigating voting-rights abuses in Mississippi and working in tandem with grassroots organizers intent on increasing opportunities for registration. The division was the product of the twentieth century's first civil rights act, in 1957, which gave Justice Department officials limited authority to implement Fourteenth and Fifteenth Amendment provisions dealing with voting rights.

The most impressive figure among the government lawyers sent

to the South in the early sixties was Wisconsin Republican John
Doar, the number two man in the civil rights division, a unit filled
with recent law school graduates dedicated to the activism espoused
by Attorney General Robert Kennedy. Though Doar was in his for-
ties, few of his more youthful associates could match his tireless
enthusiasm for his job. Instead of operating out of bureaucratic
Washington, Doar beat the backcountry bushes. He made personal
contacts with many local Blacks, listening to their grievances and
winning their trust when it became obvious that he was committed to the mission. He was the first government official to meet with
Vernon Dahmer, who by this time had been largely working in vain
to register Blacks in Forrest County. While FBI agents traveled in
Mississippi in pairs, dressed in dark suits like Mormon missionar-
ies per Director Hoover's orders, Doar often moved about by himself in informal clothing more compatible with the people he visited.
One of the first men he sought out was Dahmer, whose involvement
in voting-rights activity was well known in the area. They met at
Dahmer's farm, where Doar's host itemized a history of discrimination in Forrest County. A sense of mutual respect developed immediately. There was nothing flamboyant about either man; each went
about his business in a no-nonsense style.

Doar was also unique in that he recognized the importance of
building constructive relationships with journalists, who were
beginning to cover the movement with interest. He tried to be
responsive to their questions, and sometimes he offered inside guidance on stories. He had enough respect among the national reporters to entice them to follow his efforts in out-of-the-way places.

One of Doar's earliest targets was Forrest County. After he
learned of the repeated rebuffs encountered by each Black who
went—sometimes escorted by Dahmer—to the circuit clerk's office
in Hattiesburg to try to register to vote, Doar and his lieutenants
began compiling a dossier. With Dahmer's help, the Justice Department lawyers drew up a list of credible men and women in Forrest
County who were prepared to attest to their experiences at the hands
of the circuit clerk for the country, Theron Lynd. Doar believed he

would be able to document that these potential witnesses had given acceptable answers to Lynd's literacy test but had been failed by him without any explanation.

≈

BY MISSISSIPPI STANDARDS, Forrest County was relatively urban and cosmopolitan. It not only encompassed Mississippi Southern College and a smaller Baptist institution, William Carey College, it was the home of Camp Shelby, a giant army installation that had processed thousands of recruits during World War II and remained a major training base, which helped drive the local economy. Though Hattiesburg was one of the larger cities in the state, county officials ran the place as if it were a rural backwater where they felt free to impose any steps necessary to maintain white supremacy.

The procedure for voter registration at the Forrest County courthouse was contrived to represent an insurmountable obstacle for Blacks. Those who came to the circuit clerk's counter were disregarded or told to wait. White women among the personnel in the office were informed that they would not have to deal with any Black people; only Lynd, the elected clerk, had responsibility for seeing them, and he was invariably unavailable. When he deigned to meet with a Black applicant his manner was brusque and unyielding.

For the consumption of white voters in the county, Lynd liked to boast that no Black had been registered in Forrest County since he became circuit clerk in 1959. Lynd had run unsuccessfully for the office in 1955 against Luther Cox, the Forrest County official who had denied Dahmer's attempt to re-register as a voter following the 1949 plot to cleanse the voting rolls of all Blacks. Cox, claiming he had been able to block all but a handful of Black applicants over the years, was reelected. But after Cox's death, Lynd won a special election and set about bettering his record of intransigence.

Lynd was an exemplar of the "good ole boy" politicians of the time. He fit comfortably into the white environment of Hattiesburg, where he had played high school football. He graduated with a business degree from Mississippi State College and worked for a while for his father's gasoline-distribution firm, rising from a service station operator to an office manager, before going into politics. For respectability, he was an active Mason and a member of a Methodist church. He promised to keep preventing Blacks from voting.

Like many functionaries, Lynd had an important patron, a Hattiesburg lawyer named M. M. Roberts, a reactionary who had an influential role in the state's powerful segregationist bloc that elected Ross Barnett governor in 1959. Roberts had served as president of the state bar association in 1956 and, as a Barnett appointee, became a central figure on the board of trustees of the Institutions of Higher Learning, the "college board" that plunged the state into chaos by defying federal court orders over the integration at Ole Miss in 1962. Roberts was a veteran of fights dealing with discrimination. He had been the lead attorney representing Luther Cox when a group of disenfranchised Black men—led by Dahmer—filed a complaint as early as 1951, and he was eager to defend Lynd a decade later.

Despite Lynd's authority, he became a perfect foil for Doar and Dahmer. Not only was Lynd vulnerable to charges that he conducted the circuit clerk's affairs in a questionable fashion, he fit the physical stereotype of a southern bigot. He weighed nearly 350 pounds, his belly so massive that the top of his high-riding pants fit just below his armpits. He kept a cigar clamped between his teeth and mastered a way of talking without removing it. He favored black horn-rimmed glasses and his receding hairline revealed a bulbous, pasty forehead.

Renowned for his rudeness, Lynd seemed to take pleasure in his power to turn back a parade of Forrest County Blacks seeking to sign up as voters. Some were laborers and farmers recruited by Dahmer. Others were college-educated teachers and ministers who went to the courthouse on their own initiative. All were rejected.

"So, it's you again," Lynd snapped one day, seeing Dahmer in his office. He proceeded to lecture Dahmer on the importance of ensuring that only literate citizens held the balance of power for democracy, that elections should never be thrown into the hands of ignorant people.

Lynd may not have known it at the time, but Dahmer and his friends were producing for John Doar a number of local people prepared to testify against the circuit clerk. Meanwhile, Justice Department lawyers were collecting evidence of discriminatory practices in other places, as well, as they built a legal assault on circuit clerks in the state. In George County, just south of Forrest County, it was found that the clerk usually asked applicants to interpret Section 30 of the Mississippi Constitution—"There shall be no imprisonment for debt"—in order to pass the literacy test. Blacks were failed, regardless of their answers, but an inspection of documents showed that one white applicant had passed with a particularly interesting written interpretation of the law: "I thank that a nearger Should have 2 years in college Be for voting. Be Cause he don't under Stand."

≈

THE SITUATION IN Forrest County proved to be so outrageous that in July 1961, only six months into the Kennedy administration and four years before the voting-rights legislation passed, the Justice Department filed suit against Lynd to seek injunctive relief. Much of the evidence involved material turned over to the government lawyers by Dahmer, who had been happy to share his frustrations with sympathetic officials.

THE TRIAL BEGAN in Jackson in March 1962, and the first witness for the government was Jesse Stegall, an earnest thirty-year-old principal at a Black elementary school in Hattiesburg who had graduated from Jackson State, a leading four-year state college for Blacks. He was not only literate, he was erudite. While a student, he had met such prominent Black writers as Langston Hughes, Zora Neale Hurston, and Margaret Walker Alexander.

Stegall was one of five teachers included in the government's roster of witnesses who held advanced degrees but had flunked Lynd's literacy test. He knew that by testifying he would risk his job, which he needed to support his wife and their child. "We were not going down to the circuit clerk's office to be troublemakers," he said of his motivation. "We were going down to get our right to vote. And when you were going down to register to vote and these barricades are placed before you, you get frustrated until it really angers you."

Stegall told of an attempt he and a fellow teacher, David Roberson, made to register to vote in 1960:

> Mr. Lynd came to the counter where Mr. Roberson and I had walked and asked, "What do you boys want?"
>
> I stated, "I came to find out procedures on which to register."
>
> He said, "What's your name?" I told him my name. He asked what did I do. I told him my occupation. He asked where I lived. I told him that also. And then he said, "No, I can't register you." He said he did not have the time. I asked, when would it be possible for me to see him when he had the time. He said he did not know.

Stegall and two other teachers did not return to the circuit clerk's office until nearly a year later, when they were emboldened by knowledge that the Kennedy Justice Department was trying to facilitate voter registration. But they were again discouraged by Lynd, who told them, "I can't handle all of you at the same time. You will have some papers to fill out." It was past four in the afternoon, and Lynd said, "If you do not finish by five o'clock you will have to begin all over."

The trio left and returned early the next day. Stegall was given an application form and a section of the Mississippi Constitution to interpret that dealt with chartering corporations. Taking a half hour, Stegall provided Lynd with a clear, written interpretation of the section, a document that was introduced into evidence.

Stegall testified that a week later he went to Lynd's office to see if he had passed. Lynd told him no. Asked what part of his application had failed, Lynd said, "I can't divulge that information." He told Stegall he would have to wait another six months before applying again.

Stegall, who held a PhD, said he tried six times to register and failed each time.

Presiding over the trial was the U.S. district judge Harold Cox, a close friend of Senator Jim Eastland of Mississippi, who had prevailed on the Kennedy administration to nominate him for the judgeship. Cox was another important cog in the state's political power structure. To the Justice Department attorneys, it appeared obvious that Cox would favor Lynd and his attorney, M. M. Roberts, and give little regard to Doar, who led the government case. After Judge Cox declared a thirty-day hiatus, the Justice Department appealed the case to a more friendly venue, the Fifth Circuit Court of Appeals in New Orleans, before the trial could be completed. A three-judge panel responded with an injunction against Lynd, noting that "the witnesses produced by the government proved without question that certain serious discrimination had taken place during the term of office of the defendant Lynd."

In spite of the order to discontinue his pattern of rejecting qualified Black applicants, Lynd continued the practice. After Dahmer and his son Harold went to the courthouse to register following the injunction, they had trouble finding the circuit clerk. When they appeared at Lynd's office, they were told he was upstairs in a courtroom. The Dahmers found the courtroom empty. Coming back downstairs, they caught Lynd leaving the office. He allowed the two men to fill out an application form, but when they checked back later Lynd told them they had failed and refused to give a further explanation.

In the face of Lynd's recalcitrance, the Justice Department went back to the Fifth Circuit seeking a contempt charge against him, and setting up a new trial in September 1962, in the midst of the climactic legal battle over the integration of Ole Miss that consumed national headlines and much of the court's attention.

Finally, on July 14, 1963, Lynd was found in contempt. As part of the order, forty-three Blacks who had attempted to register after the original injunction against Lynd were put on the voting rolls. Vernon Dahmer and his son were in the group.

≈

DAHMER DREW ENERGY from the court victory. Although it came only a month after the assassination in Jackson of his friend and NAACP associate Medgar Evers, Dahmer was unintimidated and threw himself into the movement, which was gaining momentum. He and B. F. Bourn, his longtime ally in the battle in Forrest County, embraced the activities of a new generation of volunteers willing to sacrifice themselves. Although Dahmer and Bourn realized their old organization, the NAACP, was thought stodgy by many of the young volunteers coming from more radical groups such as SNCC, they developed a rapport with the activists.

Among them was Lawrence Guyot, the twenty-four-year-old activist who had been involved in the Hattiesburg Project and returned to help win support from the National Council of Churches for a voter-registration demonstration in Hattiesburg. The labors of the young Turks in the movement, combined with the groundwork carried out by local people like Dahmer, contributed to the passage of the Voting Rights Act.

Armed, at last, with federal law in 1965, Dahmer redoubled his efforts as the year came to an end. He turned his little country store, next to his home, into an unofficial clinic for voter registration. The fifty-seven-year-old farmer, who had spent the years after World War II as an obscure irritant to the white leadership in his home county, was emerging as a major figure in a state bristling with challenge and resistance by Blacks. After years of struggle, Dahmer's work had attracted not only the attention of government officials like John Doar but recognition that he was a significant player in the movement.

His renown had another effect. In the eyes of the devoted racists in the state, he had become a menace. If Dahmer could not be stopped by state laws or the whims of segregationist circuit clerks, and if the feeble efforts of the United Klans affiliates in Forrest County were unable to control him, the job fell to the White Knights in neighboring Jones County to put an end to his activities.

CHAPTER 8

A T THE APPROACH of the Christmas season, the mood among members of Landrum's circle of White Knights reflected mostly ill will, spite, and suspicion. Instead of finding himself in the fraternal organization promised by Leonard Caves—a collection of good men bonded by their desire to preserve segregation—Landrum realized that the group had many malcontents with a growing resentment for Deavours Nix.

It was also apparent to him that the FBI had infiltrated the White Knights, and many of the men had become increasingly wary of each other. Others simply dropped out of the group. Sparsely attended meetings featured not only diatribes against Blacks but in-house bickering among the members. Constable Gerald Martin's constant expressions of concern over the drunken conduct of some of the White Knights had been picked up by others. Anger at Nix finally boiled over at a December 23 meeting of Landrum's klavern, when Nix was openly criticized for the way he operated John's Restaurant. One member complained that the Klan hangout had been transformed by Nix from a family restaurant into a "beer joint" where White Knights drank too much and sometimes talked too loudly about their secret movements, bragging indiscreetly about burning down the homes of Blacks. Another Klansman observed that Nix sold beer to minors, a sure way to invite an investigation into the practices of the café.

At the same meeting, another member of Landrum's klavern, who was rethinking his decision to join the Klan, said he was uncomfortable with the rules. Landrum sensed that his criticism was directed at Nix, whose bossy manners annoyed many members. Sam Bowers's chief henchman might hold the rank of "grand director of the statewide Klan Bureau of Investigation," but Nix appeared to be appropriating power for himself that he didn't deserve.

Landrum was hardly prepared to speak out publicly against Nix, because he didn't want to alienate him further. Landrum considered the man his foremost enemy among the White Knights. Although he had been the officer to swear Landrum in, Nix had morphed into an adversary who frequently glowered at him. Meanwhile, Landrum's dislike of Nix hardened. He knew Nix was dangerous.

The Jones County units of the White Knights seemed to be breaking into cliques. Instead of a tight structure of several klaverns working in concert in a campaign to terrorize Black residents, the organization had split into factions where strong personalities prevailed. While ordinary members groused about problems, Bowers and Nix formed a two-man leadership team, meeting privately and issuing commands without wider discussion. They no longer seemed to trust many of the men they had recruited, relying on a handful of loyalists such as Cecil Sessum and a few other followers willing to accept any order Bowers handed down. Because of Nix's hostility, Landrum knew he would never be a candidate to join their small, informal fraternity, and he was relieved by that knowledge.

During some of his earlier meetings with the White Knights, Landrum had heard Bowers and others grumbling about the activities of the "Dahmer Nigger" in Forrest County. Now, in December, the talk was growing uglier, and Landrum suspected there were closed conversations taking place within the Bowers-Nix faction over what to do about the civil rights activist. But he was not privy to their thinking, and his reports to the FBI did not reflect an immediate threat.

≈

DURING THE LONG COURSE of Dahmer's activism, he and his wife Ellie had learned to live with danger. They knew that danger hung over not only them but their two children who lived with them: Bettie, their ten-year-old, and twelve-year-old Dennis, who was already helping his father on the farm and knew how to drive a car. The Dahmers took special steps to protect the youngsters, putting them in secure bedrooms with windows that were unexposed to the front of the house. More than once, windows facing Monroe Road had been shattered by rocks. There was also Dahmer's eighty-year-old aunt, Luranie Heidelberg, to be concerned about. "Aunt Ranie" managed the Dahmer store next door and lived in a room in its rear.

The Dahmers weathered the random violence—the windows broken by vandals and the hay shed torched—and they had become somewhat accustomed to the obscene telephone calls. Ellie would listen to conversations on an extension as Vernon fended off the threats: "Nigger, you're gonna get killed if you want your child in somebody's white school" or "You black nigger bastard, you might think you're white, but you're not" or "Nigger, you're going to get killed if you keep on doin' what you're doin'." Quite often the Dahmers would hear loud music and laughter in the background and concluded the calls were coming from men juiced by alcohol in redneck honky-tonks.

Occasionally, a male voice on the phone offered lurid suggestions. He called Dahmer a "queer" and proposed meeting places where homosexual needs could be fulfilled. "Man, I've got a wife and children," Dahmer told the caller. "You've got the wrong person." Ellie, who overheard them, labeled these "the freak calls, the sex calls."

The telephone messages were unsettling, but posed no physical threat. When Klansmen posted signs on trees near their home warning Dahmer of retribution for his voting-rights work, he tore them down. To him, the posters were no more capable of harm than the anonymous voices on the phone. Still, the Dahmers stayed on guard against intruders. Ellie had a theory that no southern man, even a vicious Klansman, would shoot a woman. She believed they respected womanhood, even Black women. She designated herself as the one to open the front door when a visitor knocked.

At the height of the period when they felt in jeopardy, the Dahmers slept in shifts. Ellie went to bed first, early in the evening, then woke after midnight, when Vernon would sleep. Some nights the country road outside their home carried the sound of cars that seemed to be hovering near their property and neither of them would be able to rest. Vernon was prepared for trouble. He kept a shotgun, loaded with buckshot, as well as a pistol, at his bedside. Curiously, the threatening phone calls tailed off at the end of the year, and the Dahmers decided it was safe to sleep like ordinary people.

～

ACTUALLY, the White Knights were plotting to kill him.

Dahmer became a major topic of discussion at a series of Klan meetings in December, although his name was no longer mentioned. The White Knights reverted to their rules regarding the guarded use of names. Members were to be referred to by code numbers assigned to them, and now Dahmer's name was replaced by cryptic mentions of a project "down south," a job that needed to be done in Forrest County, just south of Jones County. The secrecy was extraordinary, and although Landrum sensed that something was going on, he was excluded from the meetings.

The subject of the "job down south" was broached again at a specially called mid-December meeting held in an abandoned house on Masonite property in the Bogue Homa swamp northeast of Laurel, not far from Lawrence Byrd's farm. A select group—all of the White Knights hierarchy from Jones County—attended.

The imperial wizard was the first to speak. Bowers told the group that action was required to deal with the "big NAACP nigger" in Forrest County. "The Klan down there has done nothing to stop him, so I'm going to take the matter into my own hands to see that he is stopped," he said, and paused. "I want good men who are willing to stop him."

Nix followed Bowers and assured the group that the situation had been "thoroughly investigated" and that there was only one solution. "He has to be done away with." The two men yielded the floor to Sessum so that he could reinforce their remarks with a pep talk. "This is a job where we're going to need to take action against an individual who represents a threat to everything we stand for," Sessum declared with the conviction of one of his Sunday morning sermons directed at the devil. "It's an important job and maybe we need more than the Code Ones and Code Twos we've been enforcing around here." He looked toward Bowers and asked, "What's going to be done to the nigger?"

"That will be decided after a dry run is made," Bowers said, indicating that the operation required careful planning because it would take place in unfamiliar territory in Forrest County. "We need to case the place," he said. "No need to wait to get started. Anybody who's interested in going on a dry run should leave here immediately and meet at McCarty's Texaco station in Laurel. We'll make arrangements."

Thirty members of the White Knights were at the meeting. Six of them showed up at the service station: Henry deBoxtel, Billy Moss, Lamar Lowe, Pat Lowe, Bill Smith, and Billy Roy Pitts. When deBoxtel saw that Moss was one of the volunteers, he reconsidered. "I don't like the son of a bitch," he muttered. "Count me out."

DeBoxtel was known to be ornery, a bully whose brown eyes held little warmth. A high school dropout and an army veteran, he still styled his hair in a military buzz. He was a heavy drinker, and liked to imagine himself as a heavyweight boxer. Standing over six feet and weighing nearly two hundred pounds, he looked the part, and he enhanced that image by developing a reputation for beating up feeble drunks at a Laurel beer joint. His explosive temper made some of his Klan associates uncomfortable to be around him.

≈

A FEW DAYS LATER, Bowers visited Byrd at his radio and TV repair shop. Since Byrd had begged off the dry run on the grounds that he had back trouble, Bowers had another assignment for him. He handed Byrd two pieces of paper; each had been folded and taped. "Forrest" was written on one sheet and "Jasper" on the other, referring to problems in neighboring counties. "These need to be looked at," Bowers told Byrd.

The next Sunday night, Byrd set up a meeting in a forest near a fire tower off U.S. Highway 11, a well-traveled route between New Orleans and Washington that ran through Laurel. "I got a message from our imperial wizard," Byrd announced, "and we're gonna need some volunteers." He held up the two pieces of paper. "I got the Forrest County job, and I got something in Jasper County."

Robert Rivers, the exalted cyclops for one of the klaverns, raised his hand. He was willing to help even though he was still waiting to be reimbursed for the repair of his Volkswagen. "I got some men in my unit who live in Jasper County," Rivers said. "We can take care of it."

The Jasper County project involved a troublesome Black man who simply needed to be intimidated. The Forrest County job sounded far more serious. During a discussion about which klavern should accept responsibility, Sessum spoke up. "I'll take it and turn it over to my investigator in our group." To some, it seemed more logical to give the assignment to the klavern in Ellisville, not far from the Dahmer property. But the exalted cyclops for the Ellisville unit was elderly and afflicted with arthritis, and no one challenged Sessum.

Sessum believed that leading the operation against Dahmer would be an assignment that could turn him into a respected celebrity in the White Knights; an undertaking that would earn him Klan glory and possibly a highly publicized summons to appear before a congressional committee in Washington. Over the next couple of weeks, he wanted to be sure that the operation was planned carefully.

≈

T. WEBBER ROGERS, a barber in Laurel who cut the hair of Bowers, Nix, and Sessum, had recently been encouraged by Sessum and Nix to join their Klan. After his induction, Rogers was taken to his first White Knights meeting in the Glade community, down Highway 15 from Laurel. The new initiate was bewildered by some of the Klan procedure and unable to understand several references to the job "down south" and the importance of "getting this one done right." Rogers knew some of the men who were talking—Sessum, deBoxtel, Travis Giles, Pat Lowe, and Pete Martin—but he didn't know what they were talking about.

It was still unclear to Rogers after he heard Bowers exhorting his men about "a job down south" at another meeting in the house on Lawrence Byrd's farm. The old frame building was ideal for the secret gatherings of the White Knights. Located several hundred yards from the nearest public road, it had church pews for seating in one of the rooms.

The night was unseasonably cold, so the interior was warmed by flames from a wood-burning fireplace. Outside, Billy Roy Pitts, one of the youngest members of the White Knights, stationed himself close to the exterior chimney to catch a bit of its heat. Because of Bowers's presence, special security arrangements were in place. Pitts had been assigned duty as "sheriff of the Inner Guard," with responsibility for sweeping the site for FBI bugs and standing sentry. Straining, he could hear the voices inside.

After an opening prayer by Sessum, the "Little Preacher" introduced their leader. "It's an honor to have the imperial wizard with us tonight," Sessum said. "So without a whole lot of to-do, I'm going to turn the floor over to him because he's got something important to talk to us about."

"As some of you know," Bowers began, "I've been called to Washington early next year to testify before some House of un-American Activities, some kind of committee of congressmen, so I want to be sure some projects are taken care of down here before I go up there.

"One of those projects that we need to get moving on involves a job down south in Forrest County. There's a nigger down there who's causing a lot of problems between the whites and the blacks with his voter-registration drive. We need to show these people in

Washington that we people in Mississippi mean business. We've got to take care of problems caused by local people, and we got to show that we're tired of upstart niggers and carpetbaggers coming from the North."

Bowers's lieutenants—Nix, Sessum, deBoxtel, Byrd, and Klan lawyer Travis Buckley—listened raptly as he continued.

"The nigger I'm talking about works for the NAACP, which is a communist organization. It would be a favor to America to get rid of that whole organization, and we can do our part. So I'm calling on you all to complete this project involving this nigger before I head up to Washington."

~

THE FOCUS OF Bowers's mission became much clearer to Webber Rogers during an informal get-together of Klansmen at John's Restaurant one night later in December. By this time, Rogers realized that Nix's café was not only the favorite hangout for his friends in the organization, it served as the de facto headquarters for the White Knights. Under a haze of cigarette smoke drifting toward the ceiling, he saw Sessum murmuring with other Klansmen seated at tables in the room. The place seemed pregnant with anticipation that something momentous was about to happen. Sessum disappeared into a meeting on the second floor. Afterward, he came downstairs to report that "Sam approved the idea." Rogers assumed it had something to do with the project "down south."

Following his clandestine meeting upstairs with Bowers, Nix, and Buckley, Sessum approached Rogers and asked him to join deBoxtel and Giles outside. The four men got into Sessum's car. The sky was moonless and dark and an air of intrigue settled over the group. Although he was behind the wheel, Sessum announced, "I don't know where we're going or why." The others remained silent. He drove a short distance, then pulled to the side of the road. In a few minutes another car, with three men inside, passed. Sessum followed and the two cars moved onto Interstate 59, heading south toward Hattiesburg. Soon, Rogers saw that a third car had joined the motorcade moving slowly through the Mississippi night.

The cars turned off the interstate at an exit near Kelly Settlement. Rogers knew the territory. Peering through the darkness, he recognized the Dahmer store. He began to make a connection between this trip and a remark he had heard at an earlier Klan meeting. Someone had inadvertently used the name Dahmer in a discussion of the project "down south" and Sessum had rebuked the Klansman for the indiscretion. It seemed obvious that the Dahmer establishment was a target because Sessum and deBoxtel took note of the time required to travel from the highway to Dahmer's store. After the lead car turned around, heading back toward Laurel, its headlights blinked several times as a signal. Still, no one spoke, and Rogers remained somewhat puzzled.

Back in Jones County, Sessum dropped Rogers off at his home. They had just completed the first of several "dry runs" that Bowers wanted to make to determine the lay of the land.

≈

FOR AN ORGANIZATION descended from the original Invisible Empire and dependent on secrecy, the White Knights turned out to be clumsy practitioners of stealth, though they developed plans to cover themselves. To use a different vehicle for another "dry run" they asked George Boutwell, an engineer at Masonite, to loan his car for the drive to the Dahmer place. Boutwell was willing to help, and left his automobile with its keys inside at a Laurel service station. In case the car was identified, Boutwell thought to establish an alibi for himself by riding around Jones County that night with Gerald Martin, as his fellow Klansman made his nocturnal rounds as a peace officer. If his car were identified Boutwell had been assured that he could always say someone had stolen it.

Others involved in the operation were not as clever. No one seemed to think about the unique appearance of Boutwell's car. It was a gleaming white Buick Skylark bearing white sidewall tires and mounted with a whip antenna for his CB radio. The car was made more distinctive by a bumper sticker with the message "Visit Laurel, Mississippi." The Klansmen did not realize it, but Boutwell's car did, in fact, attract attention from other residents along Monroe Road, who were suspicious of strange cars because they knew their neighbor was being harassed.

Boutwell's Buick was driven to Kelly Settlement by Billy Moss, one of the Klansmen whom Bowers considered reliable. Sessum rode in the front passenger seat and another White Knight named Arnold Ingram was in the back. Ingram was told during the drive that he was taking part in an exercise for the project "down south" and invited to participate in the future raid. The trio completed their reconnaissance without incident, but when Ingram got home he declined the offer to become more deeply involved.

After Moss learned that deBoxtel would have command of one of the cars to be used in the operation, he dropped out. Just as deBoxtel had expressed reservations about Moss earlier, Moss complained to Byrd, "I don't trust that damned Henry deBoxtel."

It turned out that Rogers the barber would not be deemed by Sessum an appropriate accomplice for the raid. He lacked enthusiasm and experience. Little Preacher was whittling down the number of men he trusted.

＝

A FEW NIGHTS LATER a small group met in a falling-down cotton house in the middle of a field. In the absence of Bowers, Deavours Nix used the opportunity to assert his authority, repeating Bowers's insistence to finish the project "down south."

"We been talking a lot, but we still haven't done nothing," Nix hissed. "We need to take action now. We need to get rid of the problem with the nigger down south, and by doing so, we're going to be sending a message to Washington and that committee. What we need is some special, strong, handpicked men. You men who are interested in carrying out this project should be in contact with the exalted cyclops." He was referring to Sessum, the man now clearly in charge of the mission.

≈

IN EARLY JANUARY 1966, Bowers felt the time had come to strike. He called another meeting with a group of a dozen or so trusted members of the Jones County White Knights on a rugged tract of Bogue Homa swamp property owned by the Masonite corporation. The men, bundled in heavy work jackets, shivered in the cold. Even in south Mississippi, not far from the Gulf Coast, the ground was tinged with frost. With few listeners, it wasn't necessary for Bowers to shout, but he raised his voice anyway for emphasis.

"Men," he yelled, "we're about to undertake a job that is important. It's the job down south that we've been talking about. For some reason it keeps getting put off. Now is the time to do something. You all know what's involved. We've got a nigger down south that needs to be hit and hit hard. He's a troublemaker who's been working to undo everything we believe in. He's been working with the federal government—which is full of communist infiltrators—and if he gets his way he'll have every nigger in the state going to the polls and electing a bunch of apes and baboons."

Bowers appeared to be extraordinarily exercised. A vein in his neck pulsed noticeably as he spoke.

"There's been a need to control the nigger in his own county, but our friends"—he sneered at the words—"in the United Klans have been unable to do anything. This is the time for our White Knights in Jones County to go into action. We been willing to cross over to places like Jasper County and Smith County to help out in the past, and now is the time for us to go to Forrest County and show the people what a real strong organization, dedicated to keeping our society stable and free from the taint of the black man, can do. It's our opportunity to get rid of a pest—mash him like a roach—and at the same time to prove that the White Knights deserve to have the reputation as the best defender of our way of life.

"We face a job that carries a risk but needs to be done. In the next few days, I'm gonna call on each of you to take up an assignment to complete the project we been talking about. You're here tonight because each of you have earned my respect. I hope I can count on you."

The men nodded their heads in affirmation. They seemed pleased to have been singled out from the ranks of the several hundred men belonging to the White Knights in Jones County. The short list included the county's top officers and Bowers's closest associates: Nix, Sessum, Byrd, deBoxtel, and Buckley. The others on hand hoped the invitation to attend the meeting would elevate them into Bowers's inner circle. It would give them special status as members of a tightly knit gang capable of carrying out a military operation— like the Green Berets they had been hearing about in Vietnam.

CHAPTER 9

DURING THE FIRST WEEK of the new year, a radio station in the area reported in a roundup of Mississippi news that Vernon Dahmer had escalated his voter-registration activity by volunteering to handle poll-tax payments at his grocery store in order to pass them on to the circuit clerk, Theron Lynd. The five-month-old Voting Rights Act had banned literacy tests and strengthened federal oversight to guard against racial discrimination in the registration process, but it failed to strike down poll taxes for state and local elections in some southern states. In addition to providing a friendlier venue for Blacks than the Forrest County courthouse, Dahmer said he would arrange to have the two-dollar poll tax in Mississippi paid for those who could not afford it. The annual tax—a punitive measure aimed at preventing Blacks from voting—could also be assessed cumulatively, creating a greater burden on poor prospective voters who struggled to find enough income to keep their families fed.

Dahmer's initiative provoked anger among the White Knights as soon as they heard the news item. At John's Restaurant, as several members of the White Knights huddled around a counter on the second Saturday night of the new year, Henry deBoxtel snarled, "The son of a bitch thinks now that he's the goddamned circuit clerk himself." Although curse words were discouraged at Klan meetings, profanity often rent the smoke-filled air at the café.

The clatter of silverware and conversations among other diners gave cover to most of the words coming from the small knot of Klansmen. But Bob Stringer, a teenage employee of the imperial wizard, was standing nearby and could hear them clearly. The boy was a regular presence at the café. He had been working for Bowers for several years and began running errands for the White Knights after the group formed. The Klansmen recognized that the boy was treated favorably by Bowers, sort of like, one of them said, "the son Sam never had."

Stringer came from a broken family and lived with his grandparents in Laurel. When he was fourteen, he met Bowers and was hired to handle odd jobs for Sambo Amusement Company. He helped deliver vending machines and packages for Bowers. After learning that the boy could type, Bowers put him to work on the *Klan Ledger*, a mimeographed "newspaper" circulated by the White Knights and mischievously named for the *Clarion-Ledger*, the state's largest paper, a far-right daily in Jackson. The boy not only delivered the *Klan Ledger*, which consisted of a few pages filled with racist, incendiary language and stapled together in leaflet form, he typed the messages on a stencil used to reproduce each page. He laughed at some of the crude poems displayed in the *Klan Ledger*:

> Now listen, you COMMUNIST and NIGGERS and JEWS
> Tell all your buddies to spread the news.
> Your day of judgment will soon be nigh
> As the Lord in his wisdom looks down from on high
> Will this battle be lost? NEVER! I say,
> For the KU KLUX KLAN is here to stay.

Bob Stringer moved freely among the White Knights. He attended some of their rallies, appearing as something of an apprentice Klansman. He listened with interest to the conversation at the counter, which included Bowers.

For several months, Bowers had been whipping his followers into a rage over Dahmer. He had called for Dahmer to be silenced, authorizing an attack to burn down Dahmer's home as well as his store, where the voting-registration activity was taking place. The raid fell under the category of Code Three, which called for severe punishment to be meted out by the Klan. The bylaws decreed that only the imperial wizard could call for Code Four, the ultimate penalty. As the complaints about Dahmer intensified, Bowers spoke up, invoking his leadership position among the men.

"I been telling you all along, we need to do something about the Dahmer Nigger," Bowers said. "The United Klan's not going to do anything. It's up to the White Knights. And the time is now."

Bob Stringer would not forget the next words he heard. They constituted a death sentence. The boy's exciting experience in an adult world took on a chill.

He saw Bowers slap his hands on the counter and declare, "Something's got to be done about that Dahmer Nigger down south."

DeBoxtel, one of his closest associates, said, "Sam, we need to put a Code Four on him."

"You don't have to tell me that," Bowers said. "I know. I know."

≈

THE NEXT DAY was Sunday, January 9. Vernon Dahmer attended services at the Shady Grove Baptist Church, just down the road from his home. He had been estranged from the congregation earlier in the decade, but as the movement gained ground and Dahmer's voting-registration work attracted wider respect, his relationship with the church had been restored.

In the spirit of a witness attesting to good works, Dahmer rose during the long service to make an announcement. "Now you all know we've been involved in a campaign to get more folks registered to vote in Forrest County," he told his fellow worshippers. There were murmurs of approval and shouts of "Yes, Lord!"

"Now we been making great progress. The federal government is on our side. We have government lawyers on hand to make sure the Voting Rights Act is being applied, and we're getting more and more people signed up to vote." With a note of sarcasm, he added, "Our friend, Mister Theron Lynd, can't stop us now. The Justice Department lawyers are watching every move he makes. But we still got one obstacle. The state of Mississippi can still demand that we pay poll taxes. That's their last thing they can cling to, to keep colored people from voting. So we've got to make sure that our people get this tax paid. It may seem a puny thing—two dollars a year—but it's a lot of money to some people, and the state is going to demand that we pay it in order to vote.

"So we're taking special steps to follow this law. I've arranged it so that our people can come to our store—they don't have to go down to that hostile courthouse in Hattiesburg. They can come to our store and pay their poll taxes, and we'll take that money down to the courthouse for them to make sure they'll be certified to vote."

Vernon Dahmer was gratified when a member of the congregation called out, "God bless you, Brother Dahmer." Others echoed the sentiment. Dahmer felt back in the good graces of the Shady Grove Baptist Church.

≈

LATE THAT NIGHT, a small delegation that met at John's Restaurant traveled in two cars from Laurel to a house in the country near Ellisville, the other seat of government for Jones County, where Cecil Sessum had been living with his parents since he and his wife separated. Moving past the gasoline pumps outside, the men entered the front door, finding themselves in a room converted into a small store that sold miscellaneous merchandise ranging from chewing tobacco to crackers. A curtain hung in an interior doorway dividing the store from living quarters in the back. Noting that he was their host, Sessum volunteered to make coffee for the group and swept behind the curtain. The others could hear him talking with his father as he fiddled with a percolator. The group was restless.

Billy Roy Pitts, one of the youngest of the White Knights, would carry vivid memories of the night for the rest of his life:

Aside from him and Sessum, there were six other men, all heavily armed with shotguns and pistols: Henry deBoxtel, Charles Noble, Cliff Wilson, Bill Smith, who went by the nickname "Lightning," Frank Lyons, and Lester Thornton. Smith nervously racked his pump-action shotgun to make sure it worked. Most of the men had 12-gauge shotguns, weapons used for serious hunting. Some had pistols strapped on their sides.

Pitts held a job as an upholsterer and had used his talents to rig himself with a quick-draw holster. He liked Western movies and admired the cowboys who were able to employ speed to draw down on adversaries in gunfights. He had made a special leather holster, and he wore it low on his hip so that his hand could hover near the .22-caliber pistol in it. He didn't bother to install a strap for the pistol; that would have impeded his ability to pull the gun in a moment's time.

Pitts knew that he might soon be called on to use it. Earlier in the evening, Sessum had stopped by Pitts's home and told him, "Get your gun and come with me." Pitts asked where they were going. "Sam Bowers has got a job for us to do." Sessum did not elaborate. They drove to John's Restaurant, where they were joined by others. After Sessum met privately upstairs with Bowers and Nix he suggested that the group reconnoiter at his place. Pitts had the impression that they were on a mission and had received a blessing from the Klan leaders, but Bowers and Nix stayed behind at the café.

Inside the Sessums' family store, the atmosphere was hushed as Sessum brought coffee to the men. They talked idly for a few minutes, mostly about the unpleasant cold, abnormal for Jones County even in January. Eventually, Sessum offered an awkward suggestion. He asked the men if they wanted to leave a note. "What kind of note?" one of them asked.

"A note," Sessum said, "for your family in case something happens to you tonight."

"Shitfire!" one of the men barked. A couple of others grunted, but no one wanted to compose a farewell message. It was unthinkable. Before now, Pitts had not thought of the possibility of danger or death. His concern deepened, but he figured it was too late to back out.

The men loaded their shotguns into the cars, careful that the weapons' safeties were in place. Sessum carried out several empty plastic jugs while Wilson unloaded more jugs he had in the trunk of his car. In all, there were twelve king-size containers that had once held liquid soap. Most had been obtained from a friendly laundromat. Sessum took the bottles to a gas pump in front of the store and filled each one. He put the jugs in corn sacks and told the men to keep the cargo on the back floorboards of the two cars. The pale blue Pontiac Wilson was driving wound up with seven full jugs. Five were distributed to the car deBoxtel drove, a Ford belonging to a fellow Klansman, Travis Giles, who had loaned his vehicle for the project.

On their way south, Pitts finally built up the nerve to ask Sessum, "What's going on?"

"Sam Bowers has this job down south in Forrest County he wants taken care of tonight."

"I know. I already heard that. But what kind of job? I'm worried about this because I really don't know nothing about it."

"Don't get no cold feet, Billy Roy. There's nothing to worry about. This ain't gonna be no problem," Sessum assured him. "We've done dry runs on this project and we know how to do it right."

After nearly an hour, the cars passed their destination—the Dahmer home and country store. Instead of stopping, they cruised past the site, turned around, and parked beside a large country building—Shady Grove Baptist Church. The eight men climbed out of the cars and stretched. In the cold, their breath created tiny clouds. Through the darkness, they could discern a cemetery next to the church. Sessum walked to one of the graves and began urinating. The group laughed at the sport, and followed Sessum. Each of the men pissed on the gravesite.

"The only good nigger is a dead nigger," Sessum declared.

He climbed into the car with deBoxtel and told the others to wait at the church while "me and Henry check out the location of the project and make sure there ain't nobody around to interfere with us." They returned in fifteen minutes, when Sessum was ready with instructions.

DeBoxtel and the other three men in the Ford were responsible for setting fire to the Dahmer store. Sessum was riding with Pitts and Smith in the car driven by Wilson. It was a fancy Pontiac that reflected Wilson's status as a successful businessman in Laurel. Sessum said his group would take care of the Dahmer home. He told Wilson to be sure that he torched the Dahmers' car and pickup truck parked under a carport next to the house. "Make sure you shoot holes in the gas tanks so the gas will catch fire after you throw them jugs and get them lit up." Turning to Smith he said, "Bill, you shoot out the picture window in the house so we can throw the jugs inside." Pitts was assigned to cover the others as they flung the jugs. "If anybody tries to shoot at us, you shoot them. Make sure we're covered all the time."

With their headlights out, the two cars slowly approached the Dahmer property. Wilson pulled in front of the house at the same time that the Ford stopped by the store. The men emptied from the cars and began flinging the jugs of gasoline and firing their weapons. The fusillade pierced the silence of the night.

While Pitts crouched behind a brick flower box in front of the Dahmer residence, he watched as a blast from Smith's shotgun shattered the picture window while Wilson attacked the carport. Sessum, frantic with excitement, thought he heard a retaliatory roar from a shotgun fired inside the house. He ripped the jugs from their sacks, twisted off their caps, and slashed the sides with a pocket knife. He pitched two jugs, spilling gasoline, through the broken window and dashed the contents of the others against the eaves of the house. He had prepared a forked stick with a rag soaked with gasoline, but the shaking of his hands forced him to strike several matches before the device could be lit. When he threw the makeshift torch through the broken window, the room and the face of the house exploded into flames.

The four men piled back into Wilson's car. They could hear shouts of distress from the Dahmer home; they could see that the store was ablaze, too. "We got that bastard burnt out good," Sessum muttered with satisfaction. As Wilson whipped the car toward the road he veered close to the Ford as it pulled away from the store. Inexplicably, the headlights on the Ford were turned on, and Lightning Smith, riding in Wilson's Pontiac, panicked. Smith reached for his pistol and began firing at the Ford.

"What in the goddamn hell are you doing?" someone bellowed, oblivious to the ears of the minister among them, Cecil Sessum. "You're shooting at our own people, you fucking idiot!" Everyone in the car seemed to be yelling at Smith.

By this time, Smith had emptied his pistol. Suddenly chastened, he explained, "I thought it was the cops. I thought it was a trap."

The two cars careened toward a getaway, but it was obvious that deBoxtel's car could not keep up with the Pontiac. Instead of riding on rubber, the Ford sounded as though its metal tire rims were meeting the macadam of Monroe Road.

In the confusion, Billy Roy Pitts never got a chance to draw his pistol.

≈

ELLIE DAHMER AWAKENED to the bleating of a horn. Heat from the burning car had melted a wire and set off the noise. She knew instinctively something was wrong. "Vernon!" she shouted. "Get up! I believe they got us this time."

Her husband scrambled from the bed and saw flickering light from the flames in the next room. He grabbed his shotgun and yelled at his wife, "Get the children out while I try to hold 'em off!"

Bracing himself against a refrigerator in the kitchen, Dahmer fired back through the broken window. The concussions, coupled with the ungodly sound of the horn, created a terrifying din. Ellie hurried to the bedroom of her daughter, Bettie, asleep in the chaos. She pulled her from the bunk bed and tried to yank a coat hanging from the bedposts to cover her. Bettie wore only a long-sleeved nightgown, and Ellie intended to get her quickly outside, where the temperature was near freezing. Fumbling with the coat, she cast it aside; in the intense heat, she didn't have time to adjust the sleeves.

Because the window in Bettie's room was high above the ground, Ellie carried her to another window, where the drop was only a few feet. She had difficulty opening the window; her hands no longer seemed to work. She finally raised the window, but when she reached for her daughter she saw that Bettie had wrested herself away and was dancing and shrieking hysterically behind her. The window fell shut. Ellie looked for a piece of wood the family used to prop open the window in the summer; she couldn't find it. In a desperate move, she slammed her shoulder against the window. The entire fixture gave way, and she tumbled forward clumsily, through the opening and onto the ground outside. When she looked back, she saw that Vernon had their daughter in his arms. He handed her, as gently as possible, to her mother.

Meanwhile, twelve-year-old Dennis, aroused by smoke, opened his bedroom door, thinking the source of the commotion was an accident at the fireplace the family used in the winter. Startled by a gust of flame that licked into his room, he slammed shut the door and clambered out his window. Racing around the side of the burning house to alert his parents, he ran into his mother, father, and sister.

But another member of the family was unaccounted for—a twenty-six-year-old son, Harold, who had just completed a military assignment in South Korea and was living at home, sharing a bedroom with Dennis. Vernon, hobbled and weakened, was unable to climb into the boys' bedroom, so Dennis scrambled inside and woke his brother. Safely outside, the sons could see two cars speeding away from their property. One of the vehicles sounded as though it was riding on its rims.

Harold thought to ask, "Where's Aunt Ranie?"

His mother, looking toward the store that had been engulfed in flames, moaned, "Lord, have mercy! Aunt Ranie's been burned up."

A voice cried out from behind the house. "I'm over here." Aunt

Ranie had actually been the first to escape and was hiding in nearby woods.

Exposed by the light of the two burning buildings and fearing the raiders might return, the Dahmers and Aunt Ranie stumbled to a barn in the rear of the lot. Vernon, covered in ash and soot, assessed the group. Bettie appeared in immediate need of attention. Her arms were badly burned and she lay rolling on the frosted ground to get relief from the scalding pain. The whimpering child had thought she would die in the hellish room. Sitting on a bale of hay, Vernon was calm and able to talk, but reeling in agony himself. Flesh had peeled from his arms. "We got to get away from here," he said. "They might come back, and all our guns are in the house. We need to go."

Harold ran to the carport. Though the family car was being consumed by flames, the pickup truck might be functional. When he reached for the door, he recoiled from the heat but managed to open it. He slid inside, relieved to find the key in the ignition. Living in the country, the Dahmers felt secure in leaving keys in their vehicles. One of the truck's windows was missing, and hot glass sizzled in the seat, but Harold backed the truck from the carport and hurried to the home of Vernon's sister, who lived less than a quarter mile away.

After Earline Beard was awakened, she rushed to the scene in her own car. Neighbors were beginning to gather, watching helplessly from the road. In the bobbing light from the burning buildings, she saw that her brother's face and hair had been singed, and he was bleeding. Dahmer and his daughter were helped into the car, joined by Ellie and Aunt Ranie. Once the car was loaded, Earline Beard sped toward the hospital in Hattiesburg.

═

WHILE THE DAHMER FAMILY was making its way toward the barn, the Klansmen's departure faltered a half mile from the conflagration. Bill "Lightning" Smith had punctured two of the tires on the Ford with his barrage, and the limping car pulled to a stop off the road, forcing Wilson to pause the Pontiac, too.

Smith, who was being loudly derided as a fool, thought that he might have wounded one of the men in deBoxtel's car. Pitts found a first-aid kit and handed it to Smith to take to the crippled car. Smith was relieved to find that no one had been hit, but the tires were hopelessly deflated. He became the butt of new fury from his associates. Their language grew even bluer after they learned that Travis Giles, who had made the Ford available to them, had failed to pass on a key to the trunk, so they were unable to get access to a spare tire.

"We got to get the fuck away from here somehow," deBoxtel shouted in frustration. Rejecting Smith's offer of the first-aid kit, deBoxtel told him, "Get the fuck back in your own car. You've already fucked up enough for one night." Despite the flat tires, deBoxtel was determined to drive away. The two cars lumbered back onto the road, moving at a speed of less than twenty miles per hour. They were able to get across a nearby overpass above Interstate 59, but it was clear the Ford would never make it back to Jones County.

They stopped again, this time abandoning the Ford on the side of the road. Its four occupants crowded into Wilson's larger car. Now overloaded with eight nervous men, it lurched toward Laurel as the men squirmed and cursed among themselves. Billy Roy Pitts soon discovered a new reason for discomfort. His quick-draw pistol was missing. His fear that it could be traced to him overcame his reluctance to say anything to his seething companions.

"We got to go back," Pitts announced. "I think I dropped my pistol."

His announcement produced a chorus of groans, and the group's wrath was transferred from Smith to Pitts. "You got to be fucking kidding me," Pitts was told. "No way we're going back. No fucking way." The young man sat as unobtrusively as possible for the rest of the drive back to Sessum's place.

After the gang dispersed, Sessum drove Pitts home. Pitts pleaded for one stop on the way, at a trailer where Wilbur Holloway lived behind his service station in the Calhoun community. Pitts explained that Holloway was a fellow Klansman and a business associate of Sam Bowers. More importantly, Pitts said, "Wilbur bought a gun identical to mine from Rogers Trim Shop in Laurel, and I wanna borrow his gun so I can have an alibi if somebody asks me about my gun."

Sessum seemed skeptical, but Pitts insisted. "It's identical— Wilbur's gun to mine. Please, Cecil, I need to have that gun." Reluctantly, Sessum complied and the pair stopped at the trailer, where Pitts obtained the matching .22-caliber pistol from a drowsy and befuddled Holloway. It was just before dawn when Sessum left Pitts at his home, twelve hours after he had picked him up to go on the mission for Bowers. With the misadventure behind him, Billy Roy Pitts fell into a troubled sleep.

<hr>

WHEN THE DAHMERS REACHED the hospital emergency room, Bettie was assigned to one room, her father to another. The family insisted that the doctor look first at Bettie, who was wailing and seemed to be the most seriously wounded. Her hands and both arms were blistered and she had a mark on her forehead.

The physician attended to Bettie, then moved on to her father. Under the harsh fluorescent light, he could see that Vernon was also in poor condition. Loose skin was stuck to his shirt, and it was necessary to cut away the clothing to reach the wounds. It would be a painful process, and the doctor asked Ellie to leave the room because the scene might become unbearable.

Eventually, after being treated for the burns, Vernon and Bettie were moved to a hospital room they would share. Aunt Ranie, who was uninjured, was taken to a relative's home to rest. Ellie stayed at the hospital. At least, she thought, we're all alive. We managed to survive.

Around nine o'clock Monday morning, when commercial life in downtown Hattiesburg revived, Ellie felt comfortable going to a J. C. Penney store to buy clothes for members of the family. They had nothing but the torn garments, reeking with smoke, that they had fled in. But after she returned, Bettie became violently ill, spoiling her bed with vomit. In the adjacent bed, Vernon raised himself. He was able to talk, and he tried to comfort her. For a while, Ellie feared they might lose Bettie. She seemed so sick. But the nausea dissipated and the girl settled into sleep.

Dahmer was able to talk with a local reporter who came to his room seeking a brief interview. "I've been active in trying to get people to register to vote," he told his visitor, expressing some frustration. "People who don't vote are deadbeats on the state. I figure a man needs to do his own thinking. What happened to us last night can happen to anyone, white or black. At one time I didn't think so, but I have changed my mind."

Later in the long morning, Ellie left the hospital, which had become a hive of activity caused not only by the busy medical staff but by law enforcement officers and dozens of the Dahmers' friends, who were keeping a vigil in waiting rooms. Ellie felt it would be all right to leave. Her daughter and husband appeared to be resting comfortably, and she went to a cousin's home to try to get some sleep herself.

Her nap was interrupted in the afternoon by a visit from members of their church. She was told she should return to the hospital because Vernon had taken a turn for the worse. Her husband and daughter had been moved to another room, closer to the nurses' station, and Vernon had been given oxygen to help him breathe.

Ellie moved a chair so she could sit between the two beds. Bettie seemed to be sleeping soundly, but Vernon was restless. When he turned to face another direction, Ellie slid her chair so she could watch him. He dozed. Exhausted, Ellie put her head on the bed beside him. Suddenly, he sat up and loudly shouted her formal name—"Jewell"—and fell into her arms. She buzzed for a nurse while Bettie, alarmed by her father's outburst, climbed from her bed and raced for help.

Nurses brought a new oxygen tank and told Bettie and Ellie it would be best for them to move to another room. Leaving, they glanced back at the head of their household. It would be the last time they saw him alive.

The death certificate employed stark medical terms: "Peripheral vascular collapse [shock], thermal injury [burn] respiratory trac." But the reaction from Dahmer's friends, his allies in the civil rights movement, and the federal forces that had been working with him could not be reduced to clinical language. As word spread through the community that Dahmer was dead, it unleashed raw and visceral emotions. More than three hundred Blacks, no longer cowed by local authorities, marched on the courthouse, demanding action. They were led by Charles Evers, the fiery NAACP field secretary who had come home to Mississippi to fill the position held by his brother, Medgar, after he had been gunned down at his home in Jackson three years earlier. Evers called for an economic boycott of white businesses in the city. Grievance lists were prepared by Dahmer's friends in Hattiesburg to present to the city council, the Forrest County board of supervisors, the sheriff, and the local chamber of commerce.

Not lost on the public was the fact that four of Dahmer's grieving sons—Sergeant George Dahmer, Staff Sergeant Martinez Dahmer, Private Alvin Dahmer, and Master Sergeant Vernon Dahmer Jr.— were all serving in the U.S. military at distant posts and had to rush back to their home for his funeral. To dramatize their commitment to their nation—in spite of their father's murder by a force that had been at large in the country for a century—the four sons dressed in their uniforms to inspect the ruins of the Dahmer home.

~

ANOTHER MOVE TOOK PLACE out of the public eye. The FBI quietly deployed one hundred additional agents into the Piney Woods, similar to the mobilization President Johnson had ordered in outrage following the murders in Neshoba County eighteen months earlier. With a much smaller force in the area, the FBI had been pecking at the White Knights with limited success, yet their efforts had not been enough to save Dahmer. They had no informant with any knowledge in advance about the raid at the Dahmer place; aside from hearing occasional mutterings about the "Dahmer Nigger" at Klan meetings, Tom Landrum knew nothing of the plans to strike. Because of Nix's animosity, Landrum realized, he was being excluded from some of the more private, belligerent Klan meetings. That was all right with him. Yet when he learned of the attack, Landrum was appalled and consumed by guilt over his association with the White Knights. He immediately believed his Jones County faction to be responsible. At the same time, struggling with emotion, Landrum felt his resolve to help eradicate the Klan reinforced by anger.

CHAPTER 10

Lawrence Byrd heard of the strike at the Dahmer home shortly after he climbed from his bed that Monday morning. The story led the news on a local radio report at 6 a.m., a program that ordinarily featured routine items about the week's speakers at civic clubs, details of upcoming funerals, market prices for agricultural commodities, and the weather. The newscaster sounded a bit breathless, reading the wire-service account of the predawn attack, for this had the potential to attract national attention.

Byrd's first reaction was chagrin. The raid must have been carried out by the White Knights of his own county because Bowers had been urging his men to put a stop to the problem "down south" for days. Yet Byrd, the group's senator, had not been told that it was imminent, and he considered himself one of the most important officers in the structure of the Jones County Klan.

It sounded as though the raid had been botched, for if its purpose had been to eliminate the pesky Black man, Dahmer had survived, according to the report. That gave Byrd some perverse satisfaction because he had been left out of the planning. In fact, he quickly concluded, it had been an impulsive operation conducted outside the normal channels of the organization, and it was bound to have adverse repercussions.

He dressed and headed for his radio and TV repair shop in

downtown Laurel earlier than usual. He expected there would be a lot to deal with over the next twenty-four hours. En route, he learned just how badly the White Knights team had screwed up the assault on Dahmer. As he paused at an intersection, a dilapidated Buick he recognized as one belonging to deBoxtel pulled alongside his pickup. DeBoxtel's passenger, Travis Giles, waved for Byrd to pull over for a conversation.

"I'm in a hell of a shape," Giles shouted. "I loaned my car last night to go on that project Sam was talkin' about, and now I'm in deep shit because it's down there with two flat tires, down where the burning went on last night. I didn't have nothing to do with that operation, but now I'm going to be the one in trouble."

"What in the hell's going on?" Byrd asked. "I just heard on the radio the Dahmer Nigger's house got burned down and he's in the hospital."

"We can talk about all that later," deBoxtel said. "Right now we got to figure out what we can do about Travis's car."

Byrd thought of a solution. "Hell, Travis, go over to Grady Chance's service station and get his nigger, Pee Wee, to go down there and put some new tires on it."

"That ain't gonna work," Giles said, his shrill voice betraying his anxiety. "The Feds are gonna be all over the place and they're gonna be able to trace it to me. They probably already seized it. That was a damn good car, and now I'm likely to lose it. And they're gonna blame me for burning down the nigger's house."

DeBoxtel interjected his remedy for the situation. "I been tellin' Travis to report the goddamned thing stolen."

"That's a good idea," Byrd said. " I don't really know what's going on, but if you can't get to your car to fix it, you need to report it stolen. Call the Laurel police department."

"That ain't gonna work," deBoxtel snapped. "The car's not in the city, it's out in the county somewhere. Travis needs to call the sheriff's office. Tell them somebody lifted it while he was working on the night shift. He's clean since he can prove where he was."

Byrd rejected deBoxtel's idea; he thought it was dumb. "If he calls the sheriff's office, that's a tip-off he knows where the car is. Call the fucking police department, Henry. They the one's got jurisdiction at the plant where Travis is gonna say it got stole."

Giles was not so sure about any of the proposals, and he seemed to be growing more agitated.

"I'm gonna take him down to the Chow House," said deBoxtel, who managed the café for his mother. "Get him a cup of coffee. Get him to properly report the thing stolen."

As they drove off, Byrd thought: This is a fine fucking state of affairs. Whoever tried to pull off that raid couldn't direct traffic at a one-car funeral.

≈

THAT THE DIMENSIONS OF the White Knights' problems were worsening became apparent to the imperial wizard after word got back to him that not only had a car been left behind but Billy Roy Pitts had lost his pistol. Bowers thought: My organization's already full of informants for the FBI. The men I trusted and selected to go on the project failed to kill the "Dahmer Nigger." They shot up their own car. And now it turns out that one of them left his gun behind for the FBI to trace. Mulling over the situation with Nix in their aerie at John's Restaurant, Bowers told him to summon Pitts.

Pitts was shaken from his fitful sleep by the ringing telephone. "The boss wants to see you right away in my office," Nix told him. Pitts drove to the restaurant, anticipating a rebuke from Bowers and wondering, for the first time, whether he should flee Jones County.

When he arrived for the meeting, Pitts saw Bowers, Nix, and Sessum, waiting like some kind of high court ready to put a Code Four on him. Nix badgered him like a prosecutor. "Tell us, Billy Roy, what happened down at the "Dahmer Nigger's" house last night. Tell us about the pistol that we hear you lost down there. You know you have put all of us in a world of trouble." Even though Sessum had been at the scene and knew what had happened, he joined in the interrogation as if he was learning about the raid for the first time. Bowers, wearing a grim expression, began to pace the room.

Pitts explained that the pistol could not be traced to him. "I bought it from a man in Sandersville," he claimed, lying. "I don't recall no paperwork that ever went on about the gun. He just sold it to me personally. No way nobody's gonna trace it to me, and if they did, I already got the exact duplicate I can show the FBI. Cecil knows I borrowed the exact same gun from Wilbur Holloway as soon as we got back early this morning."

Before Pitts could continue, Bowers pointed a finger a few inches from his face and spit out his condemnation: "I handpicked you myself to be a replacement on this job. And you let me down. You fouled up—big time. You got us in trouble, and all of this is causing us to have to buy a car for Travis Giles."

Pitts couldn't understand why Bowers was yelling at him about Giles's car when it was Bill Smith who shot out the tires, but he didn't dare raise that point with the imperial wizard. He was relieved to be dismissed after getting a final warning from Bowers: "You keep your damned mouth shut. I don't want you talking about any of this among the men or anybody else."

～

LATER IN THE DAY, the radio station broadcast the news that Dahmer had died from his wounds, and fresh rumors and speculation ran through the ranks of the White Knights like a wildfire in the dry underbrush of the Piney Woods.

That evening, Sessum picked up Byrd to go to a meeting that representatives from each of the Jones County klaverns had been instructed to attend. Red Caldwell, the county giant, rode with them. On the way to the site, an out-of-season Boy Scouts campground, the men stopped to urinate on the side of the road. Byrd heard a limb snap in the adjacent woods and froze. "Did you hear that?" he whispered.

"Yeah," Caldwell answered, "but I didn't want to say anything because it would sound like I was running scared." They silently held their positions for several moments, thinking they might be under surveillance. The cold was biting, and when they heard nothing further, they returned to the car.

Sessum appeared more shaken than the others. "You know," he announced as though no one else knew, "the nigger died this afternoon." He was noticeably trembling and before restarting the car engine he rested his head between his arms, which cradled the steering wheel. Caldwell punched Sessum lightly on his shoulder and asked if he were OK. "I'm all right," Sessum said.

When they got to the campground, only a few men were there, blowing on their hands and stomping their feet to try to stay warm. After Sessum convened the session with a prayer he began relating his concerns to the group.

"We got problems with that job down south," he said. "I think one of our own men shot out the tires of Travis Giles's car, and Travis didn't leave a key to the trunk with our men so nobody could get to the spare tire." Sessum described the situation in the third person, as though he had not been a witness. "Our men had to leave the car behind." There were other difficulties, he said, alluding to the lost gun.

Byrd thought it was a propitious time to speak up. "The way things are turning out," Byrd said, "I think I been pushed around and put in a spot where I can be blamed, and I didn't have a damn thing to do with it. Sam Bowers and Nix bypassed me on this project. They chose the people and gave the orders and they never said a word to me about it. Ain't that right, Cecil?"

Sessum grunted an ambiguous response.

"I mean, rightfully, it was my job to pass on projects of this type," Byrd continued. "I am, after all, the senator for Jones County. But our imperial wizard, in his great wisdom, and his running mate, Deavours Nix, took it upon themselves to pull off this job. And look at the mess that's been made. I guess I'll have to take responsibility for the project," Byrd added wistfully. "I guess I'm willing to share the responsibility. But I wish they had said something to me."

By criticizing Bowers openly and referring to Nix by name, Byrd broke the Klan's rules, but neither Bowers nor Nix was there to object.

≈

THAT SAME NIGHT, the imperial wizard was making an appearance at a Klan meeting in Pachuta, a small Clarke County town about thirty miles north of Laurel, where he boasted of the Dahmer raid. "The Laurel group scored a big one," he told his followers. The mission was accomplished with only six or seven men, he said, far fewer than the number in the gang in Neshoba County. While there were problems with the "technical end," Bowers said, alluding to the abandoned car and lost pistol, "these men will never talk."

His remarks were immediately reported to the FBI by the visiting White Knights chaplain, Delmar Dennis, who had been acting for months as an undercover man for the bureau. Bowers had been pleased to be accompanied that evening by a "man of the cloth," not knowing that information Dennis had secretly supplied to the FBI earlier had been instrumental in leading to the arrests in the Neshoba County case and now would be used in the Dahmer investigation.

≈

THE NEXT NIGHT, a Tuesday, Tom Landrum attended a meeting with about a dozen members of his klavern where he heard the Dahmer attack discussed for the first time. The exalted cyclops, Speed Lightsey, seemed to know more than the others. He indicated that members of the Jones County White Knights had been involved and gave an account of how Giles's car had mistakenly been shot.

Others offered comments. Many remarks sounded outlandish, the product of rumor inflated with each telling. But some of the chatter had the ring of truth, and Landrum tried to concentrate on putting together the bits and pieces. Salient details were emerging and he wanted to remember every word that was being spoken.

When Landrum got home after midnight, he felt he needed to wake his wife. Quite often when he arrived late he would scribble a few sentences on his children's notebook paper to preserve his recollections until morning. But this night, he wanted her company. "Sweetheart, this is big," he told her. "We got to get all this down right away before I forget something important."

Without complaining, Anne left the bed and retrieved a pad and pencil to take notes that she would type surreptitiously in their courthouse office in the morning.

"The Dahmer killing was discussed and it was pulled by the Jones County Klan," Landrum's message to the FBI began.

> I have been unable to find out who did the job, but do know Giles who is Exalted Cyclops of South Group was in on the planning, and this is why his car was used while he was at work. The report that Dahmer shot the tires of Giles car is not correct according to Exalted Cyclops Speed Lightsey, who states there was a mix-up in the men who started shooting in house. Giles' car, driven by other Klansmen, made a pass by the house and circled back. The car was mistaken by Klansmen for someone coming to the aid of Dahmer family and therefore they started to shoot the car.

Landrum believed the next paragraph contained critical information, so he began with the word IMPORTANT, in capital letters:

> One of the Klansmen participating lost a .22 cal. S & W revolver. It is believed the house fell on it while burning. He was under the edge of house setting fire to it. Lightsey states this. The Klan has kept a close watch and states FBI has it staked off and gun will be found and traced to owner, which undoubtably was registered to owner.

Landrum also learned that the White Knights planned to assess each member a one-dollar fee to raise funds to repair Giles's car, in the unlikely event he would get it back. The Ford had bullet holes as well as flat tires. Red Caldwell, who fancied himself wealthier than the other Klansmen, promised to donate the tires.

Some of the scuttlebutt Landrum felt obligated to pass on to the FBI proved to be inaccurate, the product of wandering thoughts by worried men. A couple of members who were mentioned as likely suspects had nothing directly to do with the crime. But the crux of Landrum's message proved to be valuable.

~

LANDRUM'S REPORT CONFIRMED the suspicions of an FBI detail that began searching the grounds of the Dahmer property shortly after daylight on the morning of the fire, while the ruins of the home and store smoldered. Although the attack could be considered an offense under state jurisdiction, the FBI felt qualified to rush into the investigation under provisions of the Voting Rights Act.

One of the first pieces of evidence found by the agents was a .22-caliber pistol resting about ten feet from the house. No fingerprints could be lifted from the weapon because it had been exposed to intense heat, but the agents suspected it belonged to one of the assailants rather than Dahmer. The weapon was shipped to the FBI laboratory in Washington for further inspection.

The agents also collected four empty shotgun shells near the flower box in front of the house and three empty 12-gauge casings a few feet from the remains of the grocery store. One empty jug reeking of gasoline was found in the bed of Dahmer's truck that his son had backed out of the carport. There was another curious discovery, a Halloween mask that had been tossed by a tree. Plaster casts were made of tire tracks, but an examination would prove inconclusive. Material inside the house and store had been burned beyond recognition.

Within twenty-four hours Landrum met personally with Don Schaefler, one of his two local FBI controls, and another agent who had been dispatched to the scene to deal with the Dahmer case. Landrum was praised for providing the information about the lost .22-caliber pistol. The agents urged him to be especially careful now. Associating with the White Knights had become a deadly affair. At the same time, the agents encouraged Landrum to work doubly hard in obtaining more background. They told him they were on the threshold of breaking the case. Before their short meeting broke up, the agents changed code names for themselves and Landrum and chose a new location for him to hand over his written messages.

〜

MANY MEMBERS OF the White Knights were gripped anew by anxiety in the days following Dahmer's death. A fear of discovery, which had always lingered in the minds of the less boisterous Klansmen, began to spread to others.

The same day that Landrum met with the agents he drove to Speed Lightsey's service station in Sandersville. He felt comfortable engaging in a sensitive conversation with Lightsey because they had known each other for years. With little prodding, Lightsey told Landrum he felt the decision to kill Dahmer was the worst thing that could have happened to the Klan. He cited the mishaps in the bungled raid that could lead to the Jones County White Knights. Lightsey believed the operation had been conducted by a combination of men from different klaverns, but Landrum was unable to learn their identities. Customers at the service station kept interrupting their talk, and Lightsey would stray from the topic.

One of the more nervous members of the organization, pulled up to the gasoline pumps and beckoned Landrum and Lightsey to his car. "I'm scared to death," he told them. The FBI had questioned him earlier, at a time when he knew he was vulnerable after arranging repairs at his garage for a car that wound up with bullet holes during a Klan attack on a Black man's home. Now he was afraid he was being framed in a matter unrelated to the Dahmer case. The mechanic gave a rambling tale of how one of his employees—"who don't have dick for an education"—had been in contact with the FBI, seeking their help in securing him a job on the Laurel police force. The mechanic speculated that his employee would trade information about his Klan membership for the FBI's recommendation. The mechanic not only feared the FBI, he felt the White Knights might punish him for the leak.

Red Caldwell, the Jones County giant, who was usually boastful, showed rare introspection when he talked with Landrum on Wednesday. He said he was ashamed of the organization. "I'm looking for a good time to drop out," he said. Just two days earlier Caldwell had tried to appear confident when he accompanied Sessum and Byrd to the emergency Klan meeting after Dahmer died.

The White Knights were spinning out of control, Caldwell said. If the Code Four order to eliminate Dahmer had been handed down, it had been done improperly, because the chain of command had been ignored. He said Lawrence Byrd had claimed at the Monday night meeting that the incident "rested on his shoulders." Caldwell claimed Byrd had "okayed the project," ignoring the fact that Byrd actually complained that he had been bypassed.

"All this makes me and some others think Byrd is trying to take on too much power," Caldwell said. "The man glories in publicity. Byrd talks too much. I don't trust him. Speed Lightsey talks too much, too."

After Landrum said he knew nothing about the Dahmer project other than hearing about Giles's car, Caldwell passed on one other tidbit of misinformation. "One of the boys did lose his gun," he said. Then, turning to look at Landrum, Caldwell added, "That little Sessum guy seems so quiet. But then he turns around and talks too much, and it seems like he's always in on most of the stuff."

When Landrum speculated that it was Sessum who dropped the gun, Caldwell did not reply. Based on his interpretation of Caldwell's body language, Landrum reported to the FBI, "I feel almost certain that Sessum is the one who lost the gun."

In the course of their conversation, Landrum asked Caldwell if his own klavern was involved in the Dahmer raid. "If so, I'm ready to drop out," Landrum added. "I'm like you, I can't afford to be picked up by the FBI. It would ruin me."

"It was mostly the South Group," Caldwell said. "Maybe with a few others helping." He said again that he was prepared to get out of the Klan; his relationship with the organization "could destroy me, my farm, my home, everything about me."

Dropping out of the Klan was no longer an idle thought. By killing Vernon Dahmer, the Jones County gang had raised the stakes enormously. The members were no longer conspirators in mere vandalism; they faced potential charges as murderers or accessories to murder.

In spite of his connection to the FBI, Landrum was troubled by his association with the White Knights. Even if he felt confident he would never be liable to charges of murder, he would be exposed to public embarrassment if his Klan membership was revealed. At the same time, if the Klan learned he was an informant he would be subject to their vengeance.

He talked about his concern in another late-night discussion with his wife. "Anne, I don't know how much longer I can keep doing this," he told her. "This could ruin our family's reputation in Jones County, and I hate to think what some of those kluckers would do to me if they realized I was talking to the FBI."

Once again, Anne reassured him of the value of his assignment. "A lot of people in Mississippi are guilty of crimes, of doing wrong against the colored people. And a lot of other people in Mississippi are guilty of doing nothing to stop the Klan," she said. "You made a commitment to do something, and you've been following through on that commitment. What you're doing is going to be very important someday. There's more good people in Mississippi than we get credit for and you're one of those people."

Landrum was comforted by her remarks, but he still felt apprehensive.

〜

SESSUM HIMSELF appeared to be knuckling under pressure. He showed up repeatedly at Byrd's repair shop, asking if he had any news of the FBI inquiry. Byrd told him he understood they were asking about a white Buick with a whip antenna. Sessum looked relieved for a moment. "That shows how far off they are," he said, remembering the gaudy car used in a dry run. "The other car wasn't no Buick."

Travis Giles was also a frequent visitor to Byrd's shop. He said that since his car had been impounded in Forrest County he needed transportation. Giles asked the Klan senator, "I want to know what can be done to get me something."

"Hell, Travis, you need to hire you a lawyer and see if you can't get your car back by that means," Byrd suggested.

"That ain't good enough," Giles said, and left in a huff.

Knowing Giles stood implicated in the Dahmer murder, the White Knights' leadership worried that he might cooperate with the FBI out of anger and frustration over the loss of his car. Sessum told Byrd that a collection should be taken up among Klan members to buy him another automobile. "If a man has to sacrifice his car and maybe his job and his life on a Klan project, I think he's entitled to having the car replaced," Sessum reasoned.

"That's something that needs to be handled on a state level," Byrd said. "I don't handle any money. And I'm not so sure the people who are handling the money are doing so properly."

Giles returned a couple of days later to report that Bowers, Nix, and Caldwell had arranged to get him a car. He sounded pleased. But before the week was out he was back at Byrd's shop. "I'm not satisfied with that damn car they got me," he said. "The thing don't drive worth a shit. And I went down to Hattiesburg with my lawyer, like you said, and that didn't work either. I ain't ever gettin' my car back.

Hell, I don't want that old car back. I don't want my wife and kids to ever have to ride in that thing again. I'm gettin' pretty pissed."

Personal relationships inside the White Knights were on edge. And then, near the end of January, events took another unimaginable lurch when Lawrence Byrd was kidnapped.

CHAPTER 11

SHORTLY AFTER THE death of Vernon Dahmer, a decision was made in the higher echelons of the FBI that would have a profound impact on their investigation of the case. The merciless raid on the Dahmer homestead and family constituted a spit in the face of federal authority as well as civilized society. It called for forceful steps.

The civil rights community, enraged by the latest in a string of murders in Mississippi and Alabama over the past three years, had grown weary of hearing that the FBI's mandate involved "investigation, not protection." In addition to their public protests against segregation, leaders of the movement pressed the federal government for stronger security measures and for vigorous criminal prosecution that would result in convictions of those responsible for the campaign of violence by Klansmen and their segregationist sympathizers. Rather than being intimidated by the murder of their patriarch, members of Vernon Dahmer's family remained outspoken in support of his causes, and his widow, Ellie, made it clear to authorities that she was willing to openly testify in any cases brought to trial.

But local officials still showed little interest in prosecution and Mississippi's political leaders continued to throw up a perimeter of resistance to any federal attempt to enforce new laws and court decisions. Too many of the state's white citizens were unwilling to challenge the reign of the die-hard segregationists. Since the presence of the FBI was actually resented in some circles in Mississippi, the blatant attack on Dahmer represented another provocative insult to agents at work in the treacherous field. To take action on its own, the bureau chose a measure that would never be acknowledged. The FBI would meet terror with terror.

The FBI's confidence that it had immunity to break the law was the result of a highly secret and illegal program instituted ten years earlier by its director to hound groups inimical to his own personal interests. From the time he took charge of the bureau in 1924, Hoover had been obsessed with the idea of eliminating the left wing in America. In the Depression era, he targeted not only bank robbers, who gained fame by winding up on his "Ten Most Wanted" lists, but revolutionary movements he believed were led by communists—radical labor unions and leftist political organizations he despised. Hoover sharpened his assault against the communists during the Cold War that followed World War II, condoning clandestine and unconstitutional moves by his agents to spy on suspects and, if necessary, to frame them on specious charges of subversion. Hoover created a counterintelligence program in 1956 that quietly became known inside the bureau by its acronym, COINTELPRO, which gave its agents extraordinary license to use the sort of strong-arm tactics most Americans believed would be employed only in dictatorships. As Hoover built himself into a cult figure, his power increased and his surveillance widened. He deplored the coming of the civil rights movement, convinced that it, too, was communist inspired. In 1964 he publicly branded Martin Luther King as the "biggest liar in the country" and arranged illegal wiretaps on his activities. Then, in the mid-1960s, Hoover came under such pressure from the administration of Lyndon Johnson to break the Klan that he authorized his FBI to extend its campaign against "un-American" organizations to include the KKK.

The decision dovetailed with the government's acceptance of the use of torture to extract information from prisoners taken in the Vietnam War. Relying on helpful euphemisms such as "enhanced interrogation techniques . . . waterboarding . . . sleep management . . . rendition"—and, in situations calling for death, "to exterminate with extreme prejudice"—drastic measures were carried out by American servicemen and CIA officers. Sometimes the job would be shifted to American proxies at "black" locations around the globe. The Pentagon would never admit to torture, but in times of conflict would privately and grudgingly accept it as a means of saving American lives.

In Mississippi, FBI officials concluded that they were confronted with their own warlike environment. Local governmental bodies and law enforcement agencies included Klan members or sympathizers and could not be trusted. Beyond Jones County, local officials and law enforcement personnel belonged to the White Knights throughout the state. In Neshoba County, the sheriff and his chief deputy were complicit in the notorious 1964 murders there. The judicial system in the state moved with reluctance—if at all—to punish suspects in civil rights cases. Many prosecutors dithered, and juries were stacked with people friendly to the Klan who would vote to acquit or to create stalemates that led to hung juries. The FBI and the federal prosecutors who worked with them on cases were frustrated.

Through its network of informants, the FBI had been able to develop files on many of the members of the White Knights. Months before the attack on Dahmer, the bureau already knew which members were considered the most dangerous. And within hours of the attack it was apparent that Sam Bowers's operation was responsible. In the days since the murder, agents had been able to draw up a list of likely suspects after an emergency task force of more than one hundred agents went quickly into the nooks and crannies of Forrest and Jones Counties, interviewing local people, tapping reliable informants, and collecting useful material.

At the outset of the violence directed at civil rights activists earlier in the decade, FBI agents who were Mississippi natives had been criticized for being too cozy with county sheriffs and local policemen in their districts. As a result, the new corps of agents sent into the state had no long-standing ties to local lawmen. That was thought prudent. Nevertheless, Roy K. Moore, the special agent in charge of operations in the state, knew that some sort of link was necessary. As the investigation into the Dahmer raid got underway he summoned a few Mississippi prosecutors, sheriffs, and highway patrolmen whom he felt trustworthy to a meeting at the FBI's makeshift headquarters in a Holiday Inn in Hattiesburg to brief them on progress in the case and to seek their assistance.

The FBI was looking for signs of weakness in the White Knights apparatus, for men whose dedication to the organization might be fading; men who might prove vulnerable to the right kind of pressure. Based on the latest reports from Tom Landrum and other sources within the Klan, analysts had made a judgment. Since it was known that Lawrence Byrd had complained that the Dahmer raid had been conducted without his knowledge or approval and that he had been openly critical of Bowers's decision-making and handling of Klan funds, the FBI determined that he would be worth an unusual visit.

$$\approx$$

LESS THAN TWO WEEKS into the investigation, the FBI in Mississippi made an inquiry to the bureau in New York to ask if an FBI informant in the city—with the code designation NY-3461—might be available for an assignment. The request was made by an agent currently working in Mississippi who had at one time helped supervise the informant in New York. An internal teletyped FBI message on January 21 confirmed the arrangement. The FBI would provide the funds for the trip with the stipulation that the agent in New York now handling NY-3461 "should go along to be of assistance in the area where the informant would be working." According to the directions, the informant—accompanied by his wife and the New York FBI agent—would fly the coming weekend to Mobile, where hotel rooms had been reserved for them. Meanwhile, the Mississippi FBI agent was instructed to proceed immediately to meet his old informant when he arrived in Mobile, which had a major airport about one hundred miles south of Hattiesburg.

The informant was a soldier in the Colombo crime family in New York, Gregory Scarpa, who had been building a record of vicious crimes and murder in Brooklyn when arrested in 1962 for armed robbery. In exchange for his freedom, Scarpa agreed to cooperate secretly with the FBI. Free of fear of future arrests because of his deal with the federal agents, Scarpa continued to pursue his life in the mob while ratting out his associates.

The thirty-eight-year-old Scarpa was a quintessential Mafia figure. He dressed stylishly and liked to carry large sums of cash to dole out as tips to impress acquaintances. He also had a brutal side and was quite capable of violence. Louis Diamond, an attorney who once represented him, said of Scarpa, "He was crazy. He killed a lot. He was nuts. . . . Greg was an absolutely fearless man who enjoyed killing and enjoyed vengeance. And enjoyed the subtlety. He would smile at a guy, take him out to dinner, and blow his brains out." No one was sure how many murders he had committed during New York's ferocious gangland battles of the period, but there were believed to have been many. Some were carefully planned assassinations; others were spontaneous drive-by shootings. The FBI was willing to bend principles in order to utilize Scarpa's talents as a stool pigeon as well as a practitioner of intimidation.

In late January, Scarpa showed up in Laurel at Byrd's appliance store with two other men. They said they were shopping for a TV. It was closing time, and the last customers were leaving. No other employee appeared to be present. Byrd didn't recognize the men but remembered later that two of his visitors seemed to be wearing wigs. When Byrd had his back turned, he was hit over the head, frog-marched outside, and wrestled into the back seat of a car.

Byrd was not easy to overpower. Although he was forty-four, he had retained a youthful leanness on a six-foot-two frame. He was an army veteran with five years in the service during World War II. On his left forearm he had a tattoo of an American flag with the inscription "Long May It Wave," and he struggled with the intensity he had known in boot training. Yet once he was inside the car he was subdued and told to lie down and keep quiet if he wanted to survive. His captors drove a circuitous route, and Byrd was unable to follow exactly where they were going. He said afterward that he concluded he was taken to Camp Shelby, the huge military base outside Hattiesburg, where he was threatened with a gun and savagely beaten.

Byrd was a big man, but Scarpa, who weighed more than 225 pounds, was even more imposing, and he was backed up by his two accomplices. At one point, Scarpa rammed the barrel of a pistol into Byrd's mouth and warned the Klansman that he would die unless he talked. In order to get relief, Byrd agreed to submit to a series of interrogations by FBI agents, which would eventually result in an extraordinary twenty-two-page statement.

First, he would have to recover. After being released by the Scarpa trio, Byrd was admitted to a Jones County hospital, crying, highly emotional, and in pain. News of Byrd's kidnapping spread quickly. The tale was corroborated in part by a customer who had been leaving Byrd's shop when he noticed the visitors entering. He described one of them as "dark and appeared to be of Italian extraction."

≈

LIKE MOST STORIES emanating from the White Knights, details were conflicting and murky. The district attorney, W. O. "Chet" Dillard, spoke with Byrd in the hospital. He concluded that Byrd's claims that he had been "beaten within an inch of his life" were legitimate, and he described Byrd, whom he knew as a "tough guy—a big, rawboned country boy"—as a broken man. Byrd begged the district attorney not to investigate the matter. "It could get me killed," he said.

Dillard speculated that the FBI had called on two local figures—already saddled with lengthy criminal records and facing new auto-theft charges—to take part in the beating. He wondered if the quid pro quo involved a promise that their latest indictment would be dropped if they could force Byrd to talk. His suspicions about the FBI increased after he was told that Byrd's beating was believed to have taken place on federal government land—Camp Shelby, which was located near the Holiday Inn the FBI used as its outpost in Hattiesburg.

For the record, Byrd claimed he had been beaten during a robbery. He was unable to identify his assailants. The local newspaper reported that the Laurel businessman had been "kidnapped, robbed and beaten" by unidentified customers who stole a television set.

For the purpose of covering himself—and the FBI—Byrd invented a colorful account for public consumption in which he described his abduction by a stranger named "Thompson" and his accomplices. In a statement for the FBI record, Byrd claimed he had been blindfolded in the car by his kidnappers, who "put a cold gun barrel on the back of his neck." After being repeatedly threatened, Byrd said, he was turned over to occupants of another car that included a Black man brandishing a gun and a pair of females who were drinking whiskey. According to Byrd's statement, the male remarked, "We might as well do away with the white motherfucker because our troubles won't end 'til we do" and boasted to the women, "Do you believe Big Daddy can back off fifteen or twenty steps and put a bullet through his head at the temples?" At this point, Byrd claimed, the man fired a pistol near his right ear and began to beat him. The trio of captors was then said to have engaged in some bawdy repartee before giving him cigarettes and ditching him on the side of a road. In conclusion, Byrd declared, the robbers left behind the television set, which he carried with him as he walked to safety down a country lane.

The incident provoked skepticism among his confederates in the Klan. Friends thought that he might have been the victim of rogue law enforcement officers. Others believed he had been roughed up by the Klan to punish him for challenging Bowers.

Two days later, Tom Landrum reported to the FBI that Leonard Caves, the circuit clerk, felt the abduction was "a put-up deal." In a private conversation at the Jones County courthouse, the circuit clerk asked Landrum if he had heard that Byrd had been beaten by fellow Klansmen after they learned "he talked too much." Landrum said he knew nothing about the assault. The story sounded weird to him.

It never occurred to him that the FBI, which he respected, would be involved.

≈

A WEEK LATER, while the imperial wizard and Nix were fending off the long-anticipated congressional investigation in Washington into various Klan operations around the country, Byrd joined seven other members of the White Knights at a Sears, Roebuck parking lot after dark. The small group included Landrum and two of the men involved in the Dahmer raid, Sessum and Cliff Wilson. They drove to a wooded area in neighboring Jasper County to discuss several problems confronting their Klan activities.

After Sessum delivered a prayer, Byrd took charge as the ranking officer among the White Knights present. He spoke to his fellow Klansmen for the first time since his kidnapping, talking vaguely of his abduction by mysterious men and complaining that neither the Laurel police nor the FBI had any interest in the case. Byrd said that even though he "got in on the Dahmer project at the tail end" he expected to be arrested. He said he had already contacted wealthy friends who would provide him bail money. Before he finished, Byrd launched into new criticism of the absent imperial wizard. "I've got differences with Sam Bowers," he said, "but I don't want his job, and he needs to understand that." His disputes with Bowers, he said, involved the state organization's failure to reimburse members for the loss of their cars used in White Knights activity. Robert Rivers was at the meeting, and Byrd noted that he had not yet been paid for repairs needed for his Volkswagen engine that had been burned up by Bowers. Also, he pointed out, Travis Giles still had no acceptable replacement for the car abandoned during the Dahmer raid. "He's unable to pay for it," Byrd said, "and it's not fair his family's having to do without the things they need."

Byrd reported that Bowers had told him the state organization had insufficient funds to reimburse either Rivers or Giles. "We need to check where the money is going," Byrd said. More than $1,000 should have been available from collections within his own Jones County unit, he contended. But when he checked with the group's "bursar," he was told Bowers had "picked up everything but $123."

He insisted that the White Knights' constitution made provisions for distributing funds and implied that Bowers had failed to follow the rules. He recommended a meeting where state officers "will settle this matter once and for all."

A similar squabble over the organization's reluctance to reimburse Rivers and Giles had broken out at a meeting a week before. "If you feel so strongly about it, why don't you just pass the hat and take up money for it," Nix had snapped at Byrd at the time.

"I ain't gonna pass anything," Byrd retorted. "It's the state's obligation. The members are already being asked to pay too much."

In his report to the FBI following the subsequent gathering, on February 4, Landrum wrote: "There is a lot of friction between Bowers and Byrd and the county officers and state officers. Byrd stated this would break up the WKKKK."

Others in the White Knights, watching Byrd's performance, felt Byrd had lost it and was becoming mentally unbalanced.

~

AFTER HIS LATEST ERUPTION, Byrd returned to the hospital, complaining that headaches "are killing me." His sister, Dorothy Ruston, found him vomiting and speaking irrationally when she visited. She thought he was having a nervous breakdown. In a note recalling his stay in the hospital, she described the experience as a "nightmare." Complicating the situation, she said, was the constant presence of two FBI agents, J. L. Martin and William Dukes, who insisted on interviewing her brother. Sometimes, she said, they were joined by a Mississippi Highway Patrol investigator named Steve Henderson. The officers pressed Byrd to identify a car used in the Dahmer raid and warned him to be careful about saying he had been kidnapped by the FBI.

Byrd's condition appeared so fragile that his physician considered a proposal to commit him to the Mississippi state mental institution, a place commonly referred to as Whitfield, to relieve the pressure. But Byrd soon left the hospital and began playing a double role. He continued to attend meetings of the White Knights. On February 11 he hosted a group at his farmhouse, where he told members he believed the FBI had been behind his kidnapping. At the same time Byrd was now talking secretly with agents Martin and Dukes. He would meet with them as many as forty times over a two-month period.

⁓

SUSPICIONS THAT other members might be cooperating with the FBI continued to sweep through the White Knights. Red Caldwell had backed away from his vow to leave the Klan and grew belligerently defensive of the group. Always ready with volatile language, Caldwell declared at a gathering of the White Knights that "anybody saying three words to the FBI, it will be two words too many." After the men at the meeting dispersed, Byrd was pulled unexpectedly into a conversation with Deavours Nix, who told Byrd he wanted to put him in charge of a three-man committee "to take care of squealers." Byrd was not sure whether to be flattered by Nix's suggestion or to be wary of a trap. He told Nix he would think about it.

Landrum was one of those distrusted by Nix, and for months he had sensed hostility radiating from Bowers's confidant and was troubled by the prospect of a witch hunt that might ensnare him, Landrum wrote the FBI. "I feel his dislike for me is intense." Meanwhile, Landrum detected new personality conflicts within the group. There were disagreements over paying a $500 fee to a local lawyer, Bob Ridley, who represented Klansman Pete Martin. An employee of Masonite, Martin had been accused of shooting into the house of a Black physician, Dr. B. E. Murph, who held statewide office as vice president of the NAACP. More recently, Martin had been arrested after dynamite was discovered in his car. The White Knights were convinced that the explosives had been planted by the FBI in an effort to incriminate members of their group. The dispute with the lawyer was settled when Ridley agreed to take $200, which was offered as a contribution for his coming campaign for circuit judge. White Knights who were reluctant to make the payment rationalized that it might help elect another Klan-friendly judge.

At another meeting an argument broke out when a man threatened retaliation for an unauthorized cross-burning in the yard of his girlfriend. "One of these nights I'm gonna get me a shotgun and kill off a bunch," he warned. "And the Federals will thank me for it."

Aside from their wariness about each other, tensions existed among others in the group over romantic alliances. In one case, Landrum noted, three different members were competing for the favors of one woman in Jones County. In a report that described some of the squabbles, Landrum used capital letters to beg his FBI recipients: BE CAREFUL HOW THIS IS HANDLED.

"There is a great feeling of unrest in the county group," he wrote. "Cecil Sessum is fearful of being picked up and I have never heard him ask what to do before. I think he is aware that someone is on his trail."

Landrum had some sympathy for Sessum. As a self-styled minister, he had labored honestly outside the White Knights as a man of God. He was struggling with the pressures of a fractured marriage. His wife had moved with his children to the Gulf Coast, leaving Sessum using a bed at his father's home and deeply concerned he would lose custody of his children. Though Landrum noted to the FBI that Sessum "liked to talk and show how tough he is," the youth counselor felt he had a gentle side. He found it hard to equate Sessum's soft-spoken nature with his participation in the White Knights' violence.

"All are scared," Landrum wrote of the local Klansmen. "Byrd stressed that the times are trying and are going to get worse." In his next message to the FBI, Landrum reported that two members had been "sworn out" of the White Knights, leaving the group because of their own fears as well as their wives' pleas.

⟨~⟩

ONE EVENING Landrum stayed up by himself to watch a late-night movie on television. He considered the rambling home he and Anne had built on her family's land their sanctuary. Located on a country road, they had no immediate neighbors. Instead of being subjected to the obnoxious noises of loud radios and whining freight trucks, the Landrums were serenaded at night by the natural sounds of the forest, the falsetto squeals from tree frogs, and the thrumming of crickets in season. As his wife and children slept and Landrum indulged in a rare treat—the weekly *Saturday Night Movie*—he heard a snap outside, as though an intruder had stepped on a fallen tree branch and broken it. He felt the hairs on his arm quiver.

Like most families who lived outside of town, the Landrums kept a couple of dogs, a short-haired feist and a bigger shaggy hound, a mix of Lab and God-knows-what. The animals heard the noise, too, and set up howls. Landrum had one thought: it's a klucker, come to kill me, to shoot me through the window; or maybe more than one, come to burn down our house like the bastards did to the Dahmers.

He crept to another room, where he kept his hunting guns, pulled from a rack his favorite shotgun, a 12-gauge that had once been his father's, and gathered a handful of shells. Holding his breath, he maneuvered in darkness along the wall. The house was lit only by a light in the kitchen and the flickering images from the television set in the living room.

He strained to try to see outside but could detect no movement. He waited as quietly as possible. The dogs' protest quickly died down, and the only sound came from the murmurs of the TV. He held his place for several minutes before letting his guard down. By that time, he had lost the thread of the story on TV and was too unnerved to watch the rest of the movie. He went to the bedroom, but brought the shotgun with him and left it within reach on a chair. The night would wind up in ragged sleep for him, another experience that ate at his commitment to spending time with the Klan.

～

AROUND THE SAME TIME, Sessum visited Byrd at his store to discuss his concerns. Byrd asked if he thought Billy Moss, who had dropped out of the Dahmer project rather than ride with Henry deBoxtel, had talked. "It's not Moss," Sessum said dismissively. "I wouldn't go to a prayer meeting with him."

There was at least one sure suspect, Sessum indicated: Lamar "Shorty" Lowe, who had gone on one of the trial trips to scope out the Dahmer home. Lowe had suddenly disappeared from Jones County. "He's in Texas," Sessum said, "and God knows what he has told."

Billy Roy Pitts, who had lost his pistol, also appeared to have vanished, and his absence was not comforting to his mates in the White Knights.

Equally disturbing were the confrontations with the FBI. Many of the White Knights were being boldly approached by agents. They were told that they were known to be Klan members and thus potential suspects in the Dahmer murder; they also heard suggestions that it would be helpful to their future freedom to cooperate with the investigation.

Rumors about leaks had been rampant at recent Klan meetings, coupled with complaints that too much loose talk was taking place at beer joints and the Masonite plant, where many White Knights worked.

Gerald Martin, the Jones County constable, reported to members of his klavern about an attempt to intimidate him. He had been informed by FBI agents that they were keeping a book on his movements. "They know each time I've been to a meeting," he said. "That means somebody in our group is talking."

Someone yelled, "If anybody gets caught talking, he needs to be shot on the spot." The suggestion triggered a chorus of "Amens" from the group.

Landrum figured that some of his dispatches to the FBI had been the source of the information about Martin, so in his next message he suggested to the agents, "It would be better if these dates were not so specific, due to the suspicion it builds up."

≈

IN THE MIDST OF the uncertainty caused by the FBI contacts, Speed Lightsey, the exalted cyclops of Landrum's klavern, asked him to come to his service station for another chat. Landrum found Lightsey unthreatening. He was better educated than most of the White Knights and owned respectable businesses. Landrum heard that Lightsey had once led a couple of raids on Black targets in neighboring counties, but he did not consider him a hard-core Klansman willing to carry out a Code Four.

Lightsey seemed ill at ease. "The FBI is coming to talk with me every day," he whispered. "They've been asking questions about several members of our group. They've offered me money, as high as five figures, to talk." The FBI had a reputation for paying royally for information. It was well known among the members of the White Knights that their north Mississippi comrades involved in the Neshoba County murders had been arrested after the FBI bought the testimony of men familiar with the operation. "I could sure use some money," he said, "but I'm not talking. I don't want to go before a grand jury and be singled out as a snitch." Still, he was convinced several members were talking. Lightsey confided to Landrum that the FBI agents, trying to loosen his lips, had told him they had seven paid informants in the Jones County Klan.

The imperial wizard did not know it while he was off in Washington, taking some delight in defying the congressional committee investigating the Klan, but his organization was in tatters back home.

CHAPTER 12

BECAUSE OF ITS far-right and racist history, the House Un-American Activities Committee seemed an unlikely setting for an investigation of the Ku Klux Klan, but Sam Bowers and his most trusted lieutenant, Deavours Nix, traveled to Washington to appear at a hearing only three weeks after the fatal raid at Vernon Dahmer's home. For the two men from Laurel, the experience represented an opportunity to defy the hated federal government in the nation's capital while establishing a reputation for the White Knights in the company of other imperial wizards and grand dragons from older Klan groups. Bowers felt these more-established Klans engaged in little more than sinister pageantry; his White Knights had quickly proved their mettle by taking daring action that had national impact. Although he would never publicly admit responsibility for the incident, Bowers had called on his Klansmen in the waning days of 1965 to eliminate Dahmer and his voting-registration activities in order to send a message to Washington in advance of his engagement with the committee. He also liked to think that it confirmed primacy for the White Knights in the galaxy of American Klandom. Instead of approaching his date before the committee with concern, Bowers was eager to make an appearance.

The congressional investigation of the Klan groups marked a curious departure from the committee's background. Created in the

1930s as an instrument to maintain vigilance over communists, fascists, and other alleged subversives operating in the United States in the years before World War II, the committee evolved into a stage for cantankerous congressmen conducting communist witch hunts. Representative John Rankin of Mississippi, the House chamber's most obstreperous racist and anti-Semite, engineered passage of legislation authorizing the permanent committee, after being assured that Representative Martin Dies of Texas would be its chairman rather than Representative Samuel Dickstein, a Jew from New York. One historian observed, "The Committee had won the hearts of Klansmen at birth." Dies reciprocated the embrace of the Klan by describing the organization as "an old American institution." One of the reigning imperial wizards at the time responded by complimenting Dies for developing an agenda that "so closely parallels the program of the Klan that there is no distinguishable difference between them." The committee soon became known by its acronym—HUAC—famous as a haven for fools and publicity-seeking zealots.

HUAC served as an early home for an ambitious young congressman from California and his anti-communist crusades after World War II, Richard Nixon. A decade later, the committee commanded national attention during its investigation of Alger Hiss, a State Department official suspected of being a Soviet spy, and widened its net with highly publicized hearings into communist influence in the Hollywood film industry. Though Senator Joseph McCarthy of Wisconsin was never a member, the House committee reflected the spirit of his vigorous efforts to root out communists in the federal government. By the late 1950s, after it became apparent that the work of McCarthy and HUAC had greatly exaggerated the threat, enthusiasm for their investigations faded. McCarthy died a discredited man and the House committee became the butt of criticism and jokes for its parade of demagogic speeches by its members.

Still, a weakened HUAC survived into the era of the Kennedy and Johnson administrations. In 1965, with Klan terrorism on the rise, a young, liberal Democratic congressman from Atlanta named

Charles Weltner accepted a seat on the committee in order to call for a widespread investigation of the Ku Klux Klan.

After Weltner denounced the Invisible Empire and demanded congressional action in a speech on the House floor, his initiative gained momentum when a carload of Klansmen—including one FBI informant—ambushed a car shuttling civil rights demonstrators during the legendary Selma-to-Montgomery marches in the spring of that year. The driver, Viola Liuzzo, a Detroit housewife who volunteered to help in the movement, was killed. Following a spontaneous television speech by an angry President Johnson, who blamed the Klan for the murder, HUAC won a contest with the House Judiciary Committee to gain oversight of the probe.

There was more than a little irony to HUAC's investigation of the Klan. For much of the committee's life, it had portrayed communists as threats to American society and worked in its hearings to brand leftists as a dangerous "fifth column" in the country. On a parallel track, the Klan also singled out communists, as well as Blacks and Jews, for sharp criticism and attacks. To emphasize the organization's affinity with HUAC, a KKK pamphlet in 1942 had crowed, "The vicious fight on the Klan sprang from the same source which has fought the Dies committee from the day of its inception."

But with its influence ebbing, HUAC took advantage of a fresh target and the chance to rehabilitate its image. The committee's staff began a sweeping review of modern Klan outrages, collecting intelligence on various Klan operations in America. Much of the material came from the FBI, which had moved its own investigation of the Klan into high gear after the Neshoba County murders in 1964, when scores of agents were assigned to the case and began developing local informants.

A freshman Mississippi congressman, Prentiss Walker, tried unsuccessfully to dilute the impact of civil rights organizations by insisting that SNCC, CORE, and Martin Luther King's SCLC should be investigated, too. (Walker, a chicken farmer and the first Republican to represent the state in the twentieth century, had been elected in 1964 when Barry Goldwater carried Mississippi with 74 percent of the vote. Walker was a precursor of the wave of conservative southerners who would begin serving in Congress as Republicans.) However, his effort failed and the staff concentrated on such groups as the White Knights and the nation's largest congregation of Klansmen, the United Klans of America, led by its own imperial wizard, Robert Shelton of Alabama.

A five-man subcommittee headed by Representative Edwin E. Willis of Louisiana, the Democratic chairman of the full committee, began hearings in October 1965. Weltner was the lone maverick of the group. Others were thought to be reliable conservatives: Democrat Joe Pool of Texas and Republicans John Ashbrook of Ohio and John Buchanan of Alabama. But Buchanan, a freshman as well as a Baptist minister, was undergoing his own personal transformation and growing into a sharp critic of the Klan. At one point, the Alabama congressman referred to Shelton—a resident of his state—as "the Imperial Lizard."

Donald Appell, the HUAC staff member in charge of the investigation, produced hundreds of pages of evidence damning the various Klan groups. In many cases, Appell himself grilled the witnesses. By the time Bowers and Nix made their appearances, Shelton had already been eviscerated by the inquisition and faced contempt-of-Congress charges for refusing to turn over records of his organization.

Though five years younger than Bowers, Shelton got off to an earlier start in Klandom. A former tire salesman in Tuscaloosa, Alabama, Shelton founded the United Klans in 1960 and claimed to have built a membership of thirty thousand. Bowers considered Shelton a competitor rather than a brother-in-arms, and the White Knights leader took some satisfaction in the congressional hammering of Shelton. Bowers had introduced a resolution at an August 1965 gathering of his faithful in Byram, Mississippi, forbidding members of the White Knights from associating with anyone from the United Klans. In the midst of the hearings, days before

Bowers took his turn as a witness, he and his White Knights associates promoted the belief that United Klansmen were responsible for Dahmer's murder.

━━

BOWERS AND NIX were accompanied to Washington by two lawyers who were allied with the White Knights, Travis Buckley and Charles Blackwell, and a White Knights associate from Gulfport named Travis Purser. With Appell, the congressional staff investigator, leading the public interrogations, the committee warmed up with a short set of questions for Purser, who quickly invoked the defense the Mississippians would use. He declined to respond, citing "the privileges guaranteed to me by the Fifth, First and Fourteenth Amendments to the Constitution of the United States of America."

He would not answer a question about whether he had joined a group of robed Klansmen who threatened a Gulf Coast attorney at a boat dock by calling him a "nigger lawyer" and advising him to move out of the area. Nor would Purser reply to an allegation that he had asked the White Knights' state organization "to either burn or stink-bomb the Mennonite School for Wayward Girls because it was being used by COFO."

After Purser was dismissed, the committee called Nix and disposed of his testimony in short order after he, too, invoked the Fifth Amendment. Asked if he had a role in the burning of sixteen buildings in Laurel, he declined to answer. Instead of posing fruitless questions, Appell read into the record a list of charges compiled in the past few months against Nix: that White Knights business was conducted at his restaurant; that he attended a meeting where the White Knights voted to send $500 as a reward to a Klansman in Bogalusa, Louisiana, for killing a Black deputy sheriff in Washington Parish; that he had acted as a sentry, shaking down men attending a Klan rally near Jackson in search of "bugs" that might incriminate members of the White Knights; that he attended a meeting where

Bowers called his hometown "Smoke Stack City" in recognition of the homes that had been burned out there; and that he knew of the beating of a former White Knight named Billy Birdsong "because he had given Bowers more trouble than any other Klansman."

During a total of thirty-seven days of hearings spread over several months, the constant refrains of witnesses "respectfully" declining to answer questions contributed to an air of lassitude that had begun to prevail in the hearing room. Reporters lounged idly at a press table, rarely bothering to take notes. An American war in Vietnam was intensifying and news from Southeast Asia had begun to take over front-page headlines once devoted to the civil rights movement.

However, the appearance of Bowers added a charge of electricity to the proceedings, even though he, too, cited protection by the Fifth Amendment—110 times. Reporting the next day on his performance, the *Washington Post* noted that he had dressed jauntily for the occasion, wearing sunglasses, a cowboy hat, and a checked suit. Actually, Bowers came attired in a derby and a herringbone jacket. But he did appear to be enjoying himself.

Appell had a thick dossier on Bowers, and he confronted him with a number of questions. Even though he knew the imperial wizard would be unresponsive, he wanted to build a record against him—and at the same time strike some fear in Bowers by making him realize how closely authorities were watching him.

When Bowers refused to acknowledge the existence of documents relating to the White Knights that had been subpoenaed, Chairman Willis exploded. Though he was a product of the political machine created by Huey P. Long and a signatory of the Southern Manifesto, a 1956 commitment made by virtually every member of Congress from Dixie to oppose racial integration, Willis berated Bowers. "It is incredible, inconceivable, outlandish that you can say you do not now have, and never have, don't know of any records involving Klanism within your realm."

Summoned to testify before the House Un-American Activities Committee in 1966 during a national investigation of Ku Klux Klan activities, the White Knights leader Sam Bowers (center) went to Washington, accompanied by Mississippi Klan lawyers Travis Buckley (left) and Charles Blackwell. (BETTMANN / CONTRIBUTOR VIA GETTY IMAGES)

Forrest County Circuit Clerk Theron Lynd denying applications to vote from two local Black citizens on Freedom Day, January 22, 1964, in Hattiesburg, the first civil rights project scheduled for Mississippi in a year that led to Freedom Summer and a historic challenge at the national Democratic convention by the Freedom Democratic Party. (MONCRIEF PHOTOGRAPH COLLECTION, MISSISSIPPI DEPARTMENT OF ARCHIVES AND HISTORY)

Vernon Dahmer shows cotton specimens to out-of-state Freedom Summer volunteers at a Fourth of July fish fry on his farm to celebrate the passage of the Civil Rights Act of 1964 and to lift the spirits of the student activists shortly after three workers in their movement disappeared in Neshoba County, Mississippi. (HERBERT RANDALL COLLECTION, MCCAIN LIBRARY AND ARCHIVES, UNIVERSITY OF SOUTHERN MISSISSIPPI)

Visiting student volunteers and local Blacks involved in civil rights activities in Mississippi during the fateful summer of 1964 singing anthems of freedom at a gathering hosted by Vernon Dahmer on his farm. (HERBERT RANDALL COLLECTION, MCCAIN LIBRARY AND ARCHIVES, UNIVERSITY OF SOUTHERN MISSISSIPPI)

Newly widowed Ellie Dahmer being escorted to her husband's funeral at the Shady Grove Baptist Church in their Kelly Settlement community. (MONCRIEF PHOTOGRAPH COLLECTION, MISSISSIPPI DEPARTMENT OF ARCHIVES AND HISTORY)

Grieving Blacks gather at a church in Hattiesburg, preparing for a demonstration in the wake of Vernon Dahmer's murder. (MONCRIEF PHOTOGRAPH COLLECTION, MISSISSIPPI DEPARTMENT OF ARCHIVES AND HISTORY)

The imperial wizard, Sam Bowers, in federal custody again in 1968 after earlier arrests in the Dahmer case and in connection with the infamous Neshoba County murders. Bowers was not convicted for ordering the deadly "Code Four" punishment for the civil rights leader until 1998. (MONCRIEF PHOTOGRAPH COLLECTION, MISSISSIPPI DEPARTMENT OF ARCHIVES AND HISTORY)

Deavours Nix, grand director of the Klan Bureau of Investigation, proprietor of John's Restaurant, and Sam Bowers's closest confidante, following his second arrest in the Dahmer case in 1968. Nix escaped punishment with a hung jury. (MONCRIEF PHOTOGRAPH COLLECTION, MISSISSIPPI DEPARTMENT OF ARCHIVES AND HISTORY)

Henry deBoxtel, a White Knight who oper-ated the Laurel café Chow House, which also served as a hangout for the Klan. He drove the second attack car that was disabled by "friendly fire" from other Klansmen during the Dahmer raid. He was first arrested for his involvement in the case in 1966 and rearrested in 1968 but never convicted. He was a codefendant with Nix in a mistrial. (MONCRIEF PHOTOGRAPH COLLECTION, MISSISSIPPI DEPARTMENT OF ARCHIVES AND HISTORY)

The "Little Preacher," Cecil Sessum, being comforted by his mother, Velma, during a break in his 1968 trial for leading the White Knights' firebombing of the Dahmer home. He was convicted and served ten years in the state penitentiary. (Moncrief Photograph Collection, Mississippi Department of Archives and History)

Laurel's "Man of the Year," Cliff Wilson, in a jailhouse mug shot taken within hours of a local Jaycee banquet honoring him. His arrest came two years after he took part in the murderous raid on the Dahmer home. Wilson was convicted, sent to prison with a life sentence, but later released by a governor who earlier represented Wilson as a lawyer working on his appeal. (Moncrief Photograph Collection, Mississippi Department of Archives and History)

Lawrence Byrd, beaten by a New York Mafia enforcer sent to Mississippi by the FBI in order to extract a confession. As a result, Byrd became a target for execution by his fellow White Knights and eventually served prison time following his arrest and conviction in 1968. (MONCRIEF PHOTOGRAPH COLLECTION, MISSISSIPPI DEPARTMENT OF ARCHIVES AND HISTORY)

Fallen Klansman Billy Roy Pitts, who became a key witness against the White Knights in a series of trials after authorities traced the pistol he dropped during the Dahmer raid from the quick-draw holster he designed for himself. (MONCRIEF PHOTOGRAPH COLLECTION, MISSISSIPPI DEPARTMENT OF ARCHIVES AND HISTORY)

Tom Landrum, a lineman for the powerful Jones County Junior College Bobcats, before he won a football scholarship to the University of Louisville in the 1950s. (COURTESY OF THE LANDRUM FAMILY)

Newlyweds Anne and Tom Landrum.
(COURTESY OF THE LANDRUM FAMILY)

The Landrum family (first row, from left) Susan, Anne holding Mike, Tom holding Bruce; (back row, from left) David and Deb. At the time Tom was secretly enrolled in the White Knights to assist the FBI. (COURTESY OF THE LANDRUM FAMILY)

A half century after the reign of the White Knights ended, Tom and Anne Landrum posed with their friend Federal Judge Charles Pickering (right), who served as Jones County prosecuting attorney at the same time Landrum acted undercover for the FBI.
(COURTESY OF THE LANDRUM FAMILY)

BOWERS MAY HAVE produced nothing, but the committee was prepared to introduce a series of White Knights documents. One was an interesting "special edition" of the *Klan Ledger* responding to a "fanatical and incoherent TV spectacle" by Henry Bucklew, the mayor of Laurel, who went on the air in October 1965 to criticize the White Knights. The *Klan Ledger* declared that its rebuttal was not intended to "add any fuel to the fire . . . but rather as a Christian effort in the hope that it will have a calming and sobering influence on the good citizens of Jones County."

According to the broadside, Bucklew had once been a member of the Klan himself. "When Bucklew was first sworn into the White Knights, shortly before the recent election," the paper reported, "it was with the expectation that he would not only receive the political support of the Knights at the polls, but that he would also have access to the funds in the Klan treasury of Jones County." According to the report, these expectations all belonged to Bucklew. He was blocked by rules of the "Domain of the Invisible Empire" that "prevents any dipping into the till." As a result, Bucklew's "enthusiasm for the Klan began to wane."

Depicting the mayor as a greedy politician who felt jilted, the *Klan Ledger* concluded, "The conflict which now exists between the White Knights of the Ku Klux Klan and Henry Bucklew is the same, dark specter which has dogged his entire checkered public career, THE LOVE OF MONEY."

(Bucklew was often cited as a classic specimen of colorful Jones County politics. Though a generally popular figure in Laurel and perceived as anti-Klan, he was eventually brought down by questions of how he handled treasuries he controlled. Indicted for trying to bill the city of Laurel for repairs to a Jeep he used, Bucklew was convicted of attempted embezzlement and dismissed as mayor. Money continued to represent a problem for him. Though he lost the title of mayor, he retained a designation as "Reverend" and ran the Magnolia Boys Town for homeless youths on Bogue Homa Lake. An elderly couple from Virginia was so impressed by the operation that they gave Bucklew $50,000 to buy land for an adjacent "ranch" for the boys. However, funds in the account dwindled dramatically before any land was bought. Bucklew was indicted again, this time for "obtaining funds by false pretense." The Jeep conviction was overturned on appeal, and the second charge was dropped after Bucklew restored the money to the Virginians. By this time his wife had won election and occupied the office. He later won back the job of mayor for himself.)

$$\Longrightarrow$$

THE HOUSE COMMITTEE had more documents describing the White Knights as "primarily a Christian Educational body" dedicated to the preservation of a "Christian civilization" and a collection of spiritual pontifications attacking "the atheistic conspiracy of the Synagogue of Satan."

One paper referred to "communist authorities in charge of the National Government." Bowers was asked if he could name one hundred of these "communist authorities." He declined to answer. "Could you name fifty?" He declined. "Could you name twenty?" He declined. "Could you name ten?" Another decline. "Could you name five?" He would not. "Could you name one?" Bowers declined again.

He refused to talk about an assault on the business agent for the local union of the International Woodworkers of America, AFL-CIO, in Laurel, and he would not acknowledge an extensive schedule of Klan violence in Jones County, a list of more than one hundred beatings, shootings, and burnings carried out there over the past year.

He had nothing to say about an accusation that he had sent a "goon squad" to beat up the dissident White Knight Billy Birdsong. Or that his forces had used only a "small quantity of dynamite" to bomb the *Leader-Call* newspaper office to avoid damaging a bowling alley next door that housed pinball machines owned by Bowers's Sambo Amusement Company.

Appell finally asked Bowers bluntly, "As imperial wizard of the White Knights of the Ku Klux Klan of Mississippi, did you ever authorize the extermination or elimination of a human being?" Bowers paused to confer with his lawyers.

"You seem shocked by that question," the chairman injected. "Why don't you say 'no' under oath?"

Bowers whispered back and forth with his counsel again before replying, "Sir, for the reasons previously stated, I respectfully decline to answer that question." He also refused to respond to specific questions dealing with the murder of Michael Schwerner, one of the three civil rights workers slain in Neshoba County.

Near the end of Bowers's appearance, Buchanan, the Baptist minister congressman, posed a question. "Mr. Bowers, you are quoted as having said something to the effect that if it is necessary to eliminate someone, it should be done in silence, without malice, in the manner of a Christian act. Am I to understand if murder is committed in silence and without malice it can become a Christian act?"

Bowers declined to answer. At 1:30 p.m., the committee excused him and recessed for lunch.

≈

THE NEXT DAY, HUAC heard more revealing testimony, from a former member of a United Klans klavern in Pike County, another rough-and-tumble south Mississippi locale, which lay on the Louisiana state line, not far from Natchez. In 1964, the United Klans had terrorized the Black population of the county with a withering campaign of church burnings and bombings before eleven men were arrested during a federal investigation.

Emmett Thornhill, an illiterate small-time farmer who had made millions of dollars over the past decade from an oil boom in the region, was willing to talk a bit about his affiliation with the United Klans. Though his remarks were guarded, Thornhill's cooperation so excited Congressman Weltner that he bubbled, "You are the first member that has come here that has offered to testify anything about the Klan, and we have had a lot of members of the Klan here who refused to, and I appreciate your offering to tell us about it."

The fifty-seven-year-old Thornhill lived on an end-of-the-earth gravel road where snakes often slithered, outside the small town of Summit. He had no formal education and was no stranger to poverty into middle age. Yet he became one of the wealthiest men in Pike County after leasing land from property owners in order to conduct wildcat drillings. He wound up with more than two hundred oil-producing wells. Because of his widely known views on race, he was thought by many people in Pike County to be the major source of support for Klan operations when the trouble broke out in the summer of 1964. That belief was corroborated by no less an authority than the columnist Drew Pearson, whose commentary specializing in exposé was featured in hundreds of newspapers, including several in Mississippi. In his testimony, Thornhill complained that Pearson had depicted him as "the head man of the United Klans." He said he had never been an officer.

Instead, he said, he had been disturbed by the violence. "They was doing some things I didn't approve of, so I thought maybe I would get out. . . . Everybody knew that I was in the Klan and they thought I was the head of it. . . . I didn't know a thing about what was going on. . . . Everybody was accusing me of doing it anyway, and I said, well, I would just get out of it."

By the standards set by other witnesses, Thornhill was down-right voluble. He admitted he joined the Klan in early 1964. At that point Pike County was on edge over the coming Freedom Summer and new civil rights demonstrations. The county had been the scene for earlier violence, random burnings and assaults on Freedom Riders. Black activists working in the area under the direction of Bob Moses, a prominent SNCC organizer, were badly beaten during Klan attacks on them.

Thornhill described the local United Klans as a "fine organization" that did not brook violence. "If a man would get up in the klavern and bring up something like that, to go bomb a place of business and burn down a church, he wouldn't be a member long," he claimed.

According to Thornhill, his only investments in the organization were a $10 initiation fee, monthly dues amounting to $1.50, and the cost of two radio commercials and one newspaper advertisement (totaling $165) to promote a speech by Shelton, their imperial wizard, at a local fairgrounds. He also bought a ceremonial robe and attended weekly meetings on Thursday nights.

He characterized the United Klans as a benevolent group, an organization that had a "sick committee" to comfort ailing citizens, a "needy committee" to deliver groceries to hungry families, and a "book committee" to screen the libraries at public schools to ensure that no "sex books" appeared on their shelves.

Weltner asked if they also had a "wrecking crew."

"A wrecking crew?"

"A wrecking crew."

"What would they wreck?" Thornhill replied. "No, we never had no wrecking crew in my unit. Of course, I had a wrecking crew, but he wasn't in the Ku Klux Klan."

"Who was that?" Weltner asked.

"A colored boy that worked for me. He tore up three cars that I bought him. I give him a motor bike then, and he wrecked it the first week. The next week I give him another motor bike, and he got killed on it."

When confronted with the names of five Black churches that were burned in Pike County over a three-week period in the summer of 1964, Thornhill insisted, "I was out of the Klan before the bombings started, before they ever done any of the burnings." Based on his experience as a sixteen-year-old "blowing up stumps" while working on a highway project, Thornhill said he would have been more effective with dynamite than those involved in the bombings. "I believe I could have placed them sticks a little better. Dynamite blows up, not sideways."

He said he originally felt Blacks were behind the bombings in order to gain sympathy. He had offered a $1,000 reward for the apprehension of those responsible. When the eleven Klansmen were arrested, he said, he was surprised. Though he knew only two of the men, Thornhill said he and a preacher called "Brother Brown" who "had a prayer on him" visited the defendants in jail. Thornhill learned later that the minister was a member of the Klan, too.

≈

NEITHER BOWERS NOR NIX had been as forthcoming as Thornhill, but the pair returned to Jones County the same week in a triumphant manner. They appeared late at a meeting of their own Klan at the unoccupied house on Lawrence Byrd's farm. As Landrum reported to the FBI, Red Caldwell introduced Bowers and Nix as "distinguished guests." Bowers said they had been delayed because Nix had to go by the police station and sign papers against FBI agents. He told the group they had nothing to fear from the FBI as long as they kept their mouths shut.

The weather was not as cold as it had been, so the men were receptive to hearing a long-winded account of the adventure. "Our Christian militant organization will come through on top despite our enemy's force of money, brutality, and harassment," Bowers vowed. "Our fellow Klansmen conducted themselves well in Washington. And you should be proud of the fine legal counsel that represented us. Travis Buckley and Charles Blackwell are two of the smartest men I ever met." He said the White Knights would be supporting Buckley in his race for an important public office later in the year.

"I think what surprised Washington the most was the appearance of our Klansmen, all dressed up and nice," Bowers said. "They expected we were going to come up carrying whips."

Nix added his own thoughts and boasted of how he could easily handle the FBI. He said he had filed a complaint against two agents several months before and had just signed new papers against them that afternoon. The Klan should not feel inhibited by the FBI, he said. "We need to hold open meetings again and start more projects."

Landrum closed his account of the meeting with an editorial comment: "It will make you sick to hear these two 'distinguished guests' speak."

CHAPTER 13

Nix's complaint against the FBI grew out of an earlier confrontation with agents at his home on Fifteenth Avenue in Laurel. The White Knights' grand director of the Klan Bureau of Investigation said that he had been the victim of a ruthless and ill-mannered visit. In a lengthy affidavit Nix filed with the Jones County chancery clerk, he charged that he and his family had been threatened by agent Jim Webb and another officer operating out of the Jackson FBI office who was developing a reputation as a particularly tough adversary of the Klan, Jim Ingram.

Nix described a scene in which he was accosted by the two men in his front yard as he was leaving his house. The taller agent, Ingram, reportedly said, "We want to talk with you. . . . We have been waiting to get you for a long time." After the other agent "made the first of several veiled threats against my wife and three children," Nix's affidavit claimed, Ingram "then demanded that I account for my whereabouts on the night of the bombing of the Damer [sic] nigger's house in Hattiesburg."

Nix told the agents he did not trust them and asked them to leave his property. "I told them that I believed that they had masterminded a plot which caused dynamite to be planted in a Laurel citizen's car only last week, and that I was not going to have anything to do with anyone who would do a thing like that." According to the affidavit, Ingram responded with a promise to sue Nix for making that accusation and warned, "Something might happen to your wife and three children."

After another exchange, Nix said, Ingram shook his finger in his face. Nix objected to the gesture. He claimed Ingram cursed him. His affidavit used letters instead of words to fill out the sentence attributed to Ingram: "You G D S O B, I'll shake my finger at who I D well please."

When Nix asked his wife to call the police, he said, the agents hurried to their car; they were preparing to leave when Laurel officers arrived. Nix said the policemen "were nervous and appeared to be afraid of the FBI men." When it became apparent they were reluctant to make any arrests, Nix said, he went to city hall and formally charged the agents with threatening his family, disturbing the peace, and profanity.

The next day, Nix said, he followed up with a call to the police department and was told that Ingram and Webb "had escaped and could no longer be found in the city of Laurel." Nix said his experience showed "that this community is swarming with a large number of arrogant and violent men in the FBI service. These men are openly contemptuous of law and obey only some clandestine code of their own." He closed the document with his signature and a sign-off sentence: "With charity for all and malice toward none, I shall always remain a peaceful and loyal citizen of Mississippi and America."

The blowup, coming two weeks after Byrd claimed to have been abducted and beaten, dramatized a belief among the Klansmen that the bureau was ratcheting up the forcefulness of its investigation. As word came in from Landrum and other informants identifying White Knights members who might have been involved in the raid on Dahmer's home, agents were deployed in teams of two to conduct interviews with suspects, to ask where they were during the predawn hours of January 10. In some cases, these were not gentle visitations seeking cooperation, but hard-nosed attempts at intimidation.

IN JIM INGRAM'S OWN account of the encounter with Nix, which he gave later to his supervisors, the FBI agent contended that Nix had provoked the argument. "As we walked up to the house, Nix came outside and in a rage yelled at us, 'Why are you spending so much time on that nigger when you should be investigating communism?' He shouted for his wife to call the police."

After Nix was told he needed to verify where he was on January 10, he snarled, "I do not have to talk with you." He told the agents that someone had been invading his backyard recently. "If I catch somebody back there, I'm gonna kill them," he warned.

Two police cars arrived, Ingram said, and a discussion ensued. "We told the officers that the purpose of our visit was not confrontational . . . that all we wanted to do was to talk with him. The police were considerate, knowing that was the purpose of law enforcement. They refused any action, which further enraged Nix."

Nix pursued charges by contacting Bob Lee, the local FBI agent, and asking him to "assist the Laurel police in bringing Webb and Ingram to justice." He was frustrated when Lee was unwilling to intervene. Lee merely suggested that he and Nix "get together and 'talk this thing out.'"

In a formal report to Roy K. Moore, the FBI chief in Mississippi, Ingram and Webb mentioned there was an arrest warrant out for them in Jones County and suggested "that we should perhaps work in Forrest County for a while." Moore did not like the idea. Ingram later revealed that Moore told them "we should continue to work in Jones County and not be intimidated. To do otherwise would set the tone that the Klan, especially in Jones County, could do exactly as it pleased."

≈

LIKE MANY publicly elected officials in Mississippi, Chet Dillard, the district attorney for Jones County, was unhappy over the federal role in the civil rights cases. The Feds, he thought, had essentially taken over jurisdiction from the state. His concerns ignored the fact that Mississippi law enforcement and judiciary officials had shown little enthusiasm for pursuing arrests and prosecutions in the Neshoba County murders—an incident so wanton and brutal that President Johnson had felt it necessary to send former CIA director Allen Dulles as a personal emissary to Mississippi. The FBI task force had followed.

Dillard wanted to be involved in the Dahmer investigation, but considered himself preempted by the federal presence. Because the attack on Dahmer's home took place in Forrest County, another district attorney had jurisdiction for any state prosecution. But many of the suspects were residents of Jones County, so Dillard felt he had a legitimate stake in the case.

Dillard had been one of the Mississippi officials invited to Moore's FBI briefing in Hattiesburg, but he still smarted from his belief that the Feds dismissed him as either a Klan member or a sympathizer. If they had bothered to learn his background, Dillard thought, they would know it was unfair to link him to the racist organization.

A few years earlier, as a young lawyer new to the bar in Jones County, Dillard had served as a court-appointed defense attorney for a Black man, Willie Stokes, who faced a murder charge and the death penalty if convicted. Stokes was accused of fatally stabbing a white woman cashier during a robbery attempt. The defendant was uneducated and had lived in the crawl space of his aunt's house. He fumbled for words with his attorney and had nothing to say that would help his case. Dillard described Stokes as "a result of a society's failure." The attorney empathized with the defendant; he had bitter memories of seeking refuge as a child himself beneath his impoverished mother's home when authorities came to take him to an orphanage.

Knowing that the crime had created a frenzy in Jones County, Dillard sought a change in venue for Stokes's trial. Standing in the courtroom, he realized he occupied the same spot where another Black man, Willie McGee, had actually been executed. Dillard's efforts to move the trial failed, as did his attempts to plea-bargain in exchange for a life sentence. So did his arguments in the trial. After

Stokes was sentenced to death, Dillard made an unsuccessful appeal to the state supreme court.

As a last-ditch measure, he arranged a meeting with the governor at the time, Ross Barnett, whose oratory was often filled with the word "nigger." He hoped the governor might commute the death sentence to life imprisonment. Shortly after seeing Dillard personally, the governor telephoned the young attorney. Infamous for his malapropisms and non sequiturs, Barnett told the Laurel lawyer, "Ah, Brother Dillard, did you know this woman's husband was a member of the International Brotherhood of Railroad Workers?" Implying that he didn't want to upset this constituency, the governor concluded that Stokes had had a fair trial, and now he would have to go.

Before his trial, Stokes had asked Dillard what he could do. Dillard recommended prayer. "Nobody ever taught me to pray," Stokes said. "I don't know how to pray." In the days before his execution in 1961, Stokes had someone write a letter to Dillard. He assured him he had found salvation and was now prepared to die.

Given his experience with this case, the district attorney was annoyed that there might be FBI suspicions about friendships between Klan members and law-abiding people in Jones County like himself.

The latest episodes involving Lawrence Byrd and Deavours Nix led Dillard to believe that the FBI was employing strong-arm tactics that were unlawful. He had earlier expressed concerns that the bureau might be using convicted felons to do its dirty work in the abduction of Byrd, and he thought FBI agents had become heavy-handed in dealing with other suspects. Dillard also wondered if members of the Mississippi Highway Patrol, working in concert with the FBI, were complicit in some of the strange affairs going on in Jones County in the weeks since Dahmer's death.

Privately, Dillard went so far as to think that the FBI might have planted dynamite in a car belonging to Pete Martin of the White Knights. It did seem more than curious that two FBI agents happened to be observing Martin's movements when he was pulled over by Laurel police on the afternoon of January 31. After a brief exchange with Martin, the officers abruptly began to search his car. They found an empty gallon jug in his trunk and smelled it for gasoline. Then they discovered a brown paper shopping bag on the front seat. The bag contained several sticks of dynamite and a coil of fuse wires. "Somebody must have put it there," Martin protested, insisting that the package was not his. He was taken in for further questioning, and a month later he began to gush information to the FBI.

Martin acknowledged his role in the shooting incident at the home of Dr. B. E. Murph the year before. He said he used his own car for the attack and was accompanied by Frank Lyons, Lester Thornton, and Charles "Red" Noble. The guns were supplied by Nix, while Thornton and Lyons did the shooting, he said. Afterward, Noble disposed of the weapons.

Martin confessed to taking part in another operation in Hattiesburg that was arranged by Nix. The target was a Black minister's house where a party was supposed to be taking place. However, when Martin and his accomplices arrived, the home was dark. They shot up the place anyway.

Though he professed to know nothing about the Dahmer case, Martin threw out the name of Billy Ray Smith. "He hangs out at John's Restaurant and drinks heavily," Martin told the agents. "He's very close to Deavours Nix. I got no direct information that he had any connection with the Dahmer situation, but due to his association with Nix he should be considered as a suspect." Martin's mention of Smith added to confusion over two Klansmen with similar names.

Before his interrogation was over, Martin promised to continue collecting material for the FBI.

≈

AGENT JIM INGRAM'S CONTRETEMPS with Nix was just the latest in a series of brushes he had with the Klan since he moved to Mississippi as part of the FBI's increased presence in the state in 1964. A big, muscular man, Ingram realized his size could be threatening and he took advantage of it to add weight to his personal contacts with the Klan.

Ingram and Tom Landrum did not know each other, but there were similarities in their backgrounds. They were born the same year—1932—and both grew up in rural environments hard-hit by the Great Depression. While Landrum had used his hands and a mule to plow farmland in Jones County, Ingram tended livestock on his family's farm in Oklahoma. Football had been a way to a college education for both men. Ingram was first recruited by Northeastern Oklahoma A&M as a defensive end and later won a scholarship to play football for George Washington University in the District of Columbia, where his Oklahoma connections worked well with a couple of influential members of the state's congressional delegation. He was given a patronage job as an elevator operator in the Capitol by Senator Bob Kerr, the wealthy executive of the Kerr-McGee petroleum empire who became a political champion of Big Oil interests in the Senate. Though Ingram's elevator duties were humble, the job gave him daily exposure to other movers and shakers riding between floors of the building. He got to know Representative Ed Edmondson of Oklahoma, who took an interest in the young man. A former FBI agent himself, Edmondson encouraged Ingram to apply to the bureau. In the well-worked tradition of networking in Washington, Edmondson aided him with several calls to top FBI officials.

Once he became an agent, Ingram grew devoted to the longtime director. Though Hoover's domineering style was finally attracting some public criticism, Ingram said he "learned to love the man" and intended to serve him loyally. He attracted notice as a rookie while on assignment in Indiana, employing tips from informers to track down and capture an outlaw from Oklahoma who was on the FBI's "Ten Most Wanted" list. He received a personal letter from Hoover, which he treasured. In it, the director wrote to Ingram, "You demonstrated admirable resourcefulness and aggressiveness in discharging your assignment, thereby contributing to the success attained. This was a job very well done."

When people speculated over who served as the source for his critical tip, Ingram crafted a mantra for reply: "I'd love to tell you, but informants are the backbone of witness hunting. Like a good newspaper reporter, I never reveal my sources."

Ingram became so adept at dealing with inside information that he was sent to help run the collection of informants the FBI developed during its investigation of the case it code-named MIBURN, for "Mississippi Burning," following the triple murder in Neshoba County. He saw the principle of silence applied at the highest levels of the FBI after two agents arrived in Mississippi from Washington bearing a nondescript package to be turned over only to FBI inspector Joe Sullivan. The package was filled with thousands of dollars and was ultimately given to a Mississippi informant who told the FBI where the three bodies had been buried. It was not pretty work, but it got the job done. After Nicholas Katzenbach became attorney general that year, he asked Sullivan the identity of the informant. Sullivan refused on the grounds it might jeopardize the informant's life. Running informants was a perilous profession, both for the FBI agents and for those willing to talk with them.

Ingram had a parallel assignment in Mississippi, helping to ferret out police officers who belonged to the Klan. Jones and Neshoba Counties were not the only places where law enforcement agencies had been infiltrated by the Klan. Ingram discovered there were other highway patrolmen, sheriffs, deputies, constables, and policemen at various levels in jurisdictions around the state who had ties to the Invisible Empire.

When a list of untrustworthy Mississippi Highway Patrol troopers was turned over to Governor Paul B. Johnson during the 1964 investigations, Ingram felt gratified that these officers were discharged immediately. It gave him satisfaction that there were some Mississippi authorities the FBI would be able to work with.

～

WITH THE FBI fanning out to confront every known member of the White Knights with the question "Can you account for your whereabouts in the early hours of January 10?" apprehensions grew among Sam Bowers's gang in Jones County. Their dismay increased when they heard of the mysterious Byrd beating and the FBI's ominous visit to Nix's home. The White Knights went on high alert, with special attention given to detecting informants in their midst.

Suspicions about who might be talking to the FBI ran high. There were concerns about Lamar "Shorty" Lowe, who had fled town in the company of his father, another Klan member named Clifton "Pat" Lowe. The elder Lowe was known to have rented a U-Haul trailer for a one-way trip to Houston, Texas, in January.

The younger Lowe had exhibited a tendency for erratic behavior during his time in the White Knights. Months before his departure from Laurel he had incurred minor wounds when he managed to shoot himself in the leg while loading a gun. Earlier, Lowe had objected so strenuously to being stopped for speeding by Mississippi highway patrolman Tony Landrum—Tom's brother—that he wound up in jail for excessive backtalk. Before Lowe's outburst, the trooper had been prepared to let him off with a warning.

More misadventures followed in Texas. Within days he was arrested for questioning in connection with an armed robbery. Two weeks later the FBI took him into custody after he became unruly in a dispute over payments for a new Chevrolet Impala. The car was repossessed and Lowe was charged with interstate transportation of a motor vehicle. He was taken before a U.S. commissioner. According to the FBI report, Lowe "became boisterous, profane and would not listen to charge or explanation of rights." After refusing to stay quiet, he was held in contempt and thrown in the Harris County jail on February 11.

Even before he left Mississippi, the diminutive Lowe, known as "Odd Ball" as well as "Shorty," had not been considered particularly stable by his fellow Klansmen. His performance in Texas gave the FBI additional leverage to ask him about the Dahmer case.

In fact, many members of the White Knights were being questioned. Billy Roy Pitts, who had also gone to Texas, found that he could not escape the FBI badgering. He telephoned his father back in Jones County, claiming the FBI was "questioning everybody who had left Mississippi." He wanted to come home. His father sent twenty-eight dollars to make the return trip. He had worked in upholstery before leaving. He took a new job in an auto tune-up shop.

≈

IN A FEBRUARY 23 REPORT to the FBI, Landrum told of a conversation he had with Red Caldwell earlier that day. "He stated the FBI had been to him today, and he had told them to leave and not come back. He said he might have made a mistake, due to being smart with them. He said he was scared to death, and it had gotten to the point where he couldn't go to meetings without FBI knowing everything. He stated it looked to him like he would have to move or leave before it worried him to death. He stated he would drop out if he could from the Klan. He stated he had everything to lose and nothing to gain."

The White Knights county giant also told Landrum that no Jones County meetings were planned for the immediate future.

≈

THE NEXT AFTERNOON, Byrd's Radio & TV Service became the setting for a strange procession of visitors, with the entrance and exit of one character quickly followed by the arrival and departure of another character, like a scene from a stage comedy.

Deavours Nix came by first. He told Byrd that Bowers had gone into hiding, expecting to be arrested any day.

Still wounded from his beating and nursing a grudge against Bowers, Byrd expressed little sympathy. "Deavours, when our organization got in trouble up in Neshoba County and over in Natchez, Sam went around begging for money to help those men. Now that his home boys are in trouble, he's gone into hiding. That ain't no help."

"Look," Nix replied, "Sam's safe and he's in a situation where he can still help. If you want to arrange a meeting with him, we can. We got to do something about the squealers in our group, and

Sam thinks you should be the one to form a committee to discover who's leaking."

"You already mentioned that to me," Byrd said. "Seems to me it may be too late. The FBI's already closing in, going around asking us all questions, making sure we know that they're on our ass. And now you're telling me Sam's gone to ground."

"I'm telling you the FBI don't know shit," Nix said. "They don't know nothing about the Dahmer Nigger job. They just operating on a bunch of bullshit some weak members in our group may have told them. What they're doing, they're playing us off one another. One man against another. Trying to get us to talk. What we need to do is to be quiet. And to shut up any jackass who's been talking to the FBI."

In his capacity as director of the Klan Bureau of Investigation, Nix renewed his earlier suggestion and formally appointed Byrd to organize a committee to track down the informants. "I think there ought to be three members," he said. "It ought to be composed of Number Twelve and Number Seventeen. You can pick the third man." In the White Knights code, Byrd had been assigned Twelve; Number Seventeen belonged to a member named B. F. Hinton, a pudgy businessman who owned a flooring company in Laurel but had been inactive lately in the Klan.

Byrd agreed that the White Knights needed the committee and overcame his own doubts about the request. "I'll set it up," he promised. He rationalized that the task could be helpful to his own situation. Since he was already meeting secretly with the FBI, it gave him cover. He thought it also added to his standing in the Klan.

Shortly after Nix left the shop, Speed Lightsey dropped by. Byrd told him Nix had just instructed him to form an investigating committee. He asked Lightsey if he would serve.

Lightsey said he was willing and inquired, "Who's on it?"

"I can't say who's on the committee," Byrd said to Lightsey, alluding to the authority of his new position. "I can tell you there will be three members, but you won't know the identity of the others."

The next visitor was Henry deBoxtel. He complained about

pressure from the FBI, but said he refused to listen to the agents. "They've come up to me to question me several times," he said. "I just turn and walk away from them. I ain't telling them shit. Not even acknowledging my name."

"Well, we got a leak here somewhere," Byrd said. "You've been recommended to serve on a committee whose business will be to identify FBI informers. Do you want to be on it?"

"If I'm wanted, I'll be glad to serve," he said.

Within a couple of hours, Byrd's three-man committee had grown to four.

It was growing dark outside—the same time of day when the three strangers had arrived at the appliance store a few weeks earlier. This time, Cecil Sessum came through the door. Byrd dismissed his employees, suggesting that they go home early. He wanted to talk privately with Sessum, who seemed nervous.

"The FBI hasn't followed me for the past two days," Sessum said quietly to Byrd. "I'm wondering if this is the lull before the storm."

CHAPTER 14

TOM LANDRUM WAS one of the first to notice the unusual activity inside the Jones County courthouse. Leonard Caves, the circuit clerk–cum–Klansman, had strolled over to the youth counselor's office in an adjacent annex to have a cup of coffee with Landrum when he got a message to return to his own place. Caves explained to Landrum that he had to leave because Sam Bowers, reportedly "in hiding" the week before, was there and wanted to see him. Caves hurried back to find that Bowers was accompanied by Nix and Sessum. They wanted Caves to notarize a six-page, typed affidavit from Sessum that would throw a new wrinkle into the Dahmer investigation.

Landrum waited thirty minutes, then went to Caves's office to check out the situation. Bowers was still there, waiting for the circuit clerk to make five copies of the document. Since Bowers planned to circulate Sessum's affidavit, Landrum easily obtained a copy for himself and passed it on to the FBI later the same day.

Inspecting Sessum's paper, the FBI agents realized that they had on their hands yet another contradictory narrative from a ranking member of the White Knights.

First there had been the public account from Lawrence Byrd attributing his kidnapping to robbers who had nothing to do with the FBI or the Klan. Yet there existed another long statement from

Byrd, the fruit of a series of interviews agents had conducted with him over the past month since he had begun cooperating with them. It contained an account of the attack on Dahmer's property that Byrd said he had cajoled out of Sessum during a heart-to-heart talk. This confidential twenty-two-page statement implicating Sessum and others was signed March 2 and witnessed by two FBI agents, William Dukes and J. L. Martin, the same pair who had been gathering information from Byrd since the night he was forcefully taken from his store.

The latest document from a Klansman, delivered to the FBI by Landrum, was Sessum's affidavit, signed March 7, which seemed designed to refute Byrd's March 2 statement. In the new affidavit, Sessum claimed to have been set up by Byrd for an abduction in which he was terrorized by a team that included the FBI leader Roy K. Moore.

Though Sessum's bizarre affidavit had an air of credibility in light of the brutal campaign to extract confessions from suspects, it could be countered by still another secret document compiled by the FBI after agents had a dramatic interview with Sessum on March 1.

≈

IT WAS FASCINATING for the investigators to compare these dueling narratives. The various documents contained mixtures of truth, self-serving claims, and outright falsehoods. FBI agents knew that Byrd's public report of his kidnapping by robbers was a bogus one given in order to throw the Klan off any scent of his cooperation with the FBI. The agents possessed their own statement, far more valuable, that Byrd had given to Dukes and Martin, and the critical portion of his story began the evening Sessum visited him and spoke of the "lull before the storm."

According to Byrd: "I told Sessum we had to get together and he had to tell me the complete story of the Dahmer burning. Sessum wanted to know why this was necessary, and I explained to him that it was necessary in order to identify FBI informants." Byrd told

Sessum that unless he revealed what he knew about the raid, Byrd would quit his responsibilities on the Klan investigative committee, leaving Sessum with the job. The two men agreed to meet later that night.

At 8:45 p.m., Sessum telephoned Byrd at his home and told him in code, "I'm ready to pick up the merchandise." Byrd said he went to a lot used for trailer sales in Laurel, where he joined Sessum in his car. The pair drove to a wooded location. Sessum said he did not want to talk in the car, fearing that it might have been bugged by the FBI, so they walked deeper into the pine forest.

"I told Sessum that he knew I did not go on the dry run or on the job when Dahmer's place was burned and that I did not even know where the nigger lived. I told Sessum that despite this I was involved as an accessory and that my neck was on the chopping block. I told Sessum that I had to have the complete story."

He said Sessum retorted, "My neck is in the noose and I don't trust anybody." He had reason not to trust Byrd, whose erratic behavior in the days since he was hospitalized had been noted by most of the White Knights in Jones County.

Byrd feigned indignation, suggesting that Sessum should drive him back to his truck. "Or I can walk," he said. "If that's your attitude, I don't want nothing further to do with it, and you can take full responsibility for everything."

Sessum softened and agreed to fill him in on details. "Let's go back to the night when we met at the service station to go on the dry run," Sessum said. "Remember? The night you said you had a bad back and left?" After Byrd's departure, Sessum said, he met with Bowers, Nix, and deBoxtel at John's Restaurant, where the imperial wizard made a sketch of the terrain around Dahmer's place. Bowers said it was unnecessary for him and Nix to inspect the grounds because they were already familiar with the lay of the land.

Sessum said personal animosities led to departures from the project by two men. Billy Moss quit because he had been put under the thumb of deBoxtel; Moss hated deBoxtel. Sessum personally dismissed a Masonite worker named Billy Ray Smith following the trial ride to Dahmer's property because they had once argued over a girl. "I didn't trust him," Sessum said.

(The name of Billy Ray Smith would create confusion among the White Knights as well as the FBI because another member, named Bill "Lightning" Smith, actually went on the raid. Although the White Knights tried to project the image that their organization represented a close-knit band of brothers, many of the members did not know one another because they belonged to different klaverns, attended meetings infrequently, or abided by vows of secrecy.)

Following the last dry run, Bowers instructed Sessum and deBoxtel to each organize a team of three Klansmen—a total of six men—to handle the final raid on Dahmer's place. According to Byrd, Sessum told him, "I didn't know the identity of the men on Henry's team and he didn't know the identity of the men on mine."

Sessum's tale, as related by Byrd, diverged at this point from accounts coming to the FBI from other sources. By the beginning of March, nearly two months after the raid, several other members of the White Knights were cooperating with agents after being told they faced long prison sentences unless they did so. For some reason, Sessum did not mention to Byrd the name of Cliff Wilson, the Laurel businessman who drove the car Sessum rode in. Nor did he accurately identify another of the car's occupants, "Lightning" Smith, who worked by day at Wilson's store, Laurel Brace and Limb Company.

On the night of the burning, the group met at a location Sessum refused to disclose. However, he was willing to give Byrd the names of two other men in his car: Charles Noble, who went by the nickname "Red," and Billy Roy Pitts.

"Is this Billy Roy Pitts the same Pitts who went to Texas with Shorty Lowe?" Byrd asked.

"Same man," Sessum confirmed.

"Who is this guy Noble?"

"Oh, you should know Noble," Sessum said. "You'd recognize him when you saw him." (Noble was later identified by the FBI as an occupant of the car deBoxtel drove—and was not in Wilson's Pontiac. Altogether, eight men—not six—took part in the raid.)

Sessum described a scene of chaos as the White Knights fled the Dahmer property. "We drove for a while, away from the Dahmer Nigger's place, when we realized that the other car wasn't following us," Sessum told Byrd. "We turned around to go back and look for it. While we were driving back, this Pitts fellow announced he had lost his pistol at the Dahmer Nigger's house."

Sessum said Pitts started "jabbering to us about how if the FBI found his pistol, they couldn't trace it to him. Anyhow, we drove back and saw Travis Giles's car, a '63 Ford, parked beside the road with two flat tires. When we pulled up beside it, the three men who had been in it came out of the woods. All three of 'em had socks over their heads and were unrecognizable."

Sessum said the group had an excited discussion about the car. There were suggestions to have it either towed or burned. These ideas were dismissed as impractical. So the three masked men piled into the other car and the expanded group returned to Laurel. Sessum did not name any of the masked trio.

"Was one of them Henry deBoxtel?" Byrd asked. "Surely you'd recognize him, even if he had a sock over his head."

"I don't think Henry was one of them. I think he would have talked to me after we picked them up," Sessum was quoted as telling Byrd. "I did recognize the voice, though, of one of Henry's right-hand men. It was Billy Ray Smith."

Byrd said he assumed Sessum was referring to a man named Smith who worked with Cliff Wilson. He said Sessum suggested that they get together with Smith in order to identify the men in the other car.

On the night of February 27, Byrd said, he met with "Lightning" Smith and Wilson at the store for prosthetic parts before Sessum arrived:

I expressed concern that someone was talking to the FBI about the Dahmer burning. Smith then asked the purpose of the meeting that night. I told him the time had come to "come clean" and that Sessum and I were organizing an investigating committee. Smith said he had no information concerning the Dahmer matter.

Later on, Smith said he knew what was causing all the trouble and speculated that some of the men were dating the same women in Laurel and engaging in arguments among themselves which caused trouble within the Klan.

When Sessum arrived later, Byrd said he reminded them that the purpose of their meeting was to track down a leak in their organization. Byrd said he didn't know who should be suspected.

"Well, I want to know what's going to happen to the son of a bitch who is talking when we find out," Smith declared.

In his statement, Byrd claimed he offered a proposal. "We'll lecture this individual and swear him out of the Klan with the understanding that he wouldn't furnish any more information. And we'd keep him under observation."

"That's a bunch of bullshit," Smith said. "We already discussed this at our meetings and decided we'd kill the motherfucker. The person who's talkin' is going to be buried when he's identified."

At this point, according to his statement, Byrd triggered a moment of high confusion and anger when he reported that Sessum had "recognized Smith's voice as one of those individuals in the car that was shot down on the Dahmer job."

"That's a goddamned lie," Smith exploded. "I wasn't in on the Dahmer job and I don't know what goddamned car you're talkin' about." He angrily confronted Sessum. "You don't know what in the hell you're talking about. I am now facing a liar." He addressed Sessum directly: "Cecil, if you told Lawrence that, you're going to be in deep shit."

Sessum was said to have replied meekly, "I guess I am in trouble anyway. Everybody is against me and the Feds are continually after me." Byrd recalled that Sessum appeared frightened and "turned white."

According to Byrd, Sessum then contended that the voice he

heard the night of the raid belonged to a different man, named William Ray Smith, who lived on Magnolia Street in Laurel. Sessum said this man was living illegally with a woman and had earlier accused Sessum of sexually desiring his companion. He was the Klansman Sessum had vetoed as a participant in the raiding party. Sessum seemed eager to implicate his rival in romance rather than the Bill Smith standing before him. "The man is broke and has lost his car and would sell out to the Feds any day. I'm positive in my own mind that I heard William Ray Smith talking," Sessum said.

Byrd's statement continued, "It became apparent at this time that we were not going to reach an accord. Wilson suggested that we just 'let it ride' for a few days or a few weeks and see how it worked out."

═

AT THE END OF HIS lengthy statement to the FBI, Byrd described one last dramatic encounter with Sessum.

On the night of March 1, Byrd said, he received a telephone call at his home from Sessum, who said he wanted to show something to him that night. They agreed to meet in a parking lot of the Laurel hospital. According to Byrd, Sessum joined him in his station wagon and the pair traveled to Byrd's farm. They parked far from a highway, in an area where the only roads were private ones that crisscrossed his land to reach oil-drilling locations on his property. Because Sessum feared the vehicle might be bugged, they walked again into the forest to conduct their conversation.

Byrd said, "I told Sessum that I was concerned for him as well as myself." He pleaded with Sessum to talk to the FBI. "I told Sessum I had been interviewed for an hour and 45 minutes the day before by FBI agents and that it appeared obvious to me that they had the goods on the group involved in the Dahmer burning." He told Sessum to think about his children and his own future while there was time to cooperate with the authorities.

After they noticed car lights approaching from a distance, Sessum suggested that they walk deeper into a swamp. Byrd told the part-time minister he had prayed for him the night before, urging him "to tell the whole truth."

According to Byrd, Sessum replied, "This is one of them deals, and even if I did confess, it would still be used against me later, regardless of any promise that might be made to me. I only have to make peace with one person, and that's God. I took an oath that I will never reveal or betray my brother Klansmen, and I won't squeal on my brothers."

Their conversation was disrupted by the appearance of more headlights. Sessum said he believed he had been lured into a trap and slipped briefly out of sight into the darkness behind some trees. When the lights disappeared, he rejoined Byrd in his station wagon and they talked a few more minutes.

Suddenly, Byrd said, they were approached on foot by Dukes and Martin, the two agents who had been handling his case. "It's the Feds," a startled Sessum announced. "Do you have a gun?" Byrd said he had no gun. "I don't either," Sessum said. "All I got is this pocket knife." He tossed the knife on the dashboard in resignation.

After the agents identified themselves, Byrd told Sessum these were the men he had talked with the day before. Byrd said Sessum mumbled something "unintelligible which I interpreted to mean that he did not know anything." However, Sessum said he had no objection to talking to the agents. After a second car arrived, occupied by another FBI agent and a Mississippi Highway Patrol investigator, Sessum departed with Dukes and Martin. The second car followed. Byrd said he drove home alone.

Byrd signed his statement for the FBI the next morning in Hattiesburg "to set the record straight." In its final paragraph, Byrd said, "I wish to state that the oath I took when I joined the Klan, and the Klan Constitution, do not provide for me to engage in acts of violence such as that demonstrated in the Dahmer matter. I have long since realized that the violence advocated and sometimes committed by the Klan is not typical of what I thought the Klan stood for when I joined."

FOR INTRIGUE, Sessum's account of his evening with Byrd—delivered in his March 7 affidavit—rivaled the drama of Byrd's tale of being mauled by a Mafia hit man acting at the behest of the FBI. Sessum's new narrative started at the same place Byrd's statement ended, with the two men engaged in a troubled conversation at the dead end of a private road on Byrd's farm. But from that point, Sessum's statement veered wildly from the story related by Byrd.

Sessum said he agreed to join Byrd on the ride because he knew Byrd "had been sick and acting very strange since he was kidnapped and beaten several weeks previously." Sessum said he wanted "to assist him in any way that I could."

After they parked, "Mr. Byrd began talking to me about the serious emotional problem which he had and which he said was being caused by the constant harassment to which he was being subjected by the police agents of the FBI. Mr. Byrd told me that they had got him to the point where he just couldn't stand it anymore, and that he was ready to tell them anything that they wanted to hear if they just wouldn't pick him up and beat him anymore."

According to Sessum, Byrd said his abduction had been arranged by the FBI and "that they had told him they were going to put both he and I in the gas chamber for the killing of the Dahmer Nigger in Hattiesburg a couple of months ago."

Sessum claimed he tried to calm Byrd. "I told him that I did not believe that he was involved in any way with the Dahmer business, and that I was most certainly not." Assuring Byrd that they had nothing to worry about, Sessum said "these FBI men were caught up in the web of the devil and the beast system, and that persecuting the White Christian people of Mississippi was the task to which they had been assigned. I explained to him that this was our cross to bear in this time just as Jesus had borne His up in Calvary."

While they talked, Sessum said, a car with very bright lights blocked their exit. Two men jumped out with sawed-off shotguns as another car drove up.

Byrd and Sessum were ordered to get out of their vehicle "or get your heads blown off." Sessum said he was searched for a weapon, then instructed to get into a "police car." He reported that the men identified themselves as "FBI men, U.S. marshals and one Mississippi state investigator." He was unable to remember any names because they merely flashed their ID cards momentarily in the darkened car, but he felt he recognized the face of one man "who had followed me frequently" in an FBI-issued Plymouth similar to the low-budget models used by agents in Mississippi.

"Byrd and I sat in the rear of the police car, and Mr. Byrd told the officers that he believed I was the one that had killed the Dahmer Nigger, together with several men whose names he called and whom I do not know. I was very shocked at this and told the officers that Mr. Byrd was out of his head from the beating which he had received when he was kidnapped and the drugs which he had been taking since then, and I told them clearly and emphatically that I was completely innocent."

After releasing Byrd, Sessum said, the officers told him, "We're not going to fool around with you any more out here, and you are not going home." According to Sessum's affidavit, they drove to a rear entrance of a Holiday Inn in Hattiesburg. Sessum said he was taken to Room 107, where he was "brought face-to-face with the famous Mr. Roy Moore, the chief of all the FBI National Police in the whole state of Mississippi."

≈

MOORE'S FACE WOULD NOT have been known by most Mississippians, nor was his name a household word in the state. But he had become a major figure in the lives of the White Knights since J. Edgar Hoover sent him to Mississippi to supervise the rapidly expanding FBI force in the days after the murders in Neshoba County.

Born in 1914 in Oregon, Moore served in the marines and later rose in the ranks of the FBI because of his bulldog toughness. Before coming to Mississippi he gained experience in civil rights cases interrogating Klan suspects in connection with the Birmingham church bombing in 1963 that killed four young Black girls attending Sunday services. In Mississippi, Moore declared war on the Klan and drove his men relentlessly. One agent who worked under him in Mississippi said, "He'd ride a good horse to death. The more you could do and do well, the more he would expect that you'd get done."

Knowing that the outside agents would have difficulty moving around easily in a state wary of federal officials, Moore tried to team his agents with dependable members of the Mississippi Highway Patrol as they pursued the Klan during the MIBURN investigation. Following Dahmer's death, his agents were swarming again, this time in Jones and Forrest Counties. In White Knights circles, Moore was not only famous but feared.

≈

SESSUM CLAIMED Moore demanded that he "come clean" and showed him "a stack of papers almost a foot high" that contained evidence of a "clear-cut case" against Sessum despite Little Preacher's professions of innocence. Moore refused to let him call a lawyer.

"About this time," according to Sessum,

the biggest of the U.S. marshals called me a "dirty little S.O.B." and hit me in the cheek with a roundhouse right. This blow knocked me down, and my head hit the wall and dazed me momentarily. I weigh only 137 lbs. and my body is not large enough to absorb blows from a 200 lb. man. This violence took place in front of Mr. Roy Moore, who stood, watched and approved of the beating I was receiving. I told them this beating was illegal, and the big marshal picked me up again, cursed me some more and knocked me down again with a left to the jaw. This time, when I went down, I fell onto the chair in such a way that a slat in the back of the chair hit my back and injured my spine. I could not get up. Because of the shock and pain, I was almost unconscious.

Sessum said that after he revived from the blows, the marshal set upon him again with a blackjack, pounding his legs and shoulders and shouting at him, "Talk, you little S.O.B., or I'll beat you to death."

Moore watched the beating quietly, according to Sessum, who described his pain as "becoming more terrible every minute." He said he gasped at Moore that the attack was "completely illegal," only to be told by the FBI leader, "I don't see anything."

There was a pause in the confrontation while Moore and the marshal went into an adjoining room, leaving Sessum in the hands of another officer, who talked in a soothing voice and told him he wanted to "help," yet refused a plea for a lawyer. Sessum could hear typing in the adjacent room. Later Moore and the marshal returned, handing him a "confession." When he refused to sign the document, it provoked another beating by the marshal, he said. Sessum complained that he had not been able to read the paper.

"OK, read it then," he said he was told by the marshal. "But I am going to kill you if you don't sign it."

"I read Roy Moore's 'confession,'" Sessum claimed in his affidavit, "and it said a lot of lies about where I had come to them voluntarily in order to 'ease my conscience.' It went on to say that I had been in the bunch of men who had burned the Dahmer Nigger's house and named some other men as my 'accomplices' who I have never heard of."

Sessum said he was unwilling to sign the "false confession" in the face of "pain and torture" and "every kind of duress which their evil minds could design." He asked Moore for a court trial.

"This is your trial," the marshal was said to have replied, and struck him again in front of Moore.

"Finally," Sessum claimed, "the big marshal said, 'No use fooling around with this S.O.B. any longer. . . . We have gone too far with him. . . . We are going to have to take him out and kill him. . . . Let's go to the nigger graveyard.'"

Sessum continued with a lurid account of a scene in the cemetery where Dahmer had been buried.

Leaving the Holiday Inn, Sessum said, he was trundled into a two-toned tan 1965 Plymouth and driven to a country church. "The big marshal told me that he was going to kill me and leave my body by the nigger graveyard. They drove around behind the church, stopped the car and took me out." According to his account, he was forced to kneel beside an oak tree while the marshal pressed the barrel of his pistol "hard against the base of my skull, cocked it, and told me that this was my last chance to talk, and that if I did not talk now, that I would be committing suicide. I told him that my conscience was clear, and that I had nothing I could tell him about the case." The marshal instructed him to pray out loud. "As I tried to prepare myself for the moment when the bullet would enter my brain and terminate my earthly life, I remembered the example set for me by the Savior as he hung on the cross, and prayed." He said he knew God recognized that "I have done no wrong" and prayed "that you will forgive them."

Sessum said he prevailed in the confrontation after he acknowledged he was prepared to die. Instead of pulling the trigger, the marshal appeared confused and moved him back to the car. "They knew that they had got themselves into a tight spot between the law of man and the Law of God."

At 2:30 a.m., Sessum said, "they brought me back to Laurel and let me out and told me that if I ever breathed a word of any of this to anybody that they would have me killed."

～

SESSUM INSISTED he was reporting the incident publicly "in the best interest of America." The final sentences of his affidavit sounded as though they had been scripted by the imperial wizard, whose philosophy involved belief in "Christian militancy" that was essential to striking down godless federal forces prepared to bring unwanted racial integration to Mississippi.

"I want every American citizen to understand the danger in which they stand from the National Police terror of the FBI," Sessum said.

> What happened to me can and will happen to every Christian citizen of America if the anti-Christ Beast Power of the FBI is not brought under control. Roy Moore, a supposedly honorable man, like Pilate, delivered me up for death. Only the miracle of Christ preserved me.
>
> I will state that I do not believe in persecuting or harassing niggers or taking advantage of their benighted state in any way. The Dahmer Nigger has gone to his reward. I am very sorry about it. I had nothing to do with it and his family has my sympathy. But I do not see any justice in the FBI blindly casting about, picking up white Christians and torturing them in a rage of violence, and to try to appease the nigger mob leaders by getting some white Christian to throw to them. If people will just leave the good niggers and white people alone in Mississippi and quit meddling, we will be able to solve our own problems far better than can ever be done by a National Gestapo.

He signed the document. It was notarized by Leonard Caves. In the typewritten affidavit, Sessum's name was misspelled in every instance but his own signature.

⌒

SESSUM'S AFFIDAVIT lashing out at the FBI might have given his fellow Klansmen some satisfaction, but Little Preacher realized he had damned himself a few days earlier in an altogether different account of his meeting with the FBI. And he knew the FBI possessed a statement based on the encounter that would prove more truthful and contradict virtually every sentence in his new affidavit.

According to the FBI's version, Sessum agreed to go with agents Dukes and Martin to their temporary headquarters at the Holiday

Inn. As they traveled along Interstate Highway 59, Sessum noticed an exit sign for Monroe Road. Identifying himself a minister, he expressed interest in visiting the cemetery where Dahmer was buried. He was driven to the Shady Grove church.

"On observing a recent flower-decked grave," the FBI statement said, "he inquired whether this was Dahmer's grave. He was told by the agents that they did not know. Sessum at this point began to cry and wiped tears from his eyes with his handkerchief. He volunteered at this point that he had to make peace only with one person, God."

Sessum was described as in torment. Drawing on his knowledge of the Bible, he compared his plight to Jesus's agony in the Garden of Gethsemane at his hour of betrayal. He finally broke down at the Holiday Inn. He told of how his uncle had sworn him into the Klan and how he had risen to the position of exalted cyclops of Unit Five. He said his own individual Klan number was also five.

According to the FBI statement, Sessum wept quietly and wiped his eyes repeatedly. "I now realize my obligation as a minister and a Christian is stronger than my Klan oath," he told a small circle of FBI officers, which included Moore. "When I joined I didn't know we would participate in violence and death."

Sessum was asked what he knew of the burning of the Dahmer home. He was mute for a moment, then inquired about the extent of Byrd's cooperation. He was told that Byrd had provided information and had named Sessum as one of those involved. Sniffling, Sessum began to spill out recollections of events leading up to the attack: a White Knights meeting near the Bogue Homa swamp, which he began with a prayer only to be followed by Bowers's rant about "the big NAACP nigger down there" in Forrest County; a subsequent meeting upstairs at John's Restaurant between Bowers, Nix, deBoxtel, and Sessum, followed by the dry run past Dahmer's property.

Sessum began crying copiously and seemed highly agitated. "This matter has been preying on my mind," he croaked, and in a voice that was almost inaudible he admitted, "I went on the Dahmer burning."

He gave the FBI a few details. Two cars were involved, one of them the Ford loaned for the mission by Klansman Travis Giles, who was at work at Masonite so that he had an alibi. He confirmed that Giles's car was fired on by one of the Klansmen during the raid, but he would not identify the shooter. He said he felt bound by the White Knights oath never to reveal the identity of other Klansmen. Nevertheless, after Dukes asked if Billy Roy Pitts had dropped his pistol, Sessum acknowledged that Pitts had raised a question about going back to the scene to retrieve his gun.

At this point, Sessum said he could give no further information. Dukes typed a two-page statement summarizing what Sessum had said, but when it was presented to the Klansman he refused to sign it. Sessum said he would have to give the matter "further thought and prayer."

CHAPTER 15

I N THE WEEKS SINCE Vernon Dahmer's death, the strengthened force of FBI agents was joined by a number of state highway patrol investigators who served as surveillance teams. They
followed suspects in their cars or dogged their steps on the streets.
Authorities wanted the White Knights to know that they were being
watched carefully. To heighten anxiety, agents showed up to question known members at places where they worked or made unan-
nounced visits to their homes at odd hours, such as 2 a.m. "We
became very familiar with Klan members' wives," one agent noted
drolly. The tactic was designed to disrupt domestic tranquility. In
some cases, the FBI and state officers decided to "fight fire with fire,"
one law enforcement official conceded, by using extralegal methods
to rough up key figures within the Klan. But in dealing with ordinary members, the law enforcement teams simply worked to wear
down their resistance to talking.

In the case of Lawrence Byrd, he was actually facilitating their
work by convincing other Klansmen, such as Sessum, that it would
be in their best interests to cooperate. In early March, Byrd also
appealed to Billy Moss, one of the older Klansmen, to come clean.
Moss was fifty-two, had an eleventh-grade education, and operated a service station in Laurel. Fearful for his future, he agreed to
have Byrd deliver him into the hands of the FBI. Though Moss had

originally driven a car used on a trial run to the Dahmer property, he was saved from going on the murderous raid by his lingering disagreement with deBoxtel. He wanted the FBI to know he had no role in the January 10 attack on Dahmer's home.

Byrd arranged for Moss to go to Hattiesburg to talk with his contacts in the FBI. Following his meeting with the agents, Moss had second thoughts. Calling Byrd two days later and weeping loudly into the telephone, Moss said he now believed the Klan would kill both of them.

Pushing their investigation, the authorities found other White Knights who had grown tired of the violence associated with the Klan. They complained that they couldn't take the pressure any longer and agreed to tell the FBI what they knew. In a few instances, the FBI handed over money to members willing to finger suspects or share valuable tips. On top of these new informants, the FBI still had men like Tom Landrum inside the White Knights who had been reporting to them for months.

By March 7, less than two months after the Dahmer home had been burned, the FBI compiled a list of forty men who were thought to be either "involved or cognizant" of it. Bowers, Nix, and Byrd were at the top of the sheet along with the names of seven of the eight Klansmen who had actually gone on the raid.

～

WHILE THE FBI WENT about their business methodically, leaders of the Jones County White Knights fell into arguments and confrontations among themselves.

The day after Sessum signed the affidavit claiming he had been tricked by Byrd and beaten in an ordeal carried out by law enforcement figures, the imperial wizard appeared at Byrd's home. He claimed he wanted to see how Byrd was feeling.

Byrd was not particularly happy to see Bowers. "I'm feeling all right," he explained. "But I'm still very nervous and under a doctor's care for my nervous condition."

"Uh huh," Bowers murmured, as though he disbelieved Byrd or didn't really care. The two men had been sparring with each other for months at meetings, and Bowers made it clear that his visit was not a courtesy call.

"Lawrence, I've actually come to see you because I received information that you were seen entering the federal building in Hattiesburg yesterday."

"Sam, that's a lie. Who told you that?'

"You know I can't identify my sources."

"Well, under those circumstances, that makes me think you're a liar."

Bowers bristled. "You better take it easy, Lawrence. You got to pull yourself together," he said. Referring to the murders in Neshoba County, Bowers warned, "This is just like the Philadelphia case. We will be all right if we sit tight because they can't prove anything. If you can hold yourself together, everything will be all right. If you don't hold yourself together, it will hit the fan."

Byrd protested that he had no knowledge about the Dahmer case and was not talking to anybody. Unconvinced, Bowers left without another word.

Later the same day, Tom Landrum heard that Byrd had dropped out of the Klan. The White Knights' senator for Jones County had become a marked man.

≈

THE NEXT NIGHT, Landrum's klavern met at Speed Lightsey's barn. Though the cold weather had moderated by March, the fourteen members who attended continued to feel uncomfortable. This time, their discomfort was caused by the FBI investigation. After the session, Landrum reported to the FBI that Red Caldwell, one of the group's leaders, told the small group of new policies.

"The old days of nigger whipping, burnings, etcetera have got to be changed," Caldwell declared. "It's got the organization in trouble. From this day forward, it's important that we screen ourselves and

our new members and make sure we have people who are only interested in acting in a nonviolent way. We need to have men committed
to getting members to the polls and we need to raise the prestige of
the Klan. If we can dedicate ourselves to these goals, it will help." In
the meantime, Caldwell added, the White Knights should be purged
of some of its members.

For the time being, the White Knights' state organization had
recommended a moratorium on meetings. Caldwell suggested that
when the gatherings resumed they should have a hamburger supper
at Lightsey's barn and invite interested guests. He even proposed
welcoming law enforcement personnel as a goodwill gesture.

In his report to the FBI, Landrum noted wryly, "I take this means
of inviting you." He thought Caldwell sounded like a PR agent.

Caldwell met briefly with Landrum and Leonard Caves following the meeting. "I've been after them not to kill Byrd," Caldwell
said. Landrum assumed "them" referred to the state leadership of
the White Knights. "If Byrd calls you up to meet with him, by all
means don't go," Caldwell advised the pair. "Byrd called me up last
week to meet with him. I told him I would, but I didn't."

Caldwell's performance confirmed an assessment Landrum had
made of him long ago: the Klansman who posed as a big-time businessman and bon vivant was nothing more than a two-faced phony
without any real principles. He had seen Caldwell switch almost
overnight from acting as an enthusiastic exponent of Klan tactics to
being an advocate of nonviolence.

⁓

TENSION BETWEEN Bowers and Byrd escalated two days later
when the imperial wizard returned to Byrd's radio and TV repair
shop bearing an affidavit he wanted Byrd to sign. The document
stated that Byrd had been kidnapped, beaten, and drugged by the
NAACP and the FBI. Weakened by the attack, the statement alleged,
Byrd had been forced to implicate himself and others in the Dahmer

burning. The affidavit also claimed that Byrd had been led to aid the FBI in "setting a trap in which Cecil Sessum and subsequently Billy Moss were beaten by the FBI and forced to give a statement involving themselves and others in the Dahmer burning."

Byrd read the papers from Bowers, then glared at him and said, "Sam, this is all a goddamned lie. Under no circumstances am I gonna sign this thing." Although Byrd knew he had been isolated by the Klan leadership and put in some danger, he wanted to show Bowers that he was not intimidated. After all, he was a bigger man, physically, than Bowers, several inches taller and outweighing him by many pounds. Byrd also believed that Bowers was more counterfeit intellectual than tough guy.

Bowers retreated with an ultimatum. "Lawrence, I'm giving you forty-eight hours to sign your own affidavit here."

"Bullshit, Sam, I'm not signing anything," Byrd said. "You know, I got more confidence in Roy K. Moore than I got in you." He accused Bowers of having sent two men to his shop earlier in the week in an attempt to frighten him. "Sam, you send any more men here and I'm gonna shoot their ass." As Bowers began to leave, Byrd challenged him to bring Moss to a meeting at one o'clock that afternoon. "I know something I want to tell him face-to-face."

The confrontation with Moss never took place. Instead, Byrd met with his FBI handlers around 2 p.m. at his shop. The document he signed was another statement to the FBI about his encounter with Bowers. Byrd told them he knew Moss's meeting with the FBI had nothing to do with any beating.

<hr />

IN SEARCH OF credible information in the wash of rumors sweeping the White Knights, Landrum drove to Lightsey's service station for a quiet talk with him in an adjacent coffee shop.

Cupping his mug in his hands, Landrum looked across the table and whispered, "Speed, how come Sessum filed that affidavit?"

"I don't know a thing about it," Lightsey said. He responded with his own questions. "What do you know about it? What does it pertain to?"

"Well, I was at the courthouse when Cecil came into Leonard Caves's office. I know Cecil signed something that said Lawrence Byrd tricked him into coming out to his farm and had told the FBI in the presence of Cecil that Cecil and others had killed Dahmer," Landrum said. "And I know it was Deavours Nix and Sam Bowers who carried Cecil to the courthouse."

Lightsey became exercised and struggled to keep his voice down. "Now I understand the whole goddamned mess! Let me tell you some cutthroat information, and you can't breathe it to a soul. OK? Bowers and Nix had gone over Byrd's head on the Dahmer project, and Byrd didn't know shit about it until it was over. He was pissed off to have been bypassed. I didn't know anything about it either. I went to Byrd's store the afternoon after the burning to ask about it, and he said he didn't know nothing. He told me, 'Somebody sure screwed up.'"

Lightsey paused, then hissed to Landrum, "What's going on now is that Sessum was in on the deal, he was present on the project. And he and Bowers and Nix want to get Byrd in trouble to take the heat off themselves."

Lightsey leaned closer to Landrum and confided, "I got word over the weekend that a man from Philadelphia had contacted one of our group and told him that Byrd and me are to be disposed of." He let the threat sink in on Landrum for a moment. Philadelphia, Mississippi, was the home of the White Knights unit that carried out the murders in Neshoba County.

"Let me tell you, Tom, I got my .357 Magnum ready and if one of those bastards messes with me, he's a dead son of a bitch. I ain't done a thing, and I ain't taking a rap for something I didn't do."

"Well, I sure as hell don't know what's going on," Landrum said.

"Tom, you need to be careful," Lightsey said. "I know Deavours has made a statement that you are doing some talking. That means your life is in danger. What you need to do is to go get a two-way radio installed in your car so you can be in touch with people." Landrum said he couldn't afford the luxury. "Well, watch out, then," Lightsey said. "Before this is over there's gonna be some dead sons-a-bitches."

"It's a damned shame a man like Deavours Nix would try to frame people," Landrum said. "There ought to be some way to drop him from the group."

"The son of a bitch is gonna be dropped by the federal government, along with Bowers," Lightsey predicted. "Them trying to frame innocent people is what's gonna do it."

Lightsey repeated that he knew Sessum had participated in the Dahmer killing. "I don't know who else was in on the job, but I intend to find out before the day is done." He said he was so disgusted with the White Knights leadership that he would never again go to a statewide meeting and would hesitate before attending another Jones County gathering.

The conversation caused Landrum to reflect again on his own commitment. Nix had displayed open hostility toward him for weeks because of the old grievance he had with Landrum's brother; now Landrum was hearing that Nix had accused him of being an informant. He considered Nix a lowlife, and he believed he was quite capable of murder. He had no hard evidence, but suspected Nix went on the Dahmer raid. If Nix was willing to kill a man he didn't know and burn down his house, Landrum thought, he would surely be prepared to kill a spy in his midst.

On the other hand, Landrum felt he had a satisfactory relationship with Bowers and other members of the Jones County group. The imperial wizard seemed to value having another White Knight on the courthouse staff, and Bowers had never shown any animosity toward Landrum when they saw each other at meetings.

Nevertheless, Landrum's concerns reflected the temperament at the last few Klan meetings. Most members, like Landrum, had been uneasy since the attack on Dahmer's home. Though the imperial wizard had the authority to call for a Code Four assault, many members felt the mission had been carried out without the group's formal approval; few of them thought they were actually signing up for murder when they joined the White Knights. Yet murder was in the air at recent meetings, and the mood had been exacerbated by the fear that some of the Klansmen had become witnesses for the FBI.

V. L. Lee, a hot-headed member of the Jones County gang who had the nickname "Dubie," reported at a klavern meeting that he had been approached by the FBI. "I wouldn't talk with them," Lee told the group. "But I know somebody is talkin' with them. I will probably end up shootin' somebody. If I ever find out somebody's talkin', I am gonna kill him. And believe me, he won't be the first man I've killed."

Landrum weighed his options. Although his first consideration involved his responsibility for his wife and their five children, his commitment to cooperating with the FBI had been bolstered by Anne's own dedication to his task. She had never wavered. And he himself felt he had passed on valuable information about the dropped pistol. Still, it had never been a reciprocal arrangement. The FBI shared no information with him; he had no idea who else was an informant. And it was a petty annoyance that the bureau barely covered expenses he built up in mileage and dues and special Klan assessments. There were pros and cons. As always, Landrum talked these things through with his wife, and they mutually decided again that his undercover work was worth the risk.

≈

A FEW DAYS AFTER his talk with Landrum, Lightsey submitted to a short interview with the FBI. He acknowledged that he served as exalted cyclops of a Jones County klavern, and he engaged in a bit of gossip-trading with the agents. He said he heard that fellow Klansman Bill Smith "had been talking." He confirmed that another suspect, Lamar "Shorty" Lowe, had fled to Texas, but explained that Lowe was escaping a beating by another Klansman who wanted to punish him because he had "stolen some old lady's purse"—and not because of any guilt in the Dahmer case.

Lightsey identified several other leaders in the Jones County Klan but took pleasure in belittling the importance of Deavours Nix. He described Nix as a "mean bastard," and insisted he had never held the high position of statewide director of the Klan's Bureau of Investigation. When asked about Red Noble, believed to have been directly involved in the Dahmer raid, Lightsey told the agents, "I don't know nobody named Noble."

FBI agents seemed to be everywhere, buttonholing suspects and checking out any alibis they offered. Even Tom Landrum was stopped for questioning by one of the out-of-town agents who did not know of his role with the FBI.

≈

UNKNOWN TO any other member of the White Knights, there had been a breakdown within Bowers's inner circle. Henry deBoxtel had caved on March 7. Realizing that he faced possible life imprisonment for his role in the fatal raid, he began talking with the FBI. At first, he tried to limit his information. Knowing that Sessum's identity had been compromised a few days earlier, he told of a meeting where Sessum had talked about a "nigger job down south" two weeks before the Dahmer raid. DeBoxtel withheld details about the night of the actual raid, but provided the FBI with the names of the men who had accompanied him on an earlier trial run.

Two days later, deBoxtel told agents how the Klan had arranged for the use of Travis Giles's car on the raid, describing how Giles left his Ford, doomed to be disabled, with its keys still in the ignition in the parking lot at the Masonite plant while he worked his shift. Thus, Giles had an alibi. Another Masonite employee, Frank Lyons, delivered the car for the attack, he said.

DeBoxtel never acknowledged that he drove Giles's car. In this interview with the FBI, deBoxtel claimed he had not learned that the Dahmer house and store had been burned until Sessum came to deBoxtel's home at 4 a.m. and woke him with the news that "Giles's car was still down there with the wheels shot up." DeBoxtel said he went to his family's café, the Chow House, to wait for Giles, who was just getting off work, to let him know about his car. After they conferred with Lawrence Byrd, he said, they decided to report to authorities that Giles's car had been stolen.

DeBoxtel offered to the FBI the names of several people he identified as potential suspects in the raid. His list included Sessum, Lyons, Billy Roy Pitts, and Red Noble, as well as a couple of men who were innocent. Despite his cooperation, the FBI agents debriefing deBoxtel were wary about trusting him too much.

DeBoxtel did not present a picture of a man bent on good intentions. Tall and heavyset, he actually looked like a dangerous Klansman. Aside from his tough appearance, deBoxtel was not particularly smart. Though he had obtained high school equivalency credentials after serving in the army, his ambition was limited to a return to Laurel to help his mother manage the Chow House. After the White Knights were established in Jones County, deBoxtel parlayed his rough and reckless lifestyle into a role as one of Sam Bowers's favorite sidekicks.

The FBI's doubts about deBoxtel's reliability were confirmed at a subsequent meeting with him on March 25, a time when he and most of the other White Knights who had gone on the Dahmer raid sensed that the FBI was closing in on them. DeBoxtel informed the agents that he now realized he had already told them too much. He said he would deny that he had told them anything. If confronted in court with his words, he promised he would say to the judge: "Your Honor, I must have been drunk when I told those agents all that stuff."

≈

MEANWHILE, Byrd reported to the FBI that he had received a threatening telephone call. He was warned to watch what he said if he appeared before a grand jury. "What grand jury?" Byrd asked. His anonymous caller replied, "You know what grand jury, and there are at least two individuals who will bring back exactly what you say before the grand jury. You know what will happen to you if you put the finger on anybody." Byrd said he did not recognize the voice and the caller refused to identify himself.

The next day he had a final confrontation with Bowers, who reappeared at Byrd's repair shop. Byrd gave the FBI an account of an argument in which he accused Bowers of failing to follow the White Knights' constitution by releasing Sessum's affidavit. The document blamed Byrd for turning Sessum over to the FBI. Byrd said he should have been given a hearing before its release. When Byrd accused Sessum of lying, Bowers shot back that Sessum "was a good boy who lives a Christian life." Therefore, Bowers said, he believed Sessum's story.

Byrd said he told Bowers, "He may be a Christian, but he's also a damned liar." Byrd claimed he called the imperial wizard a coward. He said Bowers had "hidden out when the pressure was on" and relied on others in the White Knights to do his dirty work for him. "Don't send any of your men after me," Byrd said he warned Bowers. "If you do, they're gonna get killed."

Bowers spit out his final words: "As far as I'm concerned, Lawrence, you've formed an alliance with Satan and Roy K. Moore."

To Byrd, it sounded as though the imperial wizard was delivering a curse, or maybe a death sentence. Byrd said he accepted his fate. He told the White Knights leader, "I've chosen my side and I'll stand with it. We'll see who comes out ahead when everything is cleared up."

～

SESSUM'S SENSE OF dread deepened near the end of March, when he received a short note in the mail, addressed to him "c/o Sessum Grocery, Route 2, Ellisville, Miss." The message was from his young friend who had vanished from Jones County shortly after Dahmer's death.

"Preacher," the note began, "I am writing to tell you I had to tell them. They knew it all anyway and I was caught with the car and they were going to give me five years. If I drop out of sight they are hiding me. May god forgive me and please don't hate me." It was signed "Lamar Lowe."

It never occurred to Sessum that the FBI could have fabricated the letter.

CHAPTER 16

ELEVEN WEEKS AFTER the night riders murdered Vernon Dahmer and burned out his family, the FBI felt its high-priority investigation had amassed enough evidence for its agents to move formally against the leadership of the White Knights.

Roy Moore's forces planned over the final weekend of March for a carefully coordinated operation that began before dawn on Monday, March 28. Teams of FBI agents descended at the same hour on a dozen separate targets in Jones County, while their counterparts in Texas rounded up two suspects in Houston.

Although some Mississippi law enforcement personnel had cooperated with the FBI, the U.S. Justice Department was not yet ready to rely on Mississippi courts for a successful prosecution in the case. The arrests would be made not on state charges of murder but for federal violations of a nineteenth-century law that made it a crime to intimidate anyone pursuing their constitutional rights. Federal authorities also invoked the new Voting Rights Act, which provided criminal charges for anyone attempting to prevent people from voting.

Thirty-year-old Cecil Sessum was living at his parents' home attached to their service station near Ellisville when the agents came calling at 6 a.m. He went quietly from the same building where the raiders had gathered before heading out on their deadly mission in January.

Deavours Nix, forty-two, was taken into custody at his home in Laurel, where a photo was found of him dressed in a Klan robe and holding a pistol.

Henry deBoxtel, twenty-nine, was arrested without incident at his residence in Laurel. Like Nix, deBoxtel helped run another local café known as a hangout for Klan members.

Lawrence Byrd, the forty-four-year-old owner of the town's busy radio and TV repair shop, answered the sharp knock at the front door of his Laurel home to be greeted by a pair of FBI agents. He had been expecting the visit.

Billy Ray Smith, twenty-eight, a Masonite employee, was placed under arrest after being confronted outside his apartment building in Laurel. He protested vigorously, insisting that he was innocent, that he was a victim of mistaken identity.

Frank Lyons, another Masonite worker, submitted quietly to arrest at his home in Laurel. He was thirty-three.

Billy Roy Pitts, the self-styled cowboy who lost his pistol, yielded to FBI agents after they knocked abruptly on the door to his Laurel home. At twenty-two years of age, he was the youngest of the defendants; he worked at an auto-repair shop.

Agents quickly located Billy Moss at the gas station where he worked in Laurel. The FBI documents revealed that at fifty-two, he was the oldest Klansman arrested, and that his first name was one he never used, Emanuel.

Travis Giles, thirty-seven, was marched in handcuffs from his home in Ellisville after being aroused from his sleep. Authorities listed him as "unemployed," though he had been working at Masonite.

Pete Martin, who also worked at Masonite, stepped from his home near Laurel and into the hands of the FBI. It was his second arrest in less than two months; he had been picked up earlier after dynamite was found in his car. Those reading about his latest arrest would learn that his first name was actually Melvin and that he was thirty-three.

Charles Noble, the fifth Masonite employee taken by the FBI, was picked up at his home in Laurel. He was twenty-three, and just a few years removed from the time Tom Landrum coached him in high school football.

At the same time these men were being arrested at various locations across Jones County, FBI agents swooped down on a home in Houston, Texas, where Lamar "Shorty" Lowe, twenty-three, had sought refuge after he fled the Laurel area. Before leaving he, too, had been employed by Masonite. His father, Clifton Lowe, fifty, who worked as a handyman at a Houston motel, was taken into custody at the same time.

The FBI dragnet caught most of the men believed to have actually taken part in the raid on the Dahmer property, but some of the Klansmen recognized immediately that a mistake had been made. Though Billy Ray Smith was often seen with Nix at John's Restaurant and belonged to the White Knights, he had not been involved in the Dahmer raid. He simply had a name similar to that of Bill "Lightning" Smith, who fired the shots that blew out the window of the Dahmer home and punctured the tires of the car deBoxtel had driven that night.

Some of those arrested had already been talking to the FBI in the hope that it might ameliorate their situation if they faced charges, and it soon became apparent that their cases would never be seriously pursued.

However, the principal target in the FBI sweep, Sam Bowers, the imperial wizard, eluded their grasp that morning. The FBI had a warrant for his arrest but Bowers, anticipating the move, had gone into hiding again. In announcing the coordinated action that resulted in thirteen arrests, the FBI indicated that a hunt was on for Bowers. After being arraigned, most of the men were released the same day on bonds of $15,000 each.

Within hours of the arrests, the *Laurel Leader-Call*, an afternoon newspaper, splashed the news across its front page with a bold head-line: 14 WHITE KNIGHTS CHARGED IN VERNON DAHMER'S DEATH. The edition carried three long wire-service stories on the case and displayed photographs of all the men's faces.

The same day, FBI personnel armed with search warrants pounded their way into Bowers's cluttered living quarters at his Sambo Amusement Company at 820 South Fourth Street in Laurel. They confiscated an arsenal: a fully loaded .38-caliber pistol discovered under a pillow on Bowers's bed, a loaded nine-shot rifle beside his bed, a .30-caliber weapon equipped with two clips carrying thirty rounds each, a .44-caliber revolver loaded with six rounds of blunt-nosed cartridges.

The FBI seized several bags of coins, presumably the yield from Bowers's vending machines. They also found seven Halloween face masks, similar to the grotesque disguise found in the litter on the ground near the Dahmer home when the FBI collected evidence on the morning of the fire.

Bowers liked to pose as an erudite man, so it was no surprise to find books in his bedroom. One was a paperback entitled *The FBI Nobody Knows*. Another volume, *Race and Reason* by Carleton Putnam, dwelt on the inferiority of Blacks. ("In the next 500,000,000,000 years I would be quite prepared to concede the possibility the Negro may, through normal processes of mutation and natural selection within his own race, eventually overtake and even surpass the white race . . . when the Negro has bred out his limitations over hundreds or thousands of years.") The book was very popular among white supremacists.

Separate caches of weapons—shotguns, automatic rifles, and boxes of ammunition—were uncovered and taken away during raids at Nix's house and the Sessum dwelling. Four shotguns were seized at deBoxtel's residence.

Three days after the FBI's sweep through Jones County, Bowers turned himself in to FBI officials in Hattiesburg. He was accompanied by Travis Buckley and Charles Blackwell, the same two lawyers who had made the trip to Washington with him. The imperial wizard was arrested, fingerprinted, and had his bond set at $25,000. He was largely uncommunicative and refused to sign his fingerprint card. He failed to post bond immediately and was put in a cell in the Forrest County jail.

The FBI operation stunned the White Knights. Already divided by discord and now reeling from the arrests of its leaders, the Klan organization fell into an alarmed silence. For nearly a month, no one dared call or attend a meeting. But the White Knights were not yet dead.

Before long, Bowers arranged bond and won release. He appeared at a rally of several hundred sympathizers, who motored to a bucolic pasture in Jones County where Bowers excoriated the federal government. "The FBI made the arrests," he shouted to his flock, "to slaughter fourteen white Christians on the altar of nigger revolutionaries."

CHAPTER 17

THERE WERE DIFFERENT reactions among the White Knights to the arrests. In some cases, members retreated into inactivity, fearful of attending meetings and cowed by an intensified FBI investigation. But hard-core Klansmen reflected the bravado of Bowers's remarks, assailing the FBI and continuing to express defiance.

Three weeks elapsed between the roundup of the fourteen White Knights and the next meeting Tom Landrum attended, where he encountered sheepishness as well as a call for escalated violence. First, his courthouse comrade Leonard Caves told of how his brother had been intimidated by a recent visit by an FBI agent. The circuit clerk's sibling, R. L. Caves, was informed that the bureau knew he belonged to the White Knights because they relied on a paid spy in the Klan's midst who reported to the FBI each morning following any gathering. "We can even tell you where you sit at these meetings," the agent told R.L., who held a job in a vocational program at Jones County Junior College and feared he would be fired if officials there learned he was a member of the White Knights. His dilemma was typical of the problems others in the organization faced.

Only eleven members came to Speed Lightsey's barn for a session in late April. In the absence of klavern leaders an obstreperous Dubie Lee dominated the discussion by urging the group to carry out new projects. "We ought to be burning every night," he shouted. "If a nigger kills a white man, we should kill two niggers."

Despite Lee's angry declarations, Landrum detected a cautionary undercurrent among most in his group, a growing recognition that someone at their meeting was talking to the FBI. "Sooner or later," Lee said, "we'll find out who that man is and he'll have to go before our court. And there will be hell to pay."

Landrum found it disconcerting when another man he barely knew approached him after the meeting with a warning: "If the FBI comes to me, I'll know who's responsible." Landrum supposed the man was guessing, but it was nevertheless unnerving.

When he returned home that evening, Tom prepared his report. Once again Anne Landrum emphasized his commitment to the FBI, even as she wrote down the words she would type the next morning. "Tom, it's obvious that you're not the only one dealing with the FBI. Looks to me like there must be a lot of men talking. You knew next to nothing about the Dahmer situation or who went to that raid," she said. "Somebody else—and I'll bet it was more than one person—must have given the FBI the information that led to those arrests. I think you've got a lot of company, you just don't know it or who they are. I think there must be plenty of men in the Klan who are sick about what happened down in Hattiesburg and want nothing more to do with Sam Bowers and his people. And some of them are talking."

"It's just not easy," Tom said, "going to these meetings and hearing how I'm going to be strung up if they find out. Or to hear what they're going to do with anybody they find out has been cooperating with the FBI. Look at ole Lawrence Byrd, they think he's talking and they're ready to kill him."

"I think Lawrence Byrd is feeling the heat because he's a lot deeper into the Klan monkey business than you are," his wife said. "Seems to me there are a lot more suspects out there than you. You're a valuable source for the FBI, but I'll bet Sam Bowers and Deavours Nix and that gang are looking at others. We just need to keep up what we've been doing as quietly as possible. You need to be especially careful about how you act around them, and what you say."

Tom grunted his assent. But even in the safety of his home he was fearful. Sometimes, washing dishes in the kitchen with his back exposed to a window, he reflexively flinched at an outside noise, at the thought that a sniper might be aiming at him.

≈

A WEEK LATER, Lightsey, the host of many meetings at his barn, was a no-show on his own property. He called Landrum beforehand to say that he had a bad back. Landrum drove to the gathering of his klavern with his friend Gerald Martin, who was becoming more and more skeptical about the people in the organization. On the way, Martin groused that the Klan leadership was poor at the state level. "Sam Bowers never worked at anything other than pinball machines," he said. "And Deavours Nix has always been on the shady side."

Only five others were on hand, and none of them held leadership positions. They dispersed within forty-five minutes without conducting any business.

In his report the next day, Landrum adopted a cynical tone: "Lightsey left his phone number for me to call. I checked the number and it was Cindy's Drive-In. His back must have really been bad. Might be good if the group found out he was at Cindy's instead of being at the meeting."

Landrum also found that R. L. Caves had new doubts. "He told me he thought Lightsey was talking," he wrote. "There is suspicion among most everyone as to who is doing the talking." R.L., he said, was also troubled that the Klan would not live up to its promise to take care of the families of any members who were arrested. "This is one of the first things the Klan tells you when you join: that your family will be cared for. Caves said he had heard only one person talk about helping the families" of the men charged in the Dahmer case.

≈

LANDRUM FOUND MORE dissension among the White Knights during a long conversation in early May with Gerald Martin and Tommy Thornton, who owned a dairy by day and sometimes worked as a "security man" for the Klan at night. Thornton was in his thirties. As a contemporary of Landrum's in age and Klan membership— though they belonged to different klaverns—Thornton seemed at ease unburdening himself of his own grievances.

He told Landrum that after their mutual friend, Spec Stewart, had dropped out as an exalted cyclops, his own klavern began to lose enthusiasm and had not met recently. "We need to start meeting again, but everybody's afraid," he said. "I've been an active member, and I can see how I could have easily got into trouble. I could have been on the Dahmer project. I got several calls, but I refused to go. I told Nix and Sessum that they had better stay out of Forrest County; that Bowers didn't have any sense." Thornton referred to the imperial wizard as "Stupid Bowers."

"The first mistake was for fourteen men to go on the project. That was way too many men. Another mistake was for that boy to lose his gun. I heard the intentions were to simply burn out the property and not hurt Dahmer. Now look what they done. I'm almost sure Sessum, Billy Moss, Pete Martin, Nix, Shorty Lowe, and deBoxtel are going to end up in the pen."

Thornton rambled on. "I had guns of all types at my house at the time the fourteen men were arrested. I was keeping them for different members. That could have got me in trouble, too." He called Charles Noble, another defendant, a "good kid." Thornton said he had talked with Noble before the raid and warned him to watch his step or he would wind up arrested. "Now Pete Martin, he ain't worried about anything that's happening to him. He would go on a project tonight if asked. He's crazy enough to do anything. A day or two before he got arrested on that charge of dynamite, someone was showing around pictures of him and somebody else's wife together. It's got to where you can't trust county and state leaders. Sessum is about half crazy and real dangerous. Since he became EC of our klavern, our group has gone down. He got a lot of thugs and outlaws in our group. We need to get folks like Spec Stewart back in the fold."

Gerald Martin, who had been listening to Thornton's diatribe, interrupted to tell of his own awkward moment. "Dubie Lee called me up to come to his house. When I got there, he asked me to carry a gun to a man down around Ellisville. He got a shotgun from his hay barn and put it in my car under the rear seat. Before I could deliver it, the FBI showed up at my house. I was anxious to get rid of the FBI, who had a bunch of questions I didn't care to answer. After they left, I wanted to get rid of that gun. I don't know what it was used for, but I wanted to get rid of that gun with my fingerprints on it. I took it back to Dubie as soon as I could."

Martin was one of Landrum's few good friends in the organization, and the constable had often spoken openly to him of his reservations about Bowers. "I don't know what all these affidavits are about. They're a bunch of nonsense, and it's obvious Sam Bowers is pushing them," Martin said.

Landrum could not resist a side comment regarding Sessum's affidavit and his fevered account of his kidnapping and the threat by law enforcement officers to kill him in the Shady Grove cemetery. "If I'd been as brave in that colored graveyard as Sessum said he was, I'd have been brave enough to go to a doctor afterwards" to seek treatment for his alleged injuries, Landrum said. The others laughed.

"I think that affidavit's a bunch of bullshit," Thornton said. "I don't believe a goddamned word in it."

≈

A SPARSELY ATTENDED meeting a week later opened with a prayer coupled with the display of a Bible with an open knife beside it. Eight men were present at the home of Norman Lee, Dubie Lee's brother. There was talk of "uppity niggers" who lived in the Sandersville community, not far from Landrum's home, and suggestions that two or three houses "needed to burn."

Gerald Martin, who disapproved of the tactic of house-burning, countered, "What we need to do is to come up with some new leadership. Our group is only going to be as good as our leadership. Now, I'd like to know where Speed Lightsey is tonight. Does anybody know?"

"That's the Sixty-Four-Thousand-Dollar question," someone else said, referring to a television show that had been popular in the previous decade.

Norman Lee said he intended to meet with Lightsey soon. "We need to think about making some changes. Maybe we could meet next week and elect new officers who could run our group and build up enthusiasm. We can meet at my house again next week, and I'll try to get Sam Bowers and Deavours Nix to come."

In his report, Landrum wrote, "There seems to be more aggressiveness in Lee. It would be dangerous for someone such as he to become head of a group, and this seems to be what he is working for. Next meeting will be interesting to see what takes place between Lightsey and Lee."

It had become apparent that the Lee brothers—Norman and Dubie—were engineering a coup in Landrum's klavern in order to take over the leadership from Lightsey, the exalted cyclops.

A couple of days later, Landrum talked privately with Lightsey and then reported to the FBI: "He stated that the bylaws say that a meeting is not to be held in a home, and he was sure that Bowers didn't know about it. He stated that he didn't care if new officers are elected and he is left out of it. He stated he doubted if he would ever attend meetings at Norman Lee's house."

Others were recognizing that Lightsey, once one of the most enthusiastic members of the White Knights, appeared disillusioned with the group.

When one of Landrum's confederates in his klavern called to ask for telephone numbers for a couple of members, Landrum recommended that he contact Lightsey for the information.

The man replied that Lightsey had apparently lost power. Members of their klavern were meeting regularly at Norman Lee's house rather than Lightsey's barn, though, the caller said, the barn was actually the preferred venue. Meanwhile, he said Dubie Lee had been trying to recruit volunteers for a dangerous job that Dubie claimed had been authorized by the county giant, Red Caldwell. But Caldwell denied that he had ever approved the project, the caller reported. "Red said Dubie's a damned liar."

Lightsey eventually forced something of a showdown with Norman Lee. For a meeting of a dozen members of the klavern Lee moved the location from inside his house to his backyard. He set the scene by backing his pickup truck into the yard and placing his handgun, a knife, and a Bible on the tailgate. He was preparing to offer an opening prayer when Lightsey arrived. "Go ahead with your business," Lightsey said. "Looks like you're taking over, so go right ahead."

Startled, Lee announced, "I'm gonna need to remove our Veil of Secrecy. I need to ask our friend here what's his problem."

"I haven't got a problem. Just go ahead with your business. I want to listen."

Lee paused for a moment, then proceeded with his agenda, which included a discussion about the threat of school integration and an approaching local election in which the Klan hoped to elect a sympathetic judge.

After the meeting, Dubie Lee confronted Lightsey with an unusual question.

"Speed, how'd you like to come with me to go out and burn down a nigger house?"

"Naw," Lightsey replied. "Not interested."

"Well then, how 'bout we just shoot in one?"

"Naw, not interested in that either."

"Just thought I'd ask," Dubie said.

Landrum was troubled by the palpable tension at the meeting. The next day he drove to Lightsey's service station to talk with him.

"I was ready to resign last night," Lightsey told Landrum. "But I hate for Norman Lee to get hold of our group."

"Speed, we need for you to stay," Landrum said. "You know we got to keep the violence down. If the Lees get in charge, they're going to do nothing but cause a bunch of trouble."

Six days later, Landrum attended another meeting at Norman Lee's place. Lightsey was absent. After someone reported that several schoolteachers were referring to Klansmen as "crooks" in their classrooms, Dubie Lee advocated a campaign to burn out the educators. "I want to smell some smoke," he barked. "It's time for us to start doing something."

≈

SINCE HE HAD BECOME secretary of his klavern, Landrum learned of haphazard record-keeping that raised more questions about the Klan leadership. A member acting as a bursar for the group asked Landrum for help in straightening accounts. "I got records that are in such a mess I don't think I'll ever figure it out," the bursar told him. "I got notebooks of information on who paid money and I keep it in a brown paper bag, but it don't make no sense. I got notes, but no money. Jones County is in bad shape financially. We been paying $1.95 per member, per quarter, to the state organization. A lot of men pay initiation fees but never come to meetings or pay dues."

There were several hundred Klansmen in Jones County on the White Knights' rolls. "The county should have $500 on hand," Landrum said.

"That's right," the bursar said. "But we've had to borrow out of that to pay state dues. We don't have no money."

When Norman Lee—enjoying his new role as de facto exalted cyclops of the klavern—was asked about the discrepancies, he minimized the problem. "I think we got $22,000 in state funds," he said.

The problems between Lee and Lightsey continued to fester into the summer. One day Landrum was driving by Lee's house when he spotted him in his garden and decided to stop for a talk. "Norman, I'm not sure which group I'm supposed to be a part of," Landrum said. "I thought Speed was the EC of my group, but he seems to be dropping out and you're taking charge."

"I'm glad you brought this up, Tom," Lee said. "A new group has been formed and I'm the EC. I want you to go home and call everybody you know and tell them to come out to a meeting tonight at my house."

When Landrum informed Gerald Martin of Lee's plan, Martin scoffed. "If Norman Lee has somehow been elected EC of our group, then I'm transferring to another group."

Out of curiosity, Landrum attended the meeting that night. Only two others were there, the Lee brothers. Dubie bubbled with ideas. "We need to wait till school starts this fall, then strike at the niggers," he advised. "There's one nigger teacher who tried to register her kid in a white school. We need to burn their house. Me and two others already burned nigger houses in their neighborhood. We burned three houses in a row at the same time. Man, if you want to see a sight, that was one." He said the Klan should recruit strong men for projects like this. He mentioned one member who had followed through on instructions to commit arson in the Jones County community of Soso shortly after joining the White Knights. "Him and his son went out and burned to the ground a nigger house valued at $20,000. You have to have men like that," Dubie said.

Dispirited by the rise of the Lee brothers, Landrum had another talk with Lightsey at his service station a couple of days later. "I want to find out what group I'm supposed to attend. I'm not the only one confused. There are others in the same fix," Landrum said.

"Hell, I don't know either," Lightsey assured him. "I don't know about two groups—me being EC of one and Norman the EC of the other. I asked Red Caldwell about it, and Red didn't know anything either. There must have been some type of meeting during the week of June the thirteenth that I didn't know about. I wasn't invited. I'm totally disgusted with the whole thing. Our group was about killed when I got asked to take it over. I spent a lot of time and money building it back up in the interests of the Klan. Now it looks like I'm getting pushed out and Norman Lee is trying to take over. I'm gonna see Sam Bowers and try to find out what's going on. I know the Lees talk too much and they're gonna get us in trouble."

Lightsey confessed that he had once gone on Klan missions that could have put him in the penitentiary. "I've been lucky," he told

Landrum. "I took part in burning some of the houses in the Sanders-ville area, and I didn't get caught and wind up in the pen. Now, with all this talk of violence from Norman and Dubie Lee, they're gonna create a situation where we could all go to the pen. We're already in enough trouble over the Dahmer thing."

The White Knights were flirting with disaster, Lightsey said. "There's all this talk about killing Lawrence Byrd. Hell, Lawrence Byrd's not at fault in the Dahmer case. He didn't know about the project until it was over, and yet that's all you hear about at our meet-ings: how we got to kill Lawrence Byrd."

Four nights later, Landrum went to the next meeting at Norman Lee's place. The only other members there were the Lee brothers and the bursar who had been worried about Klan finances.

Norman Lee was vexed that no one came to his meetings. "Where's Leonard Caves?" he asked Landrum.

"I don't know."

"Looks to me like Caves is only out for the Klan to help him polit-ically," Norman said.

Then brother Dubie blurted, "Somebody should kill Lawrence Byrd 'cause he's the one who turned all our men in, and now nobody dares to come to meetings. Hell, I'm ready to go kill him myself. Anytime."

"I think Sam Bowers is the cure for the world," the bursar sug-gested, in a comment Landrum thought was particularly strange. "All the world needs is for us to let the Lord take care of it," the bur-sar added.

In his report to the FBI later that night, Landrum wrote, "I feel ridiculous being in this group of four men with a Bible and a gun in a bitterweed-infested pasture, talking about letting the Lord solve our problems."

CHAPTER 18

WHILE THE CALLS TO have Lawrence Byrd liquidated grew more clamorous within the White Knights, Byrd himself became increasingly erratic and his conduct bordered on paranoia. Even his FBI handlers, Agents Dukes and Martin, began to wonder about his behavior after he summoned them to a confidential meeting at his farm in March to tell of a threatening encounter the day before at his appliance store.

According to Byrd, he received a telephone call late in the afternoon from a stranger identifying himself as "Shorty Smith," who inquired about a television set. It was near closing time but Byrd agreed to hold his store open for him. Within a few minutes, a taxi delivered to his door a man he recognized as a fellow Klansman, Billy Ray Smith, who worked at Masonite. Within a minute, another man arrived, and Smith yielded his space as if the third man had been expected. The stranger approached Byrd and said, "You know me, don't you, Lawrence?" Byrd did not. The man said he had just called about a television set. Seeing the outline of a pistol in the visitor's pocket and noting that Smith was watching closely, Byrd concluded that the pair planned an attack on him.

Byrd believed he was saved by the appearance of one of his employees. He quickly ushered him into his private office, ostensibly to check some invoices, leaving the two visitors in the sales area. Byrd instructed his employee to take a pistol from a drawer in order to cover the "customers" if trouble erupted. After Byrd and his employee reappeared, armed, the stranger left the shop abruptly, promising to come back later, and drove away.

Byrd recalled that Billy Ray Smith stayed behind and engaged in a cat-and-mouse conversation. "How tight are the Feds on you now?" he asked Byrd. "Are you getting any sleep?"

"Hell, the Feds are in my place nearly every day," Byrd replied. "They're harassing all of us. I don't pay 'em any attention."

"What's Sessum doing?" Smith asked. "Do you ever see him?"

"I see him from time to time," Byrd said. He had a question for Smith. "Who was that fellow that was just in here?"

"That's the Pitts boy who works at Masonite," Smith said.

Byrd knew that was a lie because he knew Billy Roy Pitts and knew he didn't work at Masonite.

Staring at Byrd, Smith then posed a curious question. "Lawrence, do you know me?"

Byrd did not reveal that he knew his name. Instead, he laughed uneasily and hinted at Klan membership. "Your face is familiar, but I can't place you. You been attending any night services out yonder?"

Smith offered his own false laugh. "Yeah, I was sitting right in front of you out at your farm the night it was so cold. I was one of the guards." Smith informed Byrd his name was William Ray Smith. "But Sessum and Deavours Nix have called me Billy Ray Smith for years," he added, indicating that he had important connections with the White Knights leaders. Saying nothing else, he left the store.

≈

THREE NIGHTS LATER, the most dangerous klavern of the Jones County Klan—which included several men in the Dahmer raiding party—met in a wooded section of land inside the Laurel city limits that had been developed into a park behind an old school building.

Tom Landrum was not on hand, but another informant reported to the FBI that Sessum had warned the group, "Lawrence Byrd and Billy Moss have to be taken care of. If not, the Klan is ruined."

To torment Byrd, all of the Klansmen were urged to make at least two or three threatening telephone calls each day to Byrd and his wife. Henry deBoxtel said new efforts were being made to have Byrd committed to the state mental hospital. Byrd's associates in the White Knights had long believed he had "gone around the bend" following his kidnapping. If he were determined by medical authorities to be mentally unstable, deBoxtel said, any testimony Byrd might give in court could be invalidated. "He's had some previous mental difficulty," deBoxtel said, "and I know he's presently taking drugs."

The same week, Byrd had himself readmitted to the Laurel hospital for a "rest." He had wanted to go to a Shrine Club meeting in Meridian, some fifty miles away. The Shriners offered him a pleasant alternative to the Klan; the group enjoyed dressing in silly clothes and hats and raising money for good causes. But Byrd was persuaded not to go to Meridian by his FBI handlers. They had received indications, the agents told him, that the Klan might be planning to take some sort of action against him there.

Near the end of May, Byrd gave the FBI contradictory reports about his own peril. He confirmed that he had gotten many anonymous telephone calls warning him not to testify. If he did, Byrd was told, he "would be taken care of." A day or so later, after he mentioned these threats, he claimed to have learned that the imperial wizard had issued a statewide order to stop the harassment in order to bring Byrd back into the fold of the White Knights. Byrd said he had been called personally by Bowers and invited to attend a Klan fundraising rally on the Gulf Coast. Bowers said he would arrange for Sessum to drive Byrd to the event "to show there were no hard feelings." Byrd was dubious about the invitation, suspecting he might wind up buried in the waters of the Gulf.

Later, Byrd made it to another Shrine meeting in Meridian, where he said he met a cabdriver and "known Klansman." The man identified himself as a "representative" of Bowers and wanted to know what it would take to keep Byrd from testifying. Byrd told the FBI that he had brushed off the cabdriver with "a line and let it go."

Actually, Byrd had good reasons to be fearful. One of the Klan members visiting the Chow House found deBoxtel in the kitchen, carving a side of beef. With a malevolent grin, deBoxtel remarked, "I sure do wish this was Byrd I was cutting up."

The hostility was amplified at a countywide Klan meeting near Ellisville on the evening of May 31. Tom Landrum attended and thought the turnout was extraordinarily large—many of the men who had been indicted in the Dahmer case were there—and the meeting seemed better organized than usual. Perhaps it was because of the presence of the imperial wizard. After Red Caldwell opened with a prayer, he turned the event over to Bowers, who told the group they were faced with two issues—an upcoming election, where he hoped the Klan would have influence, and an "internal problem": Lawrence Byrd.

"Byrd has become power hungry," Bowers charged. "He has assumed too much power and caused considerable trouble. I had thought on several occasions to stop him, but I never thought it would lead to what it did: the betrayal of his fellow man. The White Knights is the only organization standing in the way of communism and Bolshevism, and Byrd has betrayed us. In his leadership role we gave him, he acted like a general and used our group for selfish purposes. He is a dangerous man. He has violated all our rules. This will cease immediately."

Though the group had been instructed to be quiet during the cover of the Veil of Secrecy, several could not resist a cheer after hearing the imperial wizard's words.

≈

LANDRUM HAD KNOWN Byrd and members of his family for several years. Though the Byrds had a respectable background and the appliance store appeared to be thriving, Landrum thought Lawrence himself was a bit shifty. He found it hard to reconcile Byrd's outwardly friendly personality with the intense anger toward Blacks that he exhibited at Klan meetings. Lately, he felt Byrd had been acting squirrelly.

In June Landrum reported to the FBI that Speed Lightsey had absolved Byrd of guilt in the Dahmer affair; therefore, Lightsey did not consider him a likely source for the agents. But others in the White Knights were unwilling to clear him. Some of the top-ranking Klansmen were convinced that Byrd was acting as an informant and deserved to die, Landrum learned. Others felt the penalty too severe and believed a mere beating might suffice.

Once again, Landrum found himself in a personal dilemma. If the Klansmen followed through on their threats and had Byrd killed, it seemed conceivable that all of the White Knights who had been present for the discussions could be implicated. The situation caused him to rethink yet again his decision to serve as a volunteer spy for the FBI. In the end, he concluded that his arrangement with Bob Lee would protect him during any investigation. And he began to believe that Byrd would be able to take care of himself. As strange and defiant as Byrd's behavior had become, the appliance store owner appeared to be more grounded than the Klansmen making idle threats about him.

～

THE CALLS TO KILL Byrd continued to be heard at the Klan meetings, so many that the FBI kept a log through the rest of the year documenting the various suggestions to put him to death.

On October 10, a source reported to the FBI that Frank Lyons, one of the men indicted in the Dahmer case, had encouraged several other members of the White Knights to take action. According to the informant, Lyons said that Byrd and one other unidentified person "needed killing." Three days later, another source attached to Unit Four of the Jones County White Knights reported that their meeting had been consumed by a discussion of how Byrd was furnishing information to the FBI. One Klansman, described as "very vocal," was said to have stressed "that the Klan take care of Byrd in some way for doing this."

During the Unit Four session, the source added, the name of Byron De La Beckwith was mentioned in connection with "a proposed project to kill Lawrence Byrd." Beckwith had been arrested in 1963 for the murder of Medgar Evers, the prominent NAACP field secretary in Mississippi, but had escaped conviction after two trials in Jackson ended with hung juries. The high-powered rifle that had been used to shoot Evers in the back outside his home had been found in a clump of briars nearby and was traced to Beckwith. But he was helped at his trial by the testimony of a Greenwood policeman, friendly with the Klan, who said he had seen Beckwith that night, more than seventy-five miles from the murder scene.

The notoriety earned Beckwith statewide recognition as a cold-blooded assassin. When ordinary citizens saw Beckwith, a traveling fertilizer salesman from Greenwood, on the streets of their Delta towns, they went out of their way to avoid him. But he had become something of an honorary figure among Klansmen, attending meetings of different groups throughout the state as if he were a celebrity. At one Klan gathering, Beckwith had boasted, "Killing that nigger gave me no more inner discomfort than our wives endure when they give birth to our children." Delmar Dennis, the Klan chaplain and FBI informant, overheard the remark and passed it on to the FBI. But in the current climate of Mississippi, it seemed unlikely that Beckwith would be tried again. In fact, Beckwith was planning to become a candidate for high office in the state.

There were suggestions that he could be brought in to do the job on Byrd. If he were marksman enough to bring down Medgar Evers with a distant shot, Beckwith would be the ideal man to rid the White Knights of Byrd's annoying presence.

During the same week that the White Knights considered calling on Beckwith, Cecil Sessum and three other members of the White Knights were reported to have driven to Byrd's farmhouse with the intention of burning it down. They had carried jugs of gasoline and other equipment to within fifty yards of the building when Sessum called off the attack. He said he "did not like the looks of things." One of the Klansmen who accompanied Sessum later explained that he agreed with Sessum's decision because they had learned the FBI knew of their plan to destroy Byrd's house.

The FBI also learned of an encounter between another Klansman and Byrd, who was by now fully estranged from the White Knights. Like an out-of-touch relative, Byrd inquired about the health of the organization but didn't bother to listen to the answer. Instead, he quickly declared that Bowers's group was "dead," and he predicted it would never rise again. "I got a raw deal from them," he complained.

Despite all the promises to kill him, Byrd continued to operate his store and move around Laurel with impunity. The Klan seemed to lack the zeal to silence him, though members continued to mutter about him, branding him a traitor. "The FBI can't guard him all the time," one member said, suggesting that they look for an opening to strike. But according to an FBI informant at the gathering, "Sessum cautioned against any action at this time." For the time being, Byrd would live as a pariah.

CHAPTER 19

I N THE SUMMER OF 1966, the annual fever of intense heat
gripped the Deep South. On Independence Day, while the rest
of the country celebrated, those in neo-Confederate circles in
Mississippi remembered with loathing that the Fourth of July a century earlier was the date that Vicksburg fell at the same hour General
Robert E. Lee's army failed at Gettysburg. Among these people, heat
exacerbated their sense of loss and frustration and kindled desire for
revenge. For evidence that the South was still being punished, they
had only to watch the mercury creep above one hundred degrees.
The afternoon sun bore down in a colorless fury, and a thin cloud
cover offered little relief. Air-conditioning units rattled inside homes
lucky enough to own such contraptions, but outside the heat seemed
to be sucking life from plants and breath from humans. Sometimes,
it caused men to think hateful thoughts and do irrational things.

The discomfort persisted into the evening of the holiday, when
Tom Landrum's unit of the White Knights gathered to discuss methods to combat federal desegregation decrees looming over the public
schools of Mississippi when classes opened in the fall. Twelve years
after *Brown v. Board of Education*—and four years after the University of Mississippi had been integrated—the political power structure in the state still refused to comply with desegregation decrees,

by citing legal loopholes and maintaining obstructionist policies. The Klan wanted to help.

Since Norman Lee's takeover, the klavern had begun meeting in his slaughterhouse, a ramshackle structure behind his home. The building reeked with the blood and dung of disemboweled animals, and Landrum felt it was an appropriate setting when Lee began to talk.

"As you all know," Lee said, "the niggers think they're gettin' ready to go to school with our children. They think they got court orders and the wisdom of the communist Supreme Court and the might of the federal government behind them, but we got our duty to prevent that. The federal government's got no right to come in and dictate to our local school boards what we should do. We need local control of our schools, not a bunch of woolly-headed jackasses that have no understanding of the situation."

Not many members had bothered to drive out to Lee's property, but there were murmurs of approval among the few who had.

"I tell you," Lee continued, "something's got to be done, and it falls to patriots like us to defend our schools. I'm ready to go all the way with anything that needs to be done. The nigger has a natural fear of the high-powered rifle, and that's one weapon that we need to use. There's a nigger preacher named Clay that's been stirrin' up trouble in his community. He's already had his house shot up to put the real fear of God in him, but he hasn't stopped. This nigger Clay needs to pay—and pay plenty—for the trouble he's caused. Somebody's going to kill that nigger."

Perspiration beaded on Lee's forehead and he grew more agitated as he exhorted the men of the klavern. "We got to be willing to use these means to save the purity of our schools. We got to be willing to use fire. Fire and guns, boys! That's what we got to use in this fight. Fire and guns! We didn't join this organization to sit around and sing hymns and listen to mealy-mouth speeches. We joined to take action."

Lee's speech provoked a feeble stirring, though Landrum withheld any audible approval. He was diverted by another matter; he detected a sour smell of sweat emanating from the men's bodies, clad in damp work clothes, and the odor hung suspended in the heavy air. He yearned to be at home instead of in a stinking slaughterhouse. Others seemed bored, too. In an effort to rally the Klansmen, Lee switched to another subject.

"Now you men are the men I trust. I trust you to be dedicated to our cause and to keep quiet about our work. I'm satisfied you wouldn't have joined up if you weren't committed to our cause. But I got to tell you there are two men I do not trust, and that's Lawrence Byrd and Speed Lightsey. Sam Bowers has been to see Lightsey four times to find out about the $500 he's got of our money, and he's been unable to find him. Lightsey's not only got our money, I hear he's been flashing thousand-dollar bills around after talking to the FBI and the federal grand jury. Something needs to be done about Lawrence Byrd and Lightsey, just as something's got to be done about the niggers."

"How come Byrd's got off without being killed?" asked one of the men.

"I couldn't answer that question," Lee said. "But Byrd's being watched closely, and I hear he's claiming that Sam Bowers and Deavours Nix have got people here in Laurel ready to kill him.

"Next Friday night," Lee continued, "we got fifty new members we're swearing in. It's nice to know that we got new people coming in that will be willing to carry out our projects. This is a time we need to show our strength. The FBI thinks they got us on the run, but we need to show them otherwise. I can tell you that we got a major project planned for the middle of the month. We need you to help out on this project. We gonna burn sixty crosses in Jones County in one night. We gonna need some lumber and some diesel fuel, and we gonna need men to light the sacred torch. When the FBI sees those flames, burning all over Jones County, they gonna be running around like a chicken with its head cut off."

WHILE NORMAN LEE and his brother remained enthusiastic about taking action, others in the White Knights believed the organization had been undone by belligerence and mismanagement, and Landrum discovered, when he began sampling opinions in conversations with fellow Klansmen, that there was no such thing as a firm consensus about the future of the organization.

Tommy Thornton, once an enthusiastic member of the dangerous East Group, told Landrum privately that Sessum, who had led members of the unit on the fatal raid at Vernon Dahmer's farm, had undermined loyalty for his klavern. He said he considered himself fortunate that he had not been a part of the Dahmer operation. Spared from that burden of guilt, Thornton said he wanted to escape any further criminal assignments. He had no plans to attend any more meetings.

Spec Stewart, once an exalted cyclops of one of the klaverns, also confided to Landrum that he intended to drop out of the White Knights. "I found out I need to look out for myself," he said. "The Klan sure as hell won't do it for me. I think the Klan is dead. There's still some loudmouths trying to hold things together, but the responsible people are dropping out." Unlike Thornton, Stewart revealed some compassion for Sessum. "The man's got a tough family situation. He's got one son living with him right now, but his wife's got custody of the other. He don't need the trouble the Klan's causing him."

Domestic difficulties were cropping up for other members of the Klan, too, and some of them were turning their attention toward preserving their marriages and away from the White Knights. "I've talked with a lot of men about getting out of the Klan," Stewart said. "They're not necessarily gonna get themselves swore out formally, they just aren't going to go to any more meetings or pay their dues. I think we all know we have to live our own lives and not worry about things going on with the Klan."

A few days later, to assess the growing number of defections, Red Caldwell, once one of the most voluble leaders of the Jones County organization, took Landrum on a meandering car ride so they could be assured no one else was listening.

"How are things going with your group?" Caldwell asked.

"We're down to about five men who can be counted on to come to our meetings," Landrum said. "But I hear they are having good turnouts with other groups."

"Naw," Caldwell said. "Things are gettin' real quiet. There's too much pressure from the FBI. Hell, Tom, even I have stopped going. I don't want the FBI all over my ass."

"No question they're having an effect."

"How many FBI agents do you reckon are in town?"

"I don't know," Landrum said, "but enough to cut the attendance in my group."

"Between the FBI and the niggers, things are at a fine howdy-do," Caldwell observed, turning the conversation toward race relations in Jones County. "I'm afraid the nigger situation might come to a boil. There's already been trouble this summer between white kids and nigger kids around the Burger Chef. The niggers had the nerve to throw bricks from off the overpass there. They knocked out one rear window and dented some other cars. One fellow who drives a chicken truck stopped and took a shot at the niggers; didn't hit nobody. Looks like the trouble is spreading. School will be starting soon. You know, Tom, some niggers are actually enrolling in the Laurel city schools. I'm gonna transfer my little girl to the county schools. I've got her enrolled at South Jones High School."

Caldwell speculated that the racial conflict might lead to an economic boycott by Jones County Blacks. Ever the car salesman, Caldwell said, "I sure hope the niggers don't boycott Laurel. My business is already off too much."

Near the end of July, Landrum went to Lightsey's service station in an effort to have another talk with him. He was told by an attendant that Lightsey no longer spent much time there. Knowing that Lightsey was now regarded to be as treacherous as Lawrence Byrd, Landrum wondered whether Lightsey had severed connections with the Klan. When Gerald Martin stopped by his office at the courthouse a couple of days later, Landrum inquired.

"I don't think Speed's quit the Klan," Martin told Landrum.

"He's just shifting his priorities. You know he had a still set up in his barn where we used to meet, don't you? Well, he's fixing to go into the legitimate whiskey business. He wants to open up a liquor store."

Thirty-three years after the end of national Prohibition, Mississippi had just become the last state in the union to legalize liquor, and entrepreneurs were rushing to invest in package stores in counties where the sale of alcohol would be approved. "Lightsey's got too much money to know what to do with it," Martin said. "Maybe that's why he bought himself a $500 dog."

≈

LANDRUM ATTENDED ANOTHER klavern meeting on August 2 at Norman Lee's slaughterhouse. Only four men were present. Lee began the ceremony by laying out a Bible and a pistol, then using his pocket knife and a meat cleaver to form a cross on a table. After uttering a short prayer he commenced his agenda with a complaint. "I had a meeting here last week, and the only ones here was me and my Bible. I don't know what it's gonna take to wake our men up. We've been taking some strong action some nights and we need support."

Lee boasted of his readiness to fight, even in hand-to-hand combat. "Lemme show you my boots." He pointed to spurs he had attached to his footwear. "I got them spurs filed down to a fine point. Any nigger who wants to mess with me, he'll be sorry." Ignoring the Klan's admonition about profanity at the meetings, Lee declared he was ready to use his fists and his spurs. "I'm ready to start tearing niggers a new asshole."

Landrum felt secure enough about his position within the Klan to raise questions. "I'm hearing all about shooting up houses; I'm hearing bragging about shooting into that Reverend Clay's house," Landrum told the little group. "I just gotta say that whoever claimed he shot into his house must have had a mighty powerful gun because his house is a long way from the highway and out of range."

Lee was indignant. "That wadn't no shotgun, let me tell you, and don't let nobody fool you about the damage that a little carbine can do. I know a man who's got a thirty-aught-six, and it can do a lot of damage." Landrum suspected he was talking about his brother, Dubie. "I can also tell you the man who was doing the shootin' wadn't doing it for no fun. He was shootin' to kill."

"I'll bet there were children in that house, and that needs to be taken into consideration," Landrum said.

"What you need to understand," Lee lectured, "is that we are involved in a war. And in a war, sometimes the innocent must suffer."

At the next meeting Norman Lee repeated his calls for violence. "One of these nights, somebody is gonna kill a nigger, and maybe that will get things started again. You know, sometimes I wake up at night and think about killing that nigger who tried to enroll his kids at our school last year. I'll be glad when our governor declares that everybody can go out hunting and get our bag limit of niggers."

The next day, Leonard Caves told Landrum he could not afford to go to any more Klan meetings. County elections were coming next year, Caves said, and it would ruin his political career if he were linked to the house shootings.

Although some men were growing faint of heart, Sessum remained resolute. He approached Landrum to see if he could use his courthouse connections to fix a jury in a forthcoming trial of a Klansman in Ellisville, the other Jones County seat of government. "I just had lunch with Sam Bowers and Deavours at Deavours's café, and we wanted to help this fellow," Sessum said.

Landrum said he did not know anyone in the Ellisville court-house well enough to intervene.

"Well, we've been having slim pickings ourselves," Sessum acknowledged. "We're having real problems getting our members involved right now." He asked about the level of interest in Landrum's unit.

"To tell the truth, we're not doing well. Attendance is down. We're having trouble getting members to attend."

"The problem," Sessum said, "is Speed Lightsey. You can't trust him. He's the kind of man who'll tear down any group." Still, Sessum expressed optimism. "I want to build a strong, aggressive group,

Tom. I'd like you to think about joining my group. My problem has been no one wants to go on projects by themselves. I have to lead them. No one else is willing to take the bull by the horns. But I'm building my group. I just brought eight new men into the Klan, and I had fourteen men at my last meeting. The FBI's not going to break me. If any man ever had pressure put on him, that's me. But I will continue to be strong-willed because I'm a Christian."

Of all the ringleaders in the White Knights, Sessum was the one Landrum found to be the most perplexing. Just as Spec Stewart had recently expressed sympathy for Sessum's troubled marital situation, Landrum continued to see a good side to the Klansman. His nature tended to be benign, and he was, after all, a man of God. Landrum had once told Anne that Sessum acted as though he had a split personality, cursed with a brain that was a thing in conflict. It was sometimes hard to believe that he could be responsible for the violence attributed to him. Landrum wondered if Sessum were torn between two jobs. He worked as a route salesman for his uncle's wholesale business and was forced into the unpleasant duty of collecting debts from customers. Sometimes he had to be hard-nosed. But on Sundays he took up the mantle of a minister and behaved too gently to be a Klansman.

Pressing Landrum for membership in his group, Sessum talked of his objectives. "There's gonna be plenty of trouble when school starts," he predicted. "I had hoped this campaign to shoot into houses would get more interest built up in our organization. So far it hasn't done as much good as I'd like. Maybe it's time for us to turn to more drastic measures—sabotage, some bombs, and some real shootings to fire our people up."

Despite his own mixed emotions about Little Preacher, Landrum was convinced he was guilty of Dahmer's murder, and when he heard Sessum advocating more deadly attacks, it was easy for him to turn down the offer to join Sessum's klavern.

Days before the new school year began, Norman Lee summoned a dwindling band of his klavern members to encourage new violence, during another session in his slaughterhouse. Landrum attended in order to report overnight to the FBI. Though the bureau policy prevented agents from providing overt protection to Black school-children and their parents, Bob Lee and his FBI colleagues in Jones County were carefully monitoring Klan activity.

Landrum passed on an account of the meeting that warned of murderous threats by the Lee brothers. According to Landrum, Norman Lee said he had attended a Klan meeting in Ellisville earlier in the week where members of another klavern vowed "to take care of" four Blacks who had registered to attend South Jones High School, a facility that the Klan had once felt would remain all white and unapproachable by any court order.

"This work needs to be done now," brother Dubie bellowed. "We need to burn down every nigger house that will burn. This will take the pressure off the men charged in the Dahmer case. We need to find men who are not scared, who are willing to do more projects than the FBI could ever hope to investigate."

Norman counseled a bit of caution. He told his brother and others, "Let's wait and see what happens when school starts. We can watch. The niggers may not show up. But I want to tell all of you, I'm not going to stand by and see any nigger go to school freely in Jones County."

Dubie raised the volume. He launched into a rant about "niggers and Lawrence Byrd" and ways to kill them. After the diatribe was finished, his brother, the klavern's self-appointed exalted cyclops, dismissed the group with a benediction, and the men shuffled their way home.

Later that night, Landrum closed his report to the FBI with an advisory paragraph: "I still feel that V. L. (Dubie) Lee is one of the most dangerous men in the Klan. He brought up again that his high-powered rifle would kill a Negro from as far away as he could see him."

TWO WEEKS LATER, the klavern gathered at the slaughterhouse to consider a new item on the agenda. Norman Lee said he had been asked by Bowers to poll his group on the question of putting Lightsey on trial. Bowers claimed that he had tried unsuccessfully to meet with Lightsey after the veteran Klansman stopped coming to meetings.

"Sam wants to know what Speed has been up to," Lee said. "He feels if our klavern will vote yes, somebody could go out and get Speed—if necessary by force—and carry him out somewhere and find out why he is spending so much time with the FBI and where he got the thousand-dollar bills he's been flashing around. We want to find out where some of our Klan money is that he never turned in, and what he's been saying to the federal grand jury."

Only five men were at the meeting—Landrum, the Lee brothers, and two others. No one seemed eager to confront Lightsey. "Listen," Landrum said, "I'm not going to take any part in any violence. I feel sure if someone would just go out to Lightsey's business and ask him some questions, we'd find out what we want without a Klan trial."

"I'm not saying any harm's gonna come to Speed," Norman Lee said. "But according to our bylaws it's got to be done by trial."

When it sounded as though the proposal for a trial would die without a vote, Dubie Lee burst into another angry monologue. "Speed Lightsey got soft," he muttered. "He can't lead no more. That's why he had to be replaced at our klavern. He's scared to go on projects that already should have been done. Scared to burn down nigger houses that should have already been burned." He paused, savoring his own words. "I know there's one thing the nigger can't stand, and that's my rifle or buckshot filling up his house. You know, I've got a rifle that came to me from mysterious sources. It may have been a gift from God. One day I found it laying on the front seat of my car, with a box of shells. I tried it out and it's got powerful force. It will shoot through a tree eight inches thick. Believe me, it's got five shots, and I put each one of those shots through an eight-inch pine tree. I had always favored a thirty-aught-six, but this rifle, I believe, is blessed. I guess I'm just going to have to do with it." He grinned maliciously, but his audience seemed more embarrassed by the tirade than whipped into action. The meeting broke up with no decision.

When Landrum telephoned Lightsey the following morning to tell him of the threat, he was surprised by Lightsey's reaction. "I already heard something about it," Lightsey said and laughed scornfully. "Dubie Lee is basically a chickenshit. He likes to talk big, but he ain't gonna do shit. I ain't got time to worry about him."

$$\approx$$

NORMAN LEE WANTED to restore order within his klavern. He moved the location of the next meeting place from his slaughterhouse to a wooded area in the southern part of Jones County, near Ellisville. Landrum, accompanied by two other members of his unit, was instructed to park his car off a highway and follow a path into the forest. It was growing dark, but the woods retained an amber light. As the men tramped through fallen pine needles, dust motes swirled overhead and insects sang in protest of the intrusion. It was September, but the summer's heat had persevered into autumn. Landrum noticed that a man he recognized as a Masonite employee emerged from a clump of bushes and began following the procession. He was carrying a shotgun and identified himself as the new "vice exalted cyclops" of the klavern. Landrum had never heard of a vice exalted cyclops; the title sounded weird. After a walk of three hundred yards, the group arrived at their destination, a clearing where Lee had set out a table and some chairs. They were joined by a few others who were not introduced.

"Men," Lee announced, "I been talking with the wizard and we are going to start having meetings that are conducted right, according to our constitution. The wizard and me have set some guidelines, and we are all gonna follow them, and if you don't like them, you can leave now."

He lowered his voice reverentially and said the group would obey the Veil of Secrecy by listening to his prayer and maintaining silence. Landrum saw that Lee had dressed the table elaborately. The top was covered with a Confederate battle flag. A Bible was opened to the Book of Romans; a sword and Lee's loaded .38-caliber pistol lay nearby.

Classes had begun in the Jones County schools, so Lee asked for a report. His new deputy said that one Black boy had enrolled at a school in Ellisville. "He came the first day, but he didn't come yesterday," the vice exalted cyclops said. "My own son is a student there, and he's gonna keep me informed as to what goes on there."

"I'd like to know the nigger's name and where he lives, because we can take care of him," Lee said. "From now on, the projects that we discuss at our meetings are going to be carried out. If you don't believe me, you can read about it in the paper."

There were discussions of ways to intimidate Black families bold enough to have their children attend previously all-white classes. From what the Klansmen were able to learn, it seemed that very few Blacks had actually despoiled the schools of Jones County. Landrum had an archaic word he liked to use for the unproductive talk among Klansmen that wandered aimlessly from one subject to another— palaver; worthless palaver.

The meeting that began with Lee's attempt at pomp broke up without purpose.

INCREASINGLY, the Klan meetings reminded Landrum of the collection of old dogs people kept around their houses, capable of menacing barks but uninterested in actually biting anyone. The public schools of Jones County continued to operate on schedule, undisturbed by any Klan action, and a small number of Black students were attending classes with whites without any major incidents. Each week, Landrum drove to meeting places to find only a couple of other Klansmen on hand; on two occasions no one other than Landrum showed up. In a brief report to the FBI, Landrum wrote: "I went by Norman Lee's house twice on the night of 10-8-66, at 8:00

and 9:15 p.m. There were no trucks parked behind the slaughter-house, or any visual sign of a meeting being held."

Norman Lee tried visiting missing members in an effort to revive his group. He went to the home of Leonard Caves, who had not come to a meeting in months, but couldn't find him. So he sought out his brother, R.L., who told Lee he himself had a state job and couldn't afford to jeopardize it. "Leonard don't need to meet with you either," he added. After all, the circuit clerk would be facing reelection before long.

Lee was disgusted with the response. "I'll bet we hear from 'Little Leonard' next year when he's needing our votes," Lee told Landrum, "and, by God, we'll remember what a weasel he was."

Landrum discovered that his courthouse associate had decided to upgrade his bigotry. Caves had become a board member of the local Citizens' Council, a statewide network of businessmen, bank-ers, and lawyers that had been formed to preserve segregation in Mis-sissippi after the Supreme Court ruling in 1954. Some critics called the Council the "country club Klan," but the power of its members gave it public respectability that the Klan could never enjoy.

Caves invited Landrum to join the Council. "I've been assigned to get two men to sign up. I can even get you put on the board."

"What good would that do?" Landrum asked.

"Tom, we need to move up. What we're doing, we're just moving the Klan from the Piney Woods up to the courthouse—and we're bringing our wives with us. We got a lot more influence than the Klan. Besides, the men who are running the Council are all Klan members anyway—Charles Blackwell, Deavours Nix, and Cecil Sessum."

Landrum snorted and spurned the opportunity to join the Cit-izens' Council. He said he needed to concentrate on the White Knights. Shortly after Caves's overture, Norman Lee enlisted Landrum in a campaign to win back the allegiance of members who had strayed. He asked him to persuade his friends Gerald Martin and Tommy Thornton to return. Both men rebuffed Landrum. Martin said he regretted his involvement with the Klan and had no intention of coming back. Thornton told Landrum that Sessum had already personally asked him to join his group—which Sessum considered a particularly prestigious klavern—and Thornton dismissed the idea. "Hell, I'm not about to get further involved with those people."

Meanwhile, Lightsey settled the quarrel over the Klan's claim to money he had been holding, but he said he would have nothing further to do with the group. He had shifted his energies toward the construction of his new liquor store. When Landrum went to see him, Lightsey talked of a theory he had developed about Bowers and Nix:

At the start of the year, he said, the two White Knights leaders felt they were losing control of their organization to their rival in the state, the United Klans. "Bowers and Deavours decided they would show the United boys what a good job they could do, so Deavours selected a bunch of his dickheads for the Dahmer project. Two or three days before they pulled off the project, I stopped by Deavours's café and all their men were in there. Billy Ray Smith was drunk as a rat. Cecil was the only one not drinking. And they were supposed to be planning the project right there. The only people who'll follow Bowers and Nix are dickheads. I blame Nix for destroying the Klan. And if that's not enough, I ran into Red Caldwell the other day and he told me, off the record, he thinks Sam Bowers is a full-fledged communist."

Making his rounds of wayward White Knights, Landrum went to talk with Lawrence Byrd, the Klan outcast. Byrd asked for their conversation to be kept confidential. After inquiring about the Klan's activities and receiving a noncommittal answer from Landrum, Byrd said, "From the reports I've been getting, the Klan is dead. I might have gotten a raw deal from them, but they look dead to me, and they'll never be built back up again." Landrum thought Byrd's boldness demonstrated the ineffectiveness of the Klan. He had listened to many members demand the killing of Byrd; yet here he was, walking around Laurel months after the threats started.

The White Knights appeared to be unraveling, and Landrum

wondered if the vehemence of people like Dubie Lee had driven men away from the Klan. Dubie had exploded again at a recent meeting, bragging of his courage. "I don't go out in the daytime unless shooting starts," he yelled, "but I'll go out anytime at night, whether it's wet or cold weather, to burn down a house or kill a man. One night we had four projects to do, and only me and a couple of other men to do the job. We flipped coins to see which one we'd do first, and by the end of the night we had taken care of all four. I tell you, if a man don't think I would kill a man or lay him out in the woods, you got another thought coming."

~

JUST BEFORE THANKSGIVING, Pete Martin, whose indictment in the Dahmer case had not diminished his ardor for the Klan, dropped by Landrum's home to tell him that Sam Bowers wanted him to come to a roadside park off Highway 11 in two hours.

"What's that about?" Landrum asked.

"I have no idea."

"Are you going?"

"Naw," Martin replied. "I gotta go to a PTA meeting."

Landrum didn't know whether Martin was joking or setting him up. Once again, he felt a ripple of fear. This was the first he had heard of any meeting with Bowers, and it came on short notice. Perhaps, he thought, they had found out about his arrangement with the FBI, and he would wind up in the Tallahala Creek tonight.

He asked Martin if anyone else was going. "A man who claimed he was acting as the bursar for the group will be there," Martin said. "Maybe you can catch a ride with him." Encouraged that he might have the company of the bursar, a relatively mild-mannered man, Landrum decided to attend the meeting with the imperial wizard.

After a rendezvous with Bowers at the park, Landrum and the bursar were directed to drive to another checkpoint near a grove of pines outside Ellisville. Eventually they followed Bowers into the woods, where they were joined by the Lee brothers; Deavours Nix;

Jesse White, the official photographer for the Klan magazine *Southern Review*; and a Laurel businessman named B. F. Hinton. Bowers asked the group to form a circle and instructed the bursar to deliver a prayer. To drop the figurative Veil of Secrecy, Norman Lee draped the Confederate battle flag on the hood of Hinton's car, then lovingly placed on the banner a Bible—turned to Romans 12—along with a knife and a pistol.

Inspired, Bowers announced, "I like the looks of that." He turned to the business at hand. The group had been summoned, he said, because he had chosen them to form a new klavern. It would be his favorite group, and it would become the strongest unit within the White Knights of Jones County, he promised. The klavern would be composed of Landrum and the bursar and the Lee brothers. The imperial wizard paused, then announced that the exalted cyclops would be Hinton. To Landrum, it sounded as though Bowers had tired of the ineptitude of the klavern during Norman Lee's short-lived reign. The move represented a rebuke to the Lee brothers, but they took the news meekly. Landrum had never seen Dubie so quiet.

After giving a short lecture on the tactics of the FBI, which he called "the Gestapo," Bowers introduced Hinton. "He's been inactive in the Klan for personal reasons, but now he's able to come back and work with us. He's going to need all the help he can get to hold this together, and I want you all to work with him."

Hinton was short and plump. He carried a soft, middle-aged belly above his belt, and he didn't look like much of a leader to Landrum. But when he was given the opportunity to speak, he made it clear that he was prepared to take over from the Lee brothers.

"First of all," he said. "I am going to be the boss. Second, anybody who goes off on a project without my permission will be on his own." He looked at Dubie Lee. "We got plenty of projects to be done, so if a man wants action he can get it. Third, our group will be the strongest, most effective group of them all. It may take a month or so to get set up, but once we do, there are some politicians and policemen and FBI agents that have caused us hardship, and we're going to get them. Fourth, we got the names of eighty-two nigger parents who signed up their children to go to white schools, and we have methods of getting them. They have creditors and charge accounts at grocery stores, and we're going to tell these folks that those niggers are bad credit risks, and that the Klan will be after them."

Hinton hitched up his trousers in a gesture meant to add to his stature. "I want to tell you that any man that double-crosses the Klan better be careful. If we feel a man might talk, we will take action, though it would be a shame to have to kill a white man. One other thing, next year is election year, and it will be prime time for us to get even with some of the politicians who've been playing games with us."

After Hinton finished his speech, the meeting drifted into a discussion about Black targets. At the mention of a potential victim named Crockett, Hinton brightened. "Oh, I was out at his house not long ago to make an estimate on a fire he had," he said. Hinton was in the flooring business.

Dubie Lee jumped into the conversation. "Did you notice his house was about eight feet off the ground in the rear? He has a little trap door under his bathroom, and I crawled under there and opened that door and poured gasoline all over the place. I'm the one that caused that damage. Me and one other man." Dubie wheezed with laughter at the recollection.

Sam Bowers's mouth puckered in distaste as if he had bitten into an overripe persimmon, and he called for the meeting to end with a short ceremony. The men formed a circle again, and each put a hand on the shoulder of the Klansman to his right. It was time to lift the Veil of Secrecy, Bowers said. The bursar dismissed the group with another prayer, and the imperial wizard extended his arm in a Nazi salute to bless his men.

⁓

BOWERS MADE ONE OTHER effort to impose order near the end of the year. He called a special meeting of Cecil Sessum's klavern to conduct a trial of Shorty Lowe, the young Klansman who had fled Mississippi for Texas days after the Dahmer murder. The members met first at a fruit stand off U.S. Highway 84 near Laurel, then crowded into three cars for a five-mile drive to an isolated gravel pit. When they arrived, they were given masks to wear at the meeting and rags to wrap around their feet. Sessum explained that these would prevent the FBI from finding footprints.

After stationing guards to watch over the proceedings, Sessum drove back to Laurel to pick up the accused, who had moved back to Mississippi with his father. Both men had been members of the East Group and were among the fourteen White Knights indicted in the Dahmer case. An hour later Sessum returned empty-handed. Lowe, he explained, had failed to meet him at the appointed place.

Shorty Lowe might have been missing, but a stream of other Klansmen showed up for the spectacle. Cliff Wilson drove up in the same Pontiac he had taken on the Dahmer raid. This time, he was accompanied by four other men in full Klan regalia. Another car, with its broken muffler spewing metallic coughs and grunts into the night, disgorged a separate cargo also wearing robes and hoods. The men in special dress had been designated to serve on the jury. After the imperial wizard arrived in the company of Deavours Nix and attorney Travis Buckley, he decreed that Lowe would be tried in absentia.

Clutching at jutting rock formations and weather-beaten shoots of bush for handholds, the men descended into the gravel pit for the formal hearing. Bowers read various charges being brought against Lowe. One involved the note Lowe had written "Preacher" Sessum from Texas, asking for Sessum's understanding for Lowe's "talking." The document was presented as a confession of complicity with the FBI, although there were suspicions that the FBI had fabricated the message. Another accusation cited Lowe for trying to sell bootleg whiskey at John's Restaurant, an illegality that jeopardized Nix's license to sell beer. After all the evidence was presented, Bowers directed his jury to convict Lowe. All but one of the men voted guilty, and Shorty Lowe, aka Odd Ball, was expelled from the Klan.

CHAPTER 20

Tom Landrum learned of another abrupt lurch in the peculiar case of Lawrence Byrd from his friend Charles Pickering, the Jones County prosecuting attorney. Pickering, sounding troubled, called Landrum in the spring of 1967 and asked if he could come to his home to discuss a growing concern. The two men had been sharing confidences since Landrum had told him of his secret arrangement with the FBI nearly two years earlier. Now Pickering had his own stunning revelation: the district attorney, Chet Dillard, who outranked Pickering, appeared to be moving with a grand jury to indict two Mississippi highway patrolmen for kidnapping Byrd. More importantly, Dillard might seek an indictment of the state's FBI chief, Roy K. Moore, for his involvement in a scheme to coerce Byrd into becoming a witness against the White Knights.

In his report to the FBI, Landrum related that Pickering said that he and the district attorney had met until 3 a.m. the night before in Dillard's office with a motley group of characters with White Knights connections, including Carl Ford and Charles Blackwell, lawyers who represented Klansmen; Klansman Pete Martin, charged with possession of dynamite; and Roy Strickland, a well-traveled felon who claimed he and a partner, Jack Watkins, had been paid by the FBI and the highway patrol to abduct Byrd. (The third person believed by Dillard to have been a participant in the kidnapping, the mysterious Mafia figure Gregory Scarpa, was not mentioned.)

The tale seemed dizzying to Landrum. The new development grew out of the arrests two weeks earlier on the Mississippi Gulf Coast of Travis Buckley, celebrated for being the imperial wizard's lawyer during the congressional hearing in Washington, and Billy Roy Pitts, notorious within the White Knights for having lost his pistol during the raid on Dahmer's home. The pair had been charged with kidnapping and beating Watkins in a Klan effort to exonerate Strickland and undermine the FBI case being built around Byrd's original statement to agents. With Buckley facing criminal charges, the team of Klan lawyers was retaliating by pressing a case against the FBI for conniving with unreliable characters in extralegal intrigue.

Almost from the beginning, Dillard had been resentful of the heavy FBI concentration in Mississippi that had taken a number of civil rights cases out of the hands of local law enforcement authorities. After talking with Byrd in the hospital a year earlier, the district attorney became convinced that the FBI had been the mastermind behind a plot to turn the Laurel TV repairman into a witness. Because the FBI shared some intelligence with local authorities, Dillard knew that Byrd had been talking regularly with FBI agents after his beating. The district attorney was also inclined to believe some of the charges included in Cecil Sessum's year-old affidavit in which he claimed that Moore had been involved in Sessum's abduction and torture at the hands of FBI agents.

Pickering told Landrum he disagreed with Dillard's conclusions. He was skeptical of the testimony of various Klansmen who insisted that they had been brutalized by the FBI, and he felt the district attorney should not be consorting with men like Strickland, believed to be the ringleader of a band of thieves in south Mississippi that stole cars and delivered them to chop shops to supply parts, or sold them cheaply on the side. Landrum didn't know if Strickland actually belonged to the White Knights, but he figured his unsavory reputation certainly qualified him for membership.

Settling into a chair at Landrum's home, Pickering asked for his friend's indulgence as he gave a bewildering account of Dillard's move against the FBI. According to Pickering, Dillard had been given a seventy-page statement in which Strickland said he was paid more than $700—plus expenses—by the FBI and the highway patrol to orchestrate the abduction of Byrd. Knowing that Byrd would recognize him, Strickland said he recruited his associate Jack Watkins and another unidentified man to overpower Byrd at his TV shop and turn him over to the highway patrolmen to apply heavy-handed pressure. Strickland added that highway patrolmen paid him to plant dynamite in Pete Martin's car.

In exchange for his services, Strickland claimed, the law enforcement officers not only paid him cash but also promised not to prosecute him on an outstanding 1965 car-theft charge. To support his argument, Strickland pointed out that his trial had been repeatedly delayed for nearly two years. (During the late-night negotiations, Dillard countered that it was Strickland himself who sought a continuance in the case, on the grounds that he had been hurt in a wreck. The prosecutor said a witness reported that he had seen Strickland deliberately ram his car into the tires of a parked 18-wheeler—not once, but twice, within minutes—in order to create the "accident.")

Strickland's case had not been resolved, Pickering told Landrum, but he remained worried. "Tom, Chet seems determined to indict two highway patrolmen on charges of intimidating Lawrence Byrd. He says he feels he's got just about enough information to indict Roy K. Moore, too. I think that would be a terrible mistake, and I'm trying to slow things down," Pickering said. "I can't imagine trusting any of these characters."

Landrum tried to fit this new information into his prior knowledge. Only three days before Pickering's visit, he had been told by other members of the White Knights that Bowers, Nix, and lawyer Carl Ford had secretly taped a conversation between Strickland and one of the patrolmen that corroborated Strickland's story of complicity in the kidnapping by the Mississippi Highway Patrol. "At the present time, Strickland is being guarded by the KKK because he feels the FBI and MHP will kill him," Landrum had written to his

FBI handlers on March 18. "Strickland is thought to know something," he added, about an unrelated case—the disappearance of a local man said to be buried in a swamp near Pascagoula.

"Dillard wants immunity for Strickland," Landrum wrote to the FBI after his latest encounter with his friend the county attorney, "but Pickering feels if one should be indicted, all should, including Strickland. Pickering is fearful for his stand. He feels that Strickland would do him harm, and also the Klan."

Pickering had reason to be fearful. He had been repeatedly castigated by Klansmen for his denunciations of the White Knights, and had learned that a Code Three—a severe beating—had been ordered for him. Still, the young county attorney remained a vocal foe of the Klan, and following his long talk with Landrum, he felt reassured that his opposition to any idea to incriminate the FBI was the wisest course.

<hr />

TO FURTHER COMPLICATE the story, the White Knights issued its own version of the Strickland affair in the Klan newsletter, the *Citizen-Patriot*. According to the two-page mimeographed paper circulated in Jones County, local citizens had been "defrauded" by Dillard, Pickering, and the FBI in an "evil plot" to implicate Strickland. The newsletter accused FBI agent Bob Lee of using pressure against defendants in a car-theft ring. "Bob Lee's motive was not so much to convict anyone in regard to the car thefts, but rather to bring additional underworld characters under FBI control where they could be used for criminal action and as stool pigeons. Roy Strickland was Bob Lee's chief target in this regard."

The Klan newsletter claimed Strickland "was out on bond doing honest work on oil rigs in Louisiana" when he was contacted by highway patrol investigators and the FBI about a plan "to kidnap and torture a confession out of Lawrence Byrd on the Dahmer case." In exchange, the law enforcement officers would ensure that Dillard, the district attorney, would not prosecute Strickland on pending charges of car theft. Strickland agreed to the deal and recruited Jack Watkins, who was "wanted for burglary and armed robbery in the Coast area," to join him in the attack on Byrd. Watkins was also given a promise of immunity, according to the story.

Byrd's kidnapping was carried out with the cooperation of the FBI, the *Citizen-Patriot* reported, with Roy K. Moore in control of the case. Afterward, Strickland became a troublesome presence in Jones County, "going on drinking binges" and creating concern that he "might reveal the whole thing to the wrong person during one of his binges." To keep Strickland quiet, the newsletter claimed Moore decided it was "safer" to send Strickland off to prison "even if this meant double-crossing him."

"Strickland began to realize that the FBI was trying to use everybody against everybody and then betray everybody for the sole benefit and advancement of the FBI," the Klan account continued. Strickland contacted the Klan attorneys "and gave them the full facts about the FBI-engineered kidnap and torture of Lawrence Byrd." The evidence was turned over to Dillard, the *Citizen-Patriot* declared, "in order to obtain a just indictment for kidnapping" against Roy K. Moore, Bill Dukes (another FBI agent), Ford O'Neil and Steve Henderson (two Mississippi Highway Patrol investigators), and Jack Watkins.

The Klan version concluded: "When first given the evidence, Dillard appeared to be interested in enforcing the law without fear or favor, but when the proper FBI pressure was applied to him he caved in like a ripe watermelon and defended the FBI men before the grand jury."

~

THE NEW IMBROGLIO within the ranks of the White Knights had been set off in early March by the arrests of Buckley, the proud Klan mouthpiece, and Pitts, after the pair were involved in a caper so bizarre that it eclipsed the usual standards of aberrant behavior by the Klan.

According to prosecutors in Jackson County, on the Mississippi Gulf Coast, Buckley and Pitts appeared one night at the Pascagoula home of Watkins, reportedly Strickland's accomplice in Byrd's beating. Introducing himself as the prosecuting attorney for Jasper County, Buckley told Watkins he "wanted him to do a job." Watkins blithely joined his visitors in their car and their conversation soon led to the subject of whiskey. Driving west toward Biloxi, Buckley stopped at the first liquor store he saw and purchased a fifth of Southern Comfort for Watkins and another fifth of Wild Turkey for Pitts. They proceeded to a service station, where Buckley bought gasoline while Watkins and Pitts purchased chasers for their drinks.

While Watkins and Pitts guzzled, Buckley made an abrupt U-turn, sending his car across the median strip and back toward Pascagoula. His new passenger paid little attention to the erratic moves until Buckley stopped in a deserted beachfront parking lot and a Ford Falcon occupied by three men pulled up behind them.

Buckley informed Watkins that he was known as one of the men who had kidnapped Lawrence Byrd and forced him to give a statement being used to prosecute some of Buckley's clients. Sobered by the accusation, Watkins denied knowing anything about the case and asked to be taken home. Instead of taking him home, Buckley drove to a dead-end road. The Ford Falcon again parked behind them.

Buckley threatened Watkins with a hunting knife and told him he would be turned over to the three men in the other car unless he made a statement that would help his clients in the White Knights. When Watkins refused, two hooded men emerged from the Falcon. They were identified as Nix and Sessum. Bowers, the imperial wizard, stayed discreetly behind in the car, observing the action as Watkins was jerked from Buckley's car and thrown to the ground. With one of his arms twisted behind his back, Watkins felt a pistol being pushed against his head. He was told it was loaded with one bullet. With each refusal to talk, Watkins heard the pistol snap on an empty chamber.

Convinced that they could not force Watkins to cooperate, Nix and Sessum told their captive they were going into the woods to dig his grave. While they were gone, Pitts pummeled Watkins with his fists. He still wouldn't talk. Disgusted by their failure, Buckley drove back to Watkins's home and dumped him there.

When called on to defend himself against kidnapping charges, Buckley claimed that he had gone to Pascagoula to seek evidence from Watkins concerning the Byrd kidnapping. As Watkins drank and they talked during their ride, Buckley said, he mentioned a burglary suspect and hoped that Watkins could beat a confession out of the man just like the one he had extracted from Byrd. Watkins replied that he had "the law on his side" in the Byrd case and was promised by authorities that he would not be prosecuted on pending car-theft charges if he took part in the assault on Byrd.

According to Buckley, after much more drinking outside the parked car, the encounter turned violent when Watkins swung at Pitts with a small knife. To disarm Watkins, Pitts hit him several times and bloodied his nose. Having consumed almost all of the Southern Comfort, Watkins then stumbled over a wire and fell. He was returned home safely, Buckley swore, and there had never been a second car or three other men present that night.

After his arrest a few days later, Buckley asked to have his case heard quickly, severed from the one against Pitts. At first, Buckley faced a relatively minor obstruction-of-justice charge. Before the month of March was over, Buckley's case in Pascagoula ended in a mistrial. But the prosecution was far from over. A grand jury soon indicted Buckley and Pitts for kidnapping. Buckley was able to make bond and retained a measure of freedom, but no one came to Pitts's rescue. Pitts languished in jail, disgruntled. His discomfort would lead to major repercussions within a year.

~

TOM LANDRUM GOT A further glimpse into the tangled Strickland story when he received a letter from a former student named Billy Ray Rucker, who asked Landrum to visit him in jail. When Landrum arrived at the Jones County facility, he was asked to wait until Klan lawyers Ford and Blackwell finished their own discussion with the inmate. Rucker was already serving a prison sentence for car theft but had been brought back to Laurel in connection with the Strickland investigation.

After the attorneys left, Landrum spoke with Rucker in his cell. Rucker confessed to his former coach that he had been associated with Strickland's auto-theft ring. Over the years, he said, he had stolen more than 150 cars, getting $800 for each one. Rucker said he had been asked by state authorities to testify against Strickland. However, Ford and Blackwell had just warned him not to say anything. They explained that Strickland had been paid by the highway patrol only to be double-crossed by the state.

Rucker told Landrum he was unwilling to cooperate in the prosecution of Strickland and expressed appreciation for Blackwell, who he said had successfully reduced his prison sentence from eleven years to seven.

"Hell, I know if I talk I'll end up in that swamp, like the other fellow," Rucker said. His old gang, he said, had already killed three people. Rucker asked Landrum: "If something happens to me, would you be willing to look out for my family if they need help?"

Landrum assured him that he would.

≈

DILLARD, who vacillated between annoyance with the FBI and a desire to cripple the Klan in Jones County, eventually decided to drop thoughts of indicting either the highway patrol investigators or the FBI leader. Instead, he arranged a trial date for Strickland.

Enraged by this turn of events, Strickland described it as another double-cross by law enforcement figures. The night before the trial, Dillard was told by an informant that Strickland, free after posting bond, was on his way to kill him. The district attorney waited with a shotgun in an upstairs room in his house until dawn, ready to defend himself, but the threat never materialized.

The trial took place on schedule and Strickland won an acquittal on April 21, 1967. Both Dillard and Pickering suspected the Klan influenced the outcome, either by landing friends on the jury or intimidating individual jurors.

≈

ON THE SAME DAY that Strickland was acquitted, a wildcat strike erupted at Laurel's Masonite plant, the largest employer in the area. The discord would bring a new wave of violence to Jones County, and the White Knights would have a major hand in it.

The flashpoint for the strike involved an incident with a forklift driver who objected to double duties that required him to unload the material he ferried through the plant with his vehicle. Upset that the company refused to change his job description, the employee walked out, eventually followed by hundreds of sympathetic co-workers.

A judge ruled that the strike violated an agreement between the International Woodworkers of America and Masonite and ordered the workers to return to their jobs. More than two thousand refused. Many were members of the White Knights; other strikers found themselves embraced by the Klan after Blacks were hired to replace them.

The Klan declared war on Masonite's new hires, men who were derided as "scabs." Hostilities escalated when it became apparent that some Black employees were given positions with seniority over whites. Weeks of conflict delivered a new dimension to the troubles besetting Jones County.

Strikers set up a makeshift field headquarters across the street from the Masonite plant, conveniently located near the lair of Sam Bowers at Sambo Amusement Company. In an unusual burst of solidarity between the strikers and right-wing extremists, who ordinarily considered the labor movement a handmaiden to communism, Klan sharpshooters fired into the homes of scabs, reportedly wounding a few workers. Railroad and gas lines serving Masonite were dynamited.

In an address to a White Knights gathering, Bowers encouraged the snipers to target Blacks. "Shooting into the white scabs' houses has to stop," the imperial wizard declared. "They have the white man's blood of the Anglo-Saxons. The niggers represent the problem. Their blood is unlike the Anglo-Saxons'. It is impure, so all of our attention should be turned to them."

≈

THREE MONTHS INTO the strike Landrum was asked by Norman Lee to help him get rid of some "Klan material" stored inside his slaughterhouse. When Landrum arrived at Lee's place the next morning the atmosphere was tingling with fear and suspicion. He noticed that Lee's wife ducked behind the building to hide, and Lee acted strange himself. In a hushed voice, he told Landrum he had some shells that needed to be thrown away. "I've also got a gun I got to destroy," Lee said.

"What have you got yourself into?" Landrum asked.

"This Masonite thing," Lee said. He went into his slaughterhouse and came out carrying a cardboard box, an attaché case, and a paper bag containing several loose shells and a clip to an M-1 carbine. He said he had already melted down one gun. Thinking that Lee was referring to an M-1, a rifle that became a staple weapon for American infantrymen during World War II, Landrum said, "I would have liked to have that gun."

"Well, I wouldn't give it to you for no amount of money," Lee replied.

While they were talking, Jesse White drove up. Lee retrieved another package for his newest visitor; it appeared to be a rifle in a black case. Wrapping a blanket around the object, he handed it to White, who peeled sharply away in his car.

"How much involved are you?" Landrum asked.

Lee did not reply. Instead, he took six cartridges from his pocket and held them toward Landrum. "I got to throw these away, too," he said.

"Put 'em in the bag with the rest of the stuff," Landrum said.

"You got to make all this stuff disappear," Lee said. "I'm not trying to rush you off, but I'd recommend that you go on now, because I'm expecting trouble and I don't know at what time."

When Landrum got home he notified the FBI that he had been given contraband apparently connected to the Masonite violence. He was told to hold on to it.

≈

TWO NIGHTS LATER, a Masonite security guard named Robert Anthony Billiot was shot and killed during a disturbance outside the plant. He had recently returned home from duty as a Green Beret in Vietnam.

Dillard and Pickering responded with the arrests of Dubie Lee and another Klansman named Andre Hendry, charging them with murder. The case was supported by a tape recording procured by Jesse White, the *Southern Review* Klansman who had long been suspected by his fellow White Knights of being an informer. The tape was played during a preliminary hearing. Lee and Hendry could be heard talking with White. In the conversation, Dubie dismissed any idea of merely shooting the guard in the legs. "Hell no," Dubie snapped. "I'm gonna shoot his fucking brains out." In the same conversation, Hendry was asked if he were troubled by Billiot's death. "Naw," he replied. "It didn't bother me a fucking bit."

Landrum had never doubted Dubie Lee's propensity for shooting people. For months at White Knights meetings he had listened to Dubie's rants and threats. The news of his arrest did not surprise him.

With the tape recording of Lee and Hendry's murderous vows as evidence, conviction in the case appeared likely. But in another demonstration of Jones County's capacity for absorbing violence, prosecutors Dillard and Pickering both left office at the end of the election year and their successors were unable to win guilty verdicts for either man.

CHAPTER 21

I N 1967, virtually every public office in Mississippi—from governor to local constable—was at stake, so the White Knights turned their attention to politics. Knowing that Blacks, newly enfranchised by the Voting Rights Act, were mobilizing as voters for the first time, the Klan began to consider strategies to counter their movement and send more of their own racist members and sympathizers into influential positions in the state capital and various courthouses.

The issue had come up for discussion at a meeting Landrum attended in mid-January when several members of his klavern expressed concern that Blacks were working harder to ensure the election of moderate whites in local elections. "The niggers have been meeting all over town," complained B. F. Hinton, who warned that a Black man might wind up holding an office in Laurel's city hall. Hinton was being assertive in his new position as an exalted cyclops after returning to the Klan's fold. Referring to the Black minister leading local political activity, Hinton added, "Some people are ready for this Reverend Clay to be moved out of Laurel, one way or another."

Landrum learned that the Jones County Klan wanted to groom Deavours Nix as a candidate for lieutenant governor. He considered it a preposterous idea, but the group's house organ, the *Southern*

Review, was already giving Nix plenty of publicity, hailing the owner of John's Restaurant as the Mississippi equivalent of Lester Maddox, the freshly elected governor of Georgia.

Maddox earned national prominence because of his refusal to serve Blacks at his Pickrick Restaurant, a fried-chicken emporium located near the Georgia Tech campus in Atlanta. Instead of merely turning away Black customers, Maddox used force, attracting network news coverage of his tactics. Brandishing wooden pickax handles that he dubbed "Pickrick drumsticks," the restaurateur and his supporters jeered at Blacks who asked to be seated. Maddox said his action, which defied the public-accommodations provisions of the Civil Rights Act of 1964, was necessary to thwart an "invasion" of his business. After a federal court found him in contempt in 1965 and began fining him $200 a day for his refusal to accept Black customers, Maddox closed the Pickrick rather than integrate it. Portraying himself as a teetotaling Baptist who was blessed with the physical ability to ride his bicycle backward and the spiritual connections to have God as his campaign manager, Maddox's zany race for governor succeeded the next year. He defeated Ellis Arnall, a former governor. A little-known state senator named Jimmy Carter finished third.

Buoyed by Maddox's victory and the presence of staunch segregationist George C. Wallace as governor next door in Alabama, the White Knights felt Mississippi would be receptive to a slate of Klan candidates whose views were more extreme than the more orthodox right-wingers who usually prevailed in state elections.

Though it all sounded outlandish to Landrum, he passed on to the FBI the political gossip he overheard. Byron De La Beckwith appeared to be emerging statewide as the favored Klan candidate for lieutenant governor. Beckwith, who had murdered Medgar Evers, was brazenly traveling through the state as a welcome speaker at racist rallies. He had a campaign slogan—"He's a straight shooter"—that he delivered with a wink at Klan appearances. From the publicity attracted by Evers's death and Beckwith's mistrials, all of Mississippi knew he was the man suspected of shooting the civil rights leader in the back.

According to one tale circulating among the White Knights that Landrum passed on to the FBI, Beckwith had approached former governor Ross Barnett, a candidate running to win the state's top office again, with a proposal that Barnett choose Beckwith as his running mate on a super-segregationist ticket. Barnett had been governor when his folly in trying to prevent the integration of the University of Mississippi led to bloody rioting and a military occupation of the campus. By state law, Barnett was unable to succeed himself after serving one term but was able to run for governor again after an interval of four years. Once a favorite of the far right, he was eager to win back the office in 1967. Though he was better known for his bumbling than his cunning, he apparently had the good sense to rebuff Beckwith. "Barnett laughed at him," Landrum wrote the FBI, drawing on Klan political intelligence. "Beckwith wanted a $10,000 campaign fund."

Despite Barnett's rejection, Klan leaders in klaverns around the state outside Jones County felt that Beckwith would be a strong candidate for lieutenant governor, so efforts were made to clear the deck for him. Nix would have to lower his ambitions and become a candidate for a lesser office.

≈

MEANWHILE, the Jones County Klan wallowed in a state of flux itself. Red Caldwell had been replaced as giant because he had stopped coming to meetings. To confirm the news, Landrum drove to Caldwell's car lot to talk with him. "Hadn't seen you in a while, Red, so I thought I'd come check on you," Landrum said in greeting.

"Naw, and you ain't gonna see me anymore," Caldwell said. "I've given up on the silly bastards."

"Well, I'm still attending some meetings, but not as regularly."

"How's the organization doing?" Caldwell inquired.

"Not a whole lot of people attending."

"I heard it had gone to pot. I have totally withdrawn from it, and

I really recommend that you do, too. With all due respect, I think there's nothing but a bunch of trash in it."

Caldwell grinned and gave Landrum a conspiratorial bit of information. "I've decided I'm going to run for sheriff of Jones County."

A week later, at a White Knights meeting where a political committee was formed to determine which candidates the Klan would support, it was announced that Nix now planned to run for sheriff. The Klansmen decided to give Nix preference over Caldwell, who was viewed as a turncoat. They also voted to go all-out for the reelection of their most prominent member in the government of Jones County, the circuit clerk Leonard Caves.

≈

IN THE MOST IMPORTANT CONTEST, the race for governor, the White Knights were able to look on the field of candidates like a sugar-craving consumer eyes a sampler box of chocolate candies. There seemed to be several attractive choices for them, and some had nutty characteristics.

Barnett enjoyed a statewide reputation for his segregationist stands and his willingness to use racial epithets in his speeches. He had been a country lawyer with a gift for florid courtroom theatrics when, in the 1950s, he curried favor with the Citizens' Council, the network of local clubs around the state dedicated to keeping schools and the public houses of power all white. He won election as governor in 1959, in part because the Council panjandrums thought him malleable to their interests. The Council leaders in Jackson—members of the Hederman family, publishers of the state's two largest newspapers—working in concert with the political organization of Senator Jim Eastland, helped elect Barnett and then showered him with bad advice when he became engaged in the confrontation with the Kennedy administration over the integration of Ole Miss. He defied the president and the U.S. Supreme Court for days before knuckling under to pressure from the administration and a criminal-contempt citation from the powerful U.S. Fifth Circuit Court of Appeals. The experience should have made Barnett a favorite of the Klansmen.

But during an appearance by Robert F. Kennedy at the University of Mississippi in 1966, the former attorney general revealed details of some of the absurd deals Barnett had sought to make with him and his brother, President John Kennedy, during the showdown over the enrollment of a Black student at the school. Suddenly, Barnett's status among the segregationists became drastically diminished. He had been caught compromising with the hated Kennedys. With Barnett discredited, there were several other popular foes of integration prepared to replace him.

Congressman John Bell Williams, a nominal Democrat, opposed the Civil Rights Act of 1964 so vehemently that he voted for Republican Barry Goldwater that year rather than Democratic president Lyndon Johnson. As a result, the party stripped him of his congressional seniority; he decided to return home from Washington to run for governor as a martyr. Williams came from the "empty sleeve" school of southern politics. He had lost an arm in a training-flight crash during World War II and mastered the role of a wounded veteran as well as that of a Mississippian mistreated in the nation's capital. With a cultivated snarl and a meanspirited speaking style that heaped ridicule on his rivals, Williams fit a profile that appealed to many Klan voters.

So did a more humble character named Vernon Brown, who campaigned as a segregationist Everyman, dressed in a worn blue suit, red tie, straw hat, and pair of workman's brogans. He was a political descendant of another obscure blue-collar candidate from south Mississippi, a welder named Robert "Blowtorch" Mason, who had been a fringe candidate in two previous elections. Like Blowtorch, Brown claimed to be a champion of the white working class, a man beholden to none of the influence flowing from country clubs and other haunts of wealthy, elitist businessmen. His problem was that he was viewed as a hapless laughingstock on the political stump.

The White Knights of Jones County finally found their darling in the figure of Jimmy Swan, a fifty-four-year-old hillbilly singer who had climbed from a childhood of desperate poverty to become a youthful fixture on the southern honky-tonk circuit. A band called Jimmy Swan and the Blue Sky Boys had a standing engagement to play every Saturday night at the Laurel Civic Center. Swan's first recording, issued by Trumpet Records in 1952, featured two songs, "Juke Joint Mama" and "I Had a Dream" (not to be confused with Martin Luther King's "I Have a Dream" speech a decade later). In a highlight moment, Swan performed with the legendary Hank Williams, whose career had been cut short by his early death in 1953.

A thin, wiry man, Swan affected the look of a country troubadour. He wore cowboy hats and hand-stitched Western shirts. Some thought he would inherit Williams's vast following, but Swan turned his interests to radio. He started working as a disk jockey and eventually became the general manager and part owner of radio station WBKH in Hattiesburg. He also shelved his musical ambitions to take up the role of full-throated exponent of white supremacy, dabbling in local politics before winning widespread recognition from far-right groups. His speeches were as fevered as the sermons of traveling evangelists; while the ministers preached that sin led to eternal damnation, Swan warned that racial "mongrelization" would destroy white civilization.

Although he appeared at Klan rallies in Mississippi, he was careful to deny membership in the secret society. Yet there was no doubt about his racial sentiments. His speeches were incendiary lamentations about the South's loss of sovereignty over its schools. With each new desegregation order, he said that "so-called Federal judges have ordered the destruction of our children." He described the judges as "thieves and outlaws" who worshipped at "the filthy, atheistic altar of integration." He branded Blacks as beasts and savages, and he soon acquired a political following.

For his 1967 campaign for governor, Swan had the help of Asa "Ace" Carter, another fiery racist who had served as an adviser for George Wallace in Alabama and claimed to have written the famous line that Wallace delivered in his first inaugural address: "Segregation now, segregation tomorrow, segregation forever." Carter's dark and bushy eyebrows contributed to a glowering expression, and he, too, became a familiar figure as he trooped through the small towns of Mississippi, making inflammatory speeches on behalf of Swan. A self-described "nigger hater," Carter boasted that he acted as a tutor for Swan, "showing him the intricacies of politics."

The musician radio-executive candidate honed his speeches for his faithful. He vowed to uphold the might of "the Christian people of this state" in order to resist the pressures from Washington of "godless communism" and integration. Swan claimed the late Mississippi politician Theodore G. Bilbo, an obstreperous white supremacist, as "a hero of mine." Bilbo had served as governor before moving to the U.S. Senate in the 1930s, where he introduced legislation designed to ship American Blacks to Africa.

As his campaign gained momentum, Swan made a promise: "Within six months from the day I take office my plan for free, private segregated schools for every white child in the state will be in operation."

Barnett, the erstwhile spokesman for segregation in the state, realized that he was losing ground to Swan. He dismissed the budding politician as "nothing but a guitar picker." Yet before the summer of 1967, political wags were claiming that every pickup truck in south Mississippi bore a Swan bumper sticker. That was an exaggeration, of course, but Swan had emerged as a force.

⌒

AT THE TIME, Mississippi politics were totally controlled by southern Democrats, a conservative wing of the national party. Few card-carrying Republicans existed in the state. The Party of Lincoln was still held responsible for Reconstruction, though Goldwater's presidential candidacy against President Johnson in 1964 had created the first modern movement toward the GOP. But elections were still effectively decided in Democratic primaries in August, three months before the general election.

Within the state Democratic Party, there were two camps: the symbolic sons of Bilbo who publicly denounced the federal government and vowed defiance, and a more "moderate" bloc whose leaders were also segregationists but mild in their comments. Lieutenant Governor Carroll Gartin, a friend of Tom Landrum's, had been a leader of the moderates and was a man with whom Landrum had felt comfortable in confiding his underground role with the White Knights shortly after he agreed to cooperate with the FBI. Gartin had his own segregationist background, but he was considered an enemy of the Klan and other extremist groups. As early as a year before the first Democratic primary, Landrum had heard Gartin denounced at a White Knights meeting. The lieutenant governor from Laurel was considered an enemy, and the White Knights of Jones County vowed they would fight Gartin on his home turf. In spite of the opposition from extremist factions, Gartin was a morning-line favorite to win the governor's office as election year approached.

But the hopes of the state's moderate bloc were dashed a week before Christmas 1966, when the fifty-three-year-old Gartin died of a heart attack hours after checking into the Jones County Community Hospital complaining of chest pains.

Gartin's death left his followers groping for a standard-bearer for 1967. A young state treasurer named William Winter eventually assumed the leadership of the Democrats' moderate branch and became a candidate. Bill Waller, a district attorney in Jackson who had dared to prosecute Beckwith for Evers's murder, also appealed for moderate votes. Yet Winter and Waller found themselves outnumbered in a campaign highlighted by racist taunts and promises to challenge federal desegregation orders. The most colorful practitioner of demagoguery was Jimmy Swan.

～

DESPITE HIS LANGUAGE on the stump, Swan remained sensitive about any public association with the Klan because he feared that the Federal Communications Commission might revoke WBKH's license if he were linked to a group held responsible for a program of terror in the area. Swan held 26 percent of the stock in the radio station. A year before he became a candidate he had initiated a strange meeting with FBI agents in Hattiesburg to disavow any relationship with Sam Bowers. It came a month after the murder of Vernon Dahmer, an incident that lacerated race relations in Swan's hometown and triggered the deployment of an army of FBI agents to the region.

Swan appeared at the FBI office without notice one Monday evening to demand an audience with a team of agents in the room. He seemed agitated and announced that he wanted to "set the record straight" about a visit he had earlier in the day from the imperial wizard, and his close associate, Nix. "I'm coming to you people because I don't want the FCC coming down on me because Sam Bowers and Deavours Nix showed up at my radio station this afternoon," Swan insisted. "I don't even know these men; it's the first time I ever saw them in my life." (An FBI account drafted shortly after Swan's appearance noted that he "appeared highly excited, distressed, and became very loud in his speech.")

Swan said that when he parked in front of the radio station he noticed a car waiting outside with two men in it. He said he "placed no significance" in the scene until his secretary told him, "We have a lot of company out there. There are a lot of FBI men around." He said he realized the men were part of a surveillance unit when he walked into his office and saw two strangers "who had made themselves at home" there. One man, he said, had the temerity to be sitting behind Swan's desk; the other was discussing business with WBKH's advertising salesman. "I swear I didn't know these people," Swan told the FBI, stating that it was his salesman who introduced him to his visitors, Bowers and Nix.

"I recognized their names as the two fellows who had gone to Washington and appeared before that congressional committee," Swan told his listeners at the FBI office. "My first thought was: I don't appreciate them being in my office. And I sure didn't appreciate Sam Bowers sitting in my chair at my desk."

Bowers confirmed to Swan that he was, indeed, the man who had gone to Washington. Bowers grinned and said, "I made some money off the government in the expenses because I took the train instead of flying." Swan was so spooked by Bowers's visit that he made up an excuse to leave the office while his salesman completed a transaction with Nix, who wanted to pay for commercials for John's Restaurant. After a few minutes, Bowers and Nix departed.

"I would sure appreciate it," Swan told the agents, "if you all would interview all the folks in my office to substantiate what I'm telling you now." He said he was troubled because agents had previously interviewed him about "my alleged affiliation" with the Klan. "I told you then, and I'm telling you again today, I'm not a member of the Klan."

Within minutes, Swan's outburst led to an interrogation from the agents in the room. He was asked if he had ever been approached about joining the organization. He admitted that he had been invited, but refused to identify who had made the overture. The agents pointed out to him that their investigation had produced information regarding dates, times, and places of Klan meetings in Forrest County as well as the identities of everyone in attendance at those gatherings. "We can tell you, Mr. Swan," one agent said, "that on more than one occasion you were identified as being in attendance."

Swan grew even more excited. "I want to take this from a year ago," he exclaimed, his voice rising. "I am not a member of the Klan."

"Well, let's talk about activities a year and a half ago," the agent replied.

"I got no information that would be of value," Swan said. Thinking of the current investigation, he blurted, "I'll be honest with you on one point. If I knew anything on the Dahmer case, I'd help you."

After he continued to deny any connections with the Klan, the agent told him, "Our information is carefully analyzed, corroborated and substantiated, and our information regarding your activities in a Forrest County klavern came from reliable sources."

"I might have gone to some meetings," Swan admitted, "but I

went as a newsman." He refused to say what had been discussed at the meetings and would not identify others who had been on hand.

"Mr. Swan, let me direct your attention to a meeting you attended where a project proposed by the Forrest County klavern was discussed. You took part in the discussion."

"I wasn't at that meeting," Swan insisted. "I was out of town on an entertainment engagement when that project was pulled." He said he believed he had been falsely fingered as a participant in the Klan planning by two individuals who were personal enemies.

Swan blamed the FBI for pitting the other co-owners of WBKH against him. "These four men came to me and said they had been contacted by the FBI. They told me the FBI had a thick file on me, and that there was a chance the FCC would take our license away from us. They even alleged I was serving as the go-between for Klan activity between Hattiesburg and Jones County, and that I had smoothed over hard feelings between Sam Bowers and a man from down here in Hattiesburg. These other owners are putting pressure on me because of these allegations about the Klan."

The agent said the FBI had not had any contact with any of the other owners of the radio station.

"Well, lemme tell you," Swan sputtered, "I never laid eyes on Sam Bowers before today, and the only way I would have recognized him would be from his picture in the newspapers."

As the discussion drifted to a conclusion, Swan wanted to end on a positive note. "I'll think over the idea of giving out some information from the secret meetings I attended as a newsman," he said, and promised to get back to the FBI if he decided to talk further. He never did. A couple of months later, he began actively campaigning for the Klan vote.

≈

IF SWAN HAD NEVER SEEN Bowers before their encounter at his radio station, they certainly began to see a lot more of each other as Swan revved up for his race for governor. The FBI learned that Swan and Bowers appeared together at a White Knights rally in Lauderdale County, where Bowers described J. Edgar Hoover as a "false god with feet of clay." Worn down by a relentless investigation of the White Knights by the FBI, Bowers made a sharp about-face in his sentiments about Hoover. He had once praised the FBI director for his battles against communism. On the same program, Swan hailed the dedication of the White Knights for their own fight with the federal government. He criticized other segregationist politicians for being too timid to attend Klan gatherings. "Any man who is ashamed to share the platform with Sam Bowers is not worthy to sit in the governor's mansion," Swan declared.

Bowers and Swan later attended a rally of the White Christian Protective and Legal Defense Fund near Jackson, where an estimated eight hundred spectators contributed $307 toward legal bills for the White Knights defendants in the Dahmer case. Six of the men charged in the murder—Deavours Nix, Cecil Sessum, Billy Roy Pitts, Billy Moss, and the Lowe father-son pair—were on hand for the event, even though the younger Lowe had been formally expelled from the Klan.

Before long, Swan campaign leaflets were being passed out at Klan meetings across the state.

~

SWAN'S RISE IN POPULARITY heartened Bowers. The imperial wizard, who dared to think that a Klansman might be elected president someday, saw that his best chances for success lay on the local level. By crafting a winning slate of Klan-backed candidates, he imagined himself an old-time boss of political affairs in Jones County. With Leonard Caves already in place in the courthouse, Bowers groomed Nix, his most trusted lieutenant, as a candidate for sheriff, another key position in county government, in which the officeholder doubled as tax collector. Nix's candidacy would checkmate Caldwell's ambitions, and if successful, it would put a Klansman in charge of law enforcement in the unincorporated areas of

Jones County and empower the state director of the Klan's Bureau of Investigation to preside over tax collection in the county as well.

Bowers plunged into political work with all of the gusto of a neo-phyte running for class presidency of the eighth grade. His strate-gies also showed eighth-grade sophistication. Landrum heard at one meeting that Bowers's political committee had "done a lot of research on elections" in order to prepare an in-house survey to determine their membership's favorite candidates for various public offices in Jones County. In a play on the name of Gallup, a respect-able national polling firm, the White Knights called their mimeo-graphed "pre-primary ballot" a "Gallop & Trot Poll."

Bowers found that 100 percent of the members responding to the survey supported Caves for circuit clerk. Nix was favored for sheriff by 98 percent of the Klansmen participating in the straw vote. They also heartily backed the candidacy of another of their own, state rep-resentative Charles Blackwell. At the same time, Bowers helped draw up a slate of Klan sympathizers to run for constable, a small-bore law enforcement office, in various subdivisions of Jones County.

In a roundup column in advance of the election, Bill Minor, the dean of Mississippi journalists, wrote in the *Times-Picayune* of New Orleans: "Jones County is believed to have the record number of Klan-backed aspirants with 27."

≈

MEMBERS OF THE White Knights were encouraged to drive to distant Swan rallies to swell the crowds. As the election year inten-sified, political discussions dominated the klavern meetings that Landrum attended. Leonard Caves returned to the embrace of the White Knights and hosted one gathering where Klansmen voiced concern about Nix's candidacy.

"Look," B. F. Hinton complained, "Deavours Nix couldn't get elected dogcatcher, much less sheriff. If we put all our marbles in his race, we're going to lose." There was consternation that Nix had identified himself as a Klan member in an appearance on local TV during a period when many members of the White Knights felt they should be adopting a lower profile.

"We need to be supporting, in our own way, every one of the men we've already endorsed for public office, especially those who can win," Hinton said.

Caves, running for reelection, agreed with Hinton's sentiment, of course, and Hinton was authorized to tell Bowers of the klavern's approval of blanket endorsements for all the Klan candidates.

Nix continued to campaign against the odds. Accompanied by the imperial wizard and Sessum, Nix appeared at a countywide meeting of the White Knights in the spring. With the season giving way to warmer temperatures, dozens of Klansmen met outdoors at the site of an abandoned oil well and heard Nix appeal for their commitment.

"Men," Nix began, "I'm running for office for one purpose, and that is to further the cause of the Klan. Some people have asked me if I would allow my fellow Klan members to make whiskey or to violate the law, and I've told them no. I tell them that good Klansmen want the law enforced. I'm proud of my record with the Klan, and I'm proud of our work here in Jones County."

Listening, Landrum thought: I've never heard such bilge. And in his memo to the FBI describing the meeting, Landrum referred sarcastically to the trio of Bowers, Nix, and Sessum as a "lovely group." At a subsequent meeting, Landrum and others were each asked to make a one-dollar contribution to Blackwell's campaign. Landrum declined.

As the first round of the primaries neared, Blackwell sought advice from Landrum on how to deal with his identification with the White Knights. "There was an article in the *Leader-Call* that labeled me a Klansman," Blackwell said, referring to the Laurel newspaper. "I wonder if I should go on TV and answer that article?"

"Charlie, I don't know what to tell you," Landrum said.

"You know I've never been a member," Blackwell insisted. "I've only acted in a professional way, representing my clients in court." Landrum was incredulous at Blackwell's protest. They had attended many Klan meetings together.

"All this is gonna kill me," the attorney moaned. "Once upon a time I had a bright political future, and now this has been hung around my neck. Even members of my own family don't trust me anymore. I know I need to break away from it, but I don't know how."

In pitiful tones, he begged Landrum "to say a good word for me. Tell people I'm gonna come out from under the Klan. I'm gonna write a speech and go on TV to show it."

Blackwell's professions of independence from the Klan failed to help. He lost his race badly. But so did Chet Dillard, the district attorney running for reelection. He had managed to anger the Klan, so Dillard's defeat brought them some solace. Meanwhile, Charles Pickering, the Klan nemesis as county attorney, attempted to move as a newly minted Republican to win another office—that of state representative. He, too, was beaten.

≈

IN THE END, Swan's candidacy fired the most enthusiasm among the Klan's true believers, and he barnstormed through the friendliest regions of the state as the campaign drew to a close. But in the aftermath of the Evers murder, the executions in Neshoba County, and the firebombing of Vernon Dahmer's home, too many Mississippians were upset over the violence, and it proved unrealistic for the Klan to dream of a political takeover.

Swan wound up with more than one hundred thousand votes statewide (and probably a majority of the white votes in Jones County)—but was eliminated in the first primary. A more exalted segregationist, Congressman Williams, was elected. Meanwhile, Beckwith, the unapologetic assassin, got thirty-four thousand votes in his race for lieutenant governor but lost, too. In Jones County, Nix and Blackwell failed, though Caves was reelected, along with a few Klan-endorsed candidates running for lesser offices.

Other incidents were roiling the White Knights, and the political losses were not the only setbacks they were suffering in the election year.

CHAPTER 22

AFTER ALL OF THE boasts about white power, racial violence, and intimidation he had heard in the two years since he joined the White Knights, Tom Landrum saw that the organization was in retreat by the fall of 1967. By this time, the problem was shared by the other Klan organizations scattered around the country. As the civil rights movement gained momentum and federal authorities increased pressure against far-right terrorist groups, various Klan groups—which had enjoyed a resurgence at the start of the decade—withered. The United Klans, the White Knights' greatest rival in Mississippi, had its back broken by an FBI roundup of members in its stronghold of McComb and the subsequent imprisonment of its national leader, Robert Shelton, in 1966. Meanwhile, a score of the White Knights had been indicted on various criminal charges, Sam Bowers's leadership was being questioned, and klavern meetings were deteriorating into bickering and complaint.

The disarray caused Landrum to reflect back to a conversation he had had with Bowers earlier in the year, when the imperial wizard had asked him about the energy level of his klavern.

Landrum had given the imperial wizard an honest reply: "I'm not sure it's ever going to get started back to what we once were. The most people we've been having at our meetings are six or seven, and sometimes you can't count on that many. We got real problems, Sam."

"I know," Bowers said. "But we done a lot of good." Bowers seemed philosophical about the weakening nature of the White Knights. "We stepped in when nobody else wanted to get involved. I know there's people no longer on board, but some of that's because we've been able to get rid of the ones been talking to the FBI. We've whittled ourselves down to a hard core of men loyal to their vows."

Landrum gave a noncommittal grunt.

"Have you been contacted by the FBI?" Bowers asked.

"Nope."

"You heard of anybody talking to the FBI?"

"Nope, haven't heard anything like that lately."

Bowers seemed satisfied with Landrum's allegiance.

When Landrum got home that evening, he dictated a new report for the FBI. He closed with an observation: "Sam did not seem as enthusiastic about the Klan. Sam had a half-smile on his face when talking about the Klan."

Landrum then elaborated on his thoughts about Bowers in a conversation he had with Anne. "You know, nothing seems 'imperial' about him these days. He seems bittersweet, like this 'Invisible Empire' he built up is falling apart. I used to hear that he was some sort of a great prophet, a strong leader, but now I'm thinking he's just a broken man."

After Anne typed the message he had dictated, Landrum followed FBI instructions to deliver it. He drove to a dark and shady spot in a park in Laurel, just a few blocks from John's Restaurant. While he waited in his car, he saw two agents, barely visible, approaching in a deep drainage ditch. Without a word, they took his two-page report and disappeared into the night.

～

THE FEDERAL GOVERNMENT was finally closing in on Bowers in connection with the 1964 murders in Neshoba County. After numerous delays—and the reluctance of state authorities to prosecute the case—the U.S. Justice Department brought more than a dozen Klan-affiliated defendants to trial in federal court in Meridian in October 1967. Unable to apply murder charges in federal jurisdiction, the prosecutors fell back on an indictment for conspiracy to violate the civil rights of the three slain men. According to Delmar Dennis, one of the informants in the case, Bowers had bragged that the operation targeting the Jewish activist Michael Schwerner and two others represented "the first time that Christians had planned and carried out the execution of a Jew." Among the defendants with Bowers were the Neshoba County sheriff, Lawrence Rainey, and his chief deputy, Cecil Price.

The government relied on its most experienced officer in the field, John Doar, an assistant attorney general for civil rights, to lead the prosecution. Doar had been the Justice Department's veteran point man in Mississippi throughout the decade, and he had cultivated a friendship with Vernon Dahmer while working to open voting rolls in Forrest County to Blacks.

Although the defendants initially felt comforted that the judge, Harold Cox, who occasionally used racial epithets in public and was a close ally of Mississippi senator Jim Eastland, would preside over the case, they soon found that not even Cox had sympathy for the Klan. It became apparent that Cox looked down on Klansmen as white-trash troublemakers whose violence had actually hastened the passage of civil rights legislation. During the trial, the judge's harshest commentary was directed at the defendants and their attorneys. After their sporadic four-year campaign of violence, the Klansmen had lost the sympathy that once cosseted them as redeemers of the southern way of life.

After nearly two weeks of testimony, the jury convicted seven of the defendants, including Bowers, Deputy Sheriff Price, and Alton Wayne Roberts, identified as the "shooter" in the executions. Another seven were acquitted. Sheriff Rainey was among those who walked from the courtroom a free man. The jury deadlocked over what to do with Edgar "Preacher" Killen, one of the many backwoods fundamentalist ministers drawn to the Klan. A mistrial was declared in Killen's case even though he had been described as the man who arranged the capture of the three Freedom Summer volunteers.

Those convicted were able to stay free on bond while they awaited formal sentencing and an appeals process. But Bowers recognized that his position as the leader of the White Knights had been further shaken. He was already under attack from within his own organization. Members of one klavern had told Bowers they were weary of his "foolishness" and were preparing to disband. Jesse White, who helped run the Klan's *Southern Review*, said he was resigning his rank as a Klan giant. White told his fellow Klansmen he was "fed up" with Bowers and felt the imperial wizard, Deavours Nix, and other state leaders had "financially ruined" him. (Even as he complained about his personal losses, White was secretly profiting as a paid informant.) Another member of Landrum's klavern confided that he wanted to transfer to a more compatible unit; otherwise he might quit. And B. F. Hinton, the new exalted cyclops of the klavern, said he wanted to form a different kind of group, where members would wear hoods and no one would know the others' identities.

Landrum invited Leonard Caves to attend a klavern meeting with him but was rebuffed. Secure in the belief that he would win in November's general election, Caves told him: "Hell, no! I'm not going to any more meetings. I know the FBI can buy people off, and I got too much to lose to worry about those sons of bitches. I don't intend to be involved anymore. I thought the Klan could help you, but I found out all they do is ruin you."

Landrum went alone to the meeting of his group, in an abandoned house in the farthest reaches of Jones County, where the password was "Mark." After a prayer, Hinton engineered a discussion that led to a unanimous vote by the ten Klansmen present to pull away from the White Knights. Landrum suggested that the group maintain control of its own money because there was no indication that funds forwarded to Bowers's state organization had been used to help defendants in the Dahmer case. The group's treasurer reported that after expending twenty-five dollars to "needy people" there was only ninety-eight dollars left in its safe-deposit box in the local bank.

Before the meeting adjourned, there was another piece of business. One of the members demonstrated how to make a gasoline bomb. He said it was easy. Simply fill an empty whiskey bottle with gasoline, then tape a Silver Salute firecracker to its side. Not for the first time, Landrum wondered: What in God's name am I doing wasting my time listening to this stuff?

Two weeks later, the group met at an isolated oil well on the property of one of the Klansmen. There was talk that Red Caldwell, the disaffected car dealer, might join the newly constituted group. Another well-known member of Laurel's business community, Cliff Wilson, was also said to be dissatisfied with the White Knights and ready to defect.

Bob Hickson, who had appalled Landrum at one of his early Klan meetings with wild ideas for Klan rampages, informed members of the klavern that he had already drawn up plans for a new organization that would be called the "Confederate Knights of the KKK." They would use such titles as "giant" and "exalted cyclops" but install different men in these positions.

According to Hickson, members of this insurgent Klan would be expected to (a) pay a ten-dollar initiation fee; (b) pay dues of four dollars each quarter, with a one-dollar fine for each month overdue; (c) be required to attend at least one meeting a month; and (d) be expected to take part in at least one project a month. There were two other rules: (e) anyone who refused to participate in a project would be tried by a six-man Klan jury; and (f) any member proved to be an informant would be shot.

Since the group seemed to be losing its lust for violence, Landrum didn't know whether to laugh or be concerned over the last item on the list.

ANOTHER MEMBER OF the White Knights had quietly broken with the organization, and his decision would prove far more critical than those of other dropouts. Billy Roy Pitts had begun cooperating with the FBI in late September. After his arrest in the Jack Watkins kidnapping, Pitts felt he had been cast away by the White Knights and left to rot in a Pascagoula jail while his cohort Travis Buckley was bailed out. He also blamed the Klan for the bungled Dahmer raid that had led to his indictment for murder. Deciding that he had little to lose, Pitts signed a twelve-page confession in front of Bob Lee and other FBI agents in the expectation that he would win some leniency for himself.

Instead of offering secondhand stories of the Klan's activity in its campaign of terror, Pitts delivered a firsthand account of the attack on Dahmer's home and gave over the names of all of the men who went on the raid. His cooperation would prove invaluable to the FBI. For more than twenty months, agents had labored to close their investigation of the Dahmer case. Working at first with leads from the lost pistol and the disabled car left behind near the scene, the FBI had been able to provoke enough loose talk to assemble evidence to secure the indictment of fourteen men within a couple of months. But some of the witnesses counted on by the government were slippery and unlikely to be reliable in courtroom testimony. Moreover, the FBI's knowledge was limited. The original indictment missed two of the major players in the attack on Dahmer's home—Cliff Wilson, who had been driving one of the cars, and Bill "Lightning" Smith, who shot out the front window of the Dahmer house and the tires of the second Klan car. Compounding the error, the wrong Bill Smith had been indicted.

In his statement, signed on September 30, 1967, Pitts underscored the risk he was taking, by referring to Klan death threats for anyone who talked about the case. After returning from torching the Dahmer home, he said, "Sessum warned the entire group to keep their mouths shut and said that anyone who decided to be a pimp would die." He added: "Bowers also told me that if anyone pimped on the deal, the pimp would hang."

After some members of the group were arrested, Pitts said, he had "personal knowledge . . . that Sam Bowers and Deavours Nix plotted to kill Lawrence Byrd, whom they believed to be the most damaging witness against them."

In subsequent interviews with authorities, Pitts acknowledged that he had accompanied Travis Buckley on the foolhardy mission to abduct Watkins, and he identified the three men who backed them up as Bowers, Nix, and Sessum. He even told authorities what he knew of White Knights terrorism in connection with the strike at Masonite.

—

KEENLY AWARE THAT Pitts's unsavory background would bring his credibility under attack in any legal proceedings, the FBI and the prosecution team realized they needed more solid evidence. In the case of Lightning Smith, now believed responsible for one of the shotgun attacks on the Dahmer property, it would be helpful to have information about his shotgun, because empty shells had been retrieved from the ground near the house.

Knowing that a number of guns would be displayed at an upcoming event in Jones County, the FBI asked Landrum for help at a "turkey shoot," an annual ritual to raise funds for charity. The event was sponsored by a local civic club and would be held in a clearing in a pine forest not far from Landrum's house. The turkey shoot was a popular affair, attracting sharpshooters and sportsmen who liked to test their aim in celebration of the Constitution's right to bear arms and the South's love of hunting. Though there were tales of the old days when contestants would shoot at the exposed heads of living turkeys pinned behind logs, modern contests were bloodless. Entrants paid fees to fire at targets of cardboard gobblers in hopes of winning prizes and local acclaim.

November 11—Armistice Day—dawned clear and crisp. Weeks after the formal beginning of autumn, a seasonal chill had finally delivered the region's first covering of frost. Since the shoot took place near his home and provided some of the gaiety of a small-town carnival, Landrum planned to take his sons: ten-year-old David, six-year-old Bruce, and Mike, the four-year-old "baby of the family." Given his new mission—to obtain a serial number and several fired shells from Smith's shotgun, if the suspect competed—Landrum called on his boys for assistance.

He instructed his sons to be on their best behavior and to help him keep the grounds clear of debris. "When I'm firing my gun, I want you to be sure to pick up the empty shells and put them in a bag," Landrum told them. "That way we don't leave a mess behind."

When they arrived at the contest, the crowd was in good humor, joking among themselves and mocking one another's failures as marksmen while loud reports from rifles and shotguns ripped the autumn air.

As he had hoped, Landrum found Smith among the contestants. He knew him from his work at Wilson's store in downtown Laurel as well as from his attendance at Klan meetings. Landrum started the conversation with praise of Smith's shotgun—"That's a good-looking piece!"—and questions about its merits. Landrum boasted about his own gun, his father's 12-gauge Winchester with a thirty-six-inch barrel. "I love this old gun, but I've been thinking of getting a new one," Landrum said. He expressed admiration again for Smith's gun. "Why don't you let me try yours out? You can shoot with mine."

Smith agreed to the proposal, and the pair swapped guns. Landrum fired five shots at the target with Smith's weapon. Then he instructed his youngest, "Mike, pick up those shells, son."

Later that day he sent the empty shells and a report to the FBI. The gun's serial number was Remington 840; the gun was a 12-gauge Magnum. Landrum also included his expenses for the day: ten dollars for five shots at two dollars each, as well as a claim for reimbursement for the six-mile round trip.

A few days later, Bob Lee told Landrum, "We know now, this was the gun."

A MONTH AFTER Jesse White's outburst questioning Bowers's leadership, suspicions that White was an informant were confirmed when he gave authorities the tape recording implicating Dubie Lee and Andre Hendry in the murder of the Masonite guard.

A White Knights meeting in November buzzed with news of White's betrayal. The onetime Klan publicist had disappeared. Baffled by his sudden departure from Jones County, the angry Klansmen demanded retribution. "No one seems to know where he is," Landrum reported to the FBI. "The consensus is that his days are numbered."

A couple of days after the turkey shoot, Landrum talked about Dubie Lee's arrest with his brother Norman, who expressed confidence that he would be acquitted if ever brought to trial. "There ain't no jury in the world that's gonna convict Dubie or any other member of a union," he said, "because those juries are gonna be made up of poor, working-class people."

"Have you seen Jesse White?" Landrum asked.

"No, but we know where he is," Lee said. "The son of a bitch bought a house in Jackson. We know the address. Some place on Azalea Drive. He also just bought a new car, obviously from the blood money he got from the FBI. Somebody is going to get that miserable son of a bitch."

≈

THE KLAN MEETINGS grew desultory. More and more members wanted to be "sworn out," to leave the organization with the equivalent of an honorable discharge. One departing Klansman asked Landrum why Leonard Caves no longer showed up at the klavern gatherings. Landrum had a ready reply. "Caves told me he didn't give a damn about the Klan any longer and was not going to let a bunch of sons of bitches get him sent to the pen."

Overhearing Landrum, another Klansman spoke bitterly of the Jones County circuit clerk, who was guaranteed another four years in office after easily winning reelection. "Caves got what he wanted from us. He got our support in the election, and now his true color is out. I never trusted the bastard anyway."

More than once, Landrum drove to the announced setting for his klavern's weekly meeting to find that no one else had bothered to come. When enough members gathered to conduct a session, Landrum felt their agenda had foolish, childish items to consider. Around Thanksgiving, he followed directions to a house adjacent to an oil rig called the "Red Well." Guarding the door was a man armed with a shotgun and wearing a black hood. Otherwise, he was attired in green work clothes, a cowboy hat perched atop his hood, and boots. A welder's torch hung from his belt. If he needed further identification, the guard's pickup truck carried the label "City Welding."

Inside, quilts were hung over the windows to provide privacy while a road flare sizzled on a table for effect. Six defused hand grenades were displayed to illustrate a rambling lecture on demolition. If filled properly, an instructor promised, each grenade could spray six thousand pieces of shrapnel when exploded. The problem for the Klan was, Landrum reckoned, that no one seemed interested in detonating bombs anymore.

～

FOR THE WHITE KNIGHTS, the year seemed to be spinning to a close in a downward trajectory, and no tale of woe better described the gloomy situation than Cecil Sessum's personal plight. His life had gone downhill in dramatic fashion, and he was dogged by a premonition that he was bound for prison, where he feared he would be physically abused by stronger men.

Though his mood was as bleak as the December weather when he came to the courthouse to talk to Landrum, Sessum found the building lit with bright Christmas decorations that seemed incongruous to him. Under indictment in the Dahmer case and in trouble in another county because of the Watkins kidnapping, Sessum wondered whether he would be welcome. But when Landrum saw

Sessum standing tentatively in his office doorway he beckoned his visitor inside.

Through all of the upheaval, Landrum continued to harbor conflicted feelings about the Klan leader. He remembered that Sessum had been protective of him when they were escaping an FBI intrusion upon a statewide White Knights meeting shortly after Landrum joined the group. And there had been other times when Sessum's friendly attitude toward him at Klan meetings served as an antidote to Deavours Nix's hostility. He also knew about Sessum's family problems. The man had experienced a staggering fall from the grace he once enjoyed when he had preached as a Baptist minister, presided over a little family, and held a good job as a salesman. Now he was effectively defrocked, his wife and children lost, and he found himself out of work.

Given the opportunity to talk with Landrum about his tribulations, Sessum uncorked a fountain of woe.

"I hardly know where to start, Tom," Sessum said. "As I figure you've heard, my wife and the children are gone, down on the Coast, and I don't know if I'll ever get them back. I thought you might have some advice, working in Youth Court with broken families and all. But right now that seems like the least of my problems.

"The only job I can get is in the oil fields, and I don't want to do that. It's backbreaking work. Meanwhile, the government is out to get me. I'm looking at a trial early next year which could put me away for the rest of my life.

"I can't prove it," Sessum went on, "but I believe all my trouble started last year when Sam got me to file that affidavit about getting beat up by the FBI. If I hadn't done that, I don't think the FBI would ever have fooled with me. But it's like I accused them of a crime, so they needed to get even with me.

"Now I got more charges being laid against me than I can handle. They got this thing with Travis Buckley down on the Coast, and they got this wild accusation from Webber Rogers in the Dahmer thing. Rogers been out to get me since the time he got shot in Covington County. You know about that?"

Landrum shook his head. He had heard about a distant dispute between Webber Rogers and some Klansmen, and now there were rumors that Rogers was one of the witnesses lined up to testify in the Dahmer case. But he didn't know what Sessum was talking about.

Sessum appeared grateful for the chance to elaborate, and he related a ludicrous story. Listening, Landrum added it to his growing collection. Someday, he thought, he might compile a book called *The Mysterious Tales of the White Knights*.

Rogers, Sessum began, was a "ne'er-do-well barber." Though Sessum admitted that he recruited Rogers for the Klan, the fellow soon became a source of trouble. "I think he went on a dry run at the Dahmer home and started talking about the case even though he didn't know much about it. Then he bailed out of the Klan and got arrested on some other charge. He asked Jesse White and me to go on his bond. Okay? So we put up the bond money and Webber goes free and then don't show up for a hearing, so they're gonna revoke our bond. And that won't do. Jesse picks me up and we drive up to Covington County to find Webber and make a citizen's arrest. We got a guy named Billy Carr to go with us. You following me?"

"Trying to," Landrum said.

"So we find Webber and pile him in the car and are driving back to put him in jail in Jones County when an argument breaks out in the back seat. Webber jumps out of the car. This guy Carr shoots him in the leg with a small-caliber pistol. It knocks Webber to the ground, but he gets up and pulls a gun himself. Turns out to be a toy gun, but Carr don't know it, so he shoots him again. Webber is moaning and saying there's gonna be hell to pay. So we drive the idiot to the hospital. Instead of being grateful, he files charges against not only Carr but Jesse and me, too.

"We had to go to trial in Covington County last summer, for assault and battery or something. It wound up a hung jury, so we're free. But now I hear Webber's gonna be a witness in the Dahmer case, gonna claim a lot of stuff against us, stuff he doesn't know nothing about."

Sessum paused for a moment, then resumed his lamentation.

"Now I hear we got Billy Roy Pitts ready to testify against us in the Travis Buckley case. Billy Roy and I used to be the best of friends. Then he started running around with this woman, and I warned him she was a sorry person. He wound up marrying her, and he knows I called her 'sorry.' I think he resents that, and that's why he's trying to involve me in the case where he and Travis Buckley kidnapped that fellow on the Coast."

Sessum said he could trace most of his problems "to the fact that I tried to help out my friends. Now I'm hoping I got enough friends and enough people who got faith in me to get me out of all my trouble."

≈

ON DECEMBER 29, Bowers learned the depth of his own troubles. Judge Cox, the erstwhile segregationist, came down hard on the imperial wizard. For his conviction on the conspiracy charge, Cox sentenced Bowers to ten years in prison, a term similar to that given to the Neshoba shooter, Alton Wayne Roberts. The deputy sheriff Cecil Price was ordered to serve six years.

Realistically, Bowers knew he had little chance of overturning the conviction, but his team of lawyers was prepared to postpone the immediate prospect of prison with a series of appeals. For the time being, Bowers remained free, determined to fight, like a dedicated Confederate soldier, to the last ditch.

CHAPTER 23

RMED WITH Billy Roy Pitts's detailed account of the firebombing, authorities began to fill the holes that had been
gaping in their investigation since it started nearly two
years before in the ashes of the Dahmer home. Their original theory
that only six men went on the raid had been advanced by Klan informant Delmar Dennis, whose reports were helpful in the Neshoba
case and other probes of the White Knights. However, Dennis had
not been present for the Dahmer operation and based his information on what he had heard. Pitts, on the other hand, had participated
in the attack and was able to re-create the scene during his long,
cooperative talks with the FBI. Pitts and five of the other raiders had
been indicted in 1966. Now he was implicating two others directly
involved in the assault: Bill "Lightning" Smith (clearing Billy Ray
Smith, who had been arrested by mistake) and his employer, Cliff
Wilson, the respected Laurel businessman.

Even as investigators built their case against Wilson, the local
Junior Chamber of Commerce—blind to Wilson's activities as a
Klansman—planned to honor him as their "Man of the Year" at an
elaborate banquet early in 1968. The thirty-five-year-old Wilson's
résumé fit nicely into a model idealized by the Jaycees, an organization filled with enthusiastic young men eager to make names for
themselves. He was a former president of the Laurel Jaycee chapter

and served as one of a dozen vice presidents in the state network of Jaycees. In addition to Wilson's work constructing artificial limbs at his impressive brick office in the town's medical complex, he was known for his busy volunteer schedule as a Little League baseball coach, a leader of a Cub Scout pack, a board member with the PTA, and a fundraiser for several charities. Wilson seemed to represent the quintessence of a Jaycee.

But two years earlier, Pitts was now telling investigators, Wilson had driven one of the two cars used in the Dahmer raid. When the second auto was disabled by the "friendly fire" of Lightning Smith, all eight members of the White Knights assault team had piled into the blue Pontiac driven by Wilson to rush from the burning buildings.

An exemplary citizen by day, a terrorist by night, Wilson had kept up his Klan activities for another two years. A few days after the Jaycees announced the banquet to anoint him Man of the Year, Wilson met with Vic West, a member of Landrum's klavern, to urge the group to take greater interest in the White Knights. "We had a really good county meeting last week," Wilson told West. "Sam Bowers was there and everybody was impressed with the attendance. Everybody but your Group One was represented. You need to get in touch with the faithful members of your group and get them lined up for the next meeting."

West, whose enthusiasm for the Klan had been fading, was non-committal. But he thought to congratulate Wilson for the Jaycee tribute, and added a prophetic warning about his continued role in the White Knights: "After this nice honor, I'd hate to see you get into trouble."

After learning that the banquet for Wilson would probably coincide with his indictment by a grand jury meeting secretly at the same time, Bob Lee, the resident FBI agent, wanted to figure out a way to persuade the Jaycees to hold off their affair. He hinted that Wilson would be an inappropriate choice, but could be no more specific without breaching confidentialities.

The elaborate dinner took place on schedule, with the Reverend Bob Marsh, the pastor of Laurel's First Baptist Church and a talented after-dinner speaker, delivering the keynote address. Marsh chose as his theme "The Essence of a Good Community" and rolled out the rhetoric for the evening's honoree. While more than two hundred Jaycee boosters and their wives listened raptly, Marsh declared, "The essence of a good community is people like Clifford Wilson, people who relate to their fellow man and take an active interest in civic affairs, people who have a constructive influence on society, whose lives are driven by an intangible, invisible force that emanates from their personality."

At the conclusion of the evening, a smiling Wilson, holding his bronze plaque, thanked the speaker for his remarks and the Jaycees for their honor. He asked for the audience's support when he would represent Laurel as their nominee for a greater accolade, "Mississippi's Outstanding Young Man," to be awarded at a statewide event in Jackson the following month.

Instead, Wilson was arrested within hours on charges of murder and arson. The Jaycees were mortified, and Rev. Marsh, the up-and-coming minister of Laurel's largest church, was so shattered by the experience that he fell into a deep depression.

≈

WILSON AND LIGHTNING SMITH were the new names among thirteen Klansmen indicted when the state took an unprecedented initiative in the case and pressed charges of murder and arson. The FBI and Justice Department officials, limited largely to pursuing conspiracy charges, agreed to yield the prosecution to Mississippi authorities and to turn over their evidence to the district attorney in Forrest County.

In addition to the eight men identified as members of the raiding party, the state indicted Bowers, Nix, Buckley, Byrd, and Travis Giles, the owner of the abandoned car, for arson.

The legal action promised new business for attorneys representing the White Knights, but Buckley, the best-known Klan lawyer in the state, had his hands full defending himself, not only in the Dahmer case but in the Watkins abduction on the Gulf Coast. Within days of the new indictments, Buckley went on trial in Pascagoula for kidnapping. The bumbling attorney discovered that the key witness against him would be the man he had enlisted to accompany him on the mission to intimidate Watkins, Billy Roy Pitts.

In his testimony, Pitts reiterated the story he had told the FBI, how he and Buckley—with the aid of the hooded Nix, Sessum, and Bowers in a second car—drove Watkins to a remote location, where he was pummeled and threatened with a gun. Watkins, the other major prosecution witness, corroborated Pitts's account but had to concede on the stand that he had previously been convicted of armed robbery, burglary, and auto theft.

During the trial, Buckley was jailed briefly by the judge for contempt of court during the jury selection. Then he and his defense lawyer, Albert Sidney Johnston III—the namesake of the famous Confederate general mortally wounded at Shiloh—were held on charges of jury tampering.

On top of the relatively minor misdemeanor charges, the jury convicted Buckley on February 4, 1968, on the kidnapping charge. He was sentenced to ten years in prison and disbarred. Buckley immediately appealed, but the conviction of the Klan lawyer by a Mississippi jury dealt the White Knights another setback.

≈

TOM LANDRUM DIDN'T KNOW Buckley very well, but thought of him as something of a fool. In his Youth Court job, Landrum came into contact with many lawyers, and he felt Buckley was one of the least distinguished he encountered. His legal presentations were rambling and rarely to the point, and Landrum believed Buckley's reputation had been tarnished by his close association with Bowers.

After word of Buckley's conviction on the Gulf Coast reached Laurel, Landrum reflected on the situation at home one night with Anne. "This is just the latest nail in the coffin for the Klan," he told his wife. "The kluckers are going to hell in a handbasket. As far as I can tell, there's no interest or activity going on. Everybody I talk to tells me they're not going to mess with the Klan anymore. Some of the young people are getting out, fixing to go back to college. They want to get out before they ruin their lives."

"Do you hear any word about the Klan taking revenge on the people who've turned on them?" Anne asked. "People like Billy Roy Pitts or Jesse White?" Implicit in her question was her concern that her husband might also be accused someday of betraying the Klan.

"Naw, I don't hear much talk anymore. Everybody is sort of hunkered down, waiting to hear what happens next. The arrest of Cliff Wilson had a lot of impact. It's one thing for Sam Bowers and Deavours Nix to get indicted, but it's another thing altogether when a community leader like Cliff winds up facing murder charges.

"There's a whole lot of unrest in the organization. People no longer want to be involved, and people no longer trust Bowers. Vic West talks to Jimmy Swan a lot, and he told me the other day that Swan said there was a movement for him to replace Sam as imperial wizard. This indictment of Sam in the Dahmer case and his conviction up in Neshoba County puts him in big trouble. Hard to think he's going to be able to stay in charge. The thing is, Vic told me, that Jimmy Swan wants to stick to politics and was going to turn down any offers to take over for Sam.

"Right now, the White Knights are like a rudderless ship. People are afraid to hold meetings, and there's nobody to rally much interest."

≈

THE WHITE KNIGHTS absorbed another punishing blow in March, when Sessum became the first of the Klan defendants to go on trial in Hattiesburg on a charge of murder in the Dahmer case. As the testimony began, Sessum did his best to appear as a meek Missionary Baptist minister, forcing a bland smile and chewing gum placidly.

Once again, Pitts served as the state's principal witness, this time giving an agonizing version of the predawn assault on the Dahmer estate, where he said Sessum led a team that firebombed the home while deBoxtel was in charge of torching Dahmer's store. A week before his testimony, Pitts had pleaded guilty to murder; Sessum's lawyers depicted him as a liar attempting to reduce his time in prison, but an all-white jury composed mostly of working-class men believed the turncoat Klansman. It took them only two hours to reach their verdict, and the judge immediately imposed a life sentence. Sessum, dazed by the decision, became the first white man in Mississippi history to be successfully prosecuted by the state for murder in a civil rights case.

Writing in the next day's *Hattiesburg American*, reporter Elliott Chaze noted in his second paragraph, "The question now is whether Pitts, the state's star witness, can be kept alive long enough to testify in 20 additional trials scheduled by the state" in connection with Dahmer's death. Chaze reported that Sessum's lawyer, Lawrence Arrington, had observed that Pitts had been a valuable asset to the prosecution. "He's worth a lot to them—alive." The lawyer claimed there were twenty-one U.S. marshals on the scene, Chaze wrote, "to see that Billy Roy continued breathing and talking."

≈

BY AN EXTRAORDINARY COINCIDENCE, the day after Sessum's conviction, Dr. Martin Luther King Jr. appeared in Jones County for another stop on his tour to win support for a Poor People's March on Washington he planned to lead that spring. King had been invited by Rev. Allen Johnson, whose home had been bombed by the White Knights the year before. King visited Johnson's renovated house, then spoke to a congregation of hundreds at the local minister's church.

Instead of heralding the outcome of Sessum's trial in neighboring Forrest County, the spiritual leader of the nation's civil rights movement concentrated on his mission on behalf of impoverished Americans. It was time, he told the overflow crowd, to change a system where the privileged lived in houses with "wall to wall carpet" while exploiting those who dwelt in shacks infested with "wall to wall rats and roaches." He vowed to go "to Washington to demand—not to beg—that something be done immediately to improve the lives of our poor people."

King had been under criticism by some of his allies in the movement as well as by President Johnson for moving away from the traditional civil rights movement in order to oppose the war in Vietnam and to embrace unusual approaches such as his Poor People's March. Nevertheless, King appeared imbued with messianic zeal and remained bold in his travel schedule. But fearing that danger lurked in his path, his followers made sure that he was escorted in a motorcade from Laurel to Hattiesburg by heavily armed Black men. Some of them had been trained by the militant Deacons for Defense and Justice, a group of Black men who had taken up arms and openly clashed with Klan units in nearby Bogalusa, Louisiana, earlier in the decade.

Hundreds waited into the night to hear King when he arrived at the Holy Rosary Church, another outpost for movement activities. Within a few days, King would be diverted from his Poor People's program, called to Memphis to support striking sanitation workers in the city on a bluff overlooking the Mississippi River. There, on April 4, the modern prophet had an appointment at his personal Golgotha.

＝

KING'S DEATH HAD A profound effect on Black communities across America, and in the Piney Woods region of Mississippi that had briefly offered him a sanctuary, the reaction demonstrated strong new outrage, anger, and determination to overcome a history of discrimination and indignity. The assassination also introduced another shock element to the local white population. By now, even lifelong segregationists had been worn down by a seemingly ceaseless parade of violence by the White Knights, directed first at the civil rights upheaval and now at the lingering Masonite dispute.

At last, there seemed to be a growing desire among people of both races to put an end to the terror. Following Sessum's conviction and the adverse reaction to the murder in Memphis, the shift in mood became obvious to Landrum. Tolerance toward the White Knights had worn out, and he watched as local Klansmen scrambled in greater numbers to leave the organization and protect themselves from prosecution.

≈

NORMAN LEE, once the blustering exalted cyclops of Landrum's klavern, approached him about finding a job. He said his wife was ill and he wanted to close the slaughterhouse adjacent to his home. He wondered if he could find a position on the Mississippi Highway Patrol. Landrum was not encouraging, but gave him the name of someone to call. Lee and his brother, Dubie, also worried about the impending trial for the murder of the Masonite guard. Dubie Lee told Landrum that the authorities "got nothing on me other than some evidence they bought."

Wary of the investigation into the shootings at Masonite, Norman Lee asked Landrum if he could get back the ammunition and other material he gave him for safekeeping. Thinking quickly, Landrum told him, "I hid it. Now I have to go back and see if it is still there." Lee lost interest in retrieving the cache, but continued to press Landrum for help in finding a job. Since Lee lacked a high school diploma, Landrum made an appointment for him to take a GED test. He flunked and expressed general disgust at his personal situation. He reopened his butchering business, but it was not doing well either.

By the end of April, Landrum had lost count of the number of times Norman Lee had pestered him about one thing or another. Then Lee came to him with a new request. "You remember them robes and stuff I give you some time back? There's a man who thinks he's got a pretty good group of men who want to come in, and he needs some robes for them."

"Aw, hell, Norman, I gave those robes to Vic West to keep."

"Well, could you see Vic and get them for us? If we're gonna have any new blood in our group, we need to get them outfitted properly."

Landrum sighed, and said he would talk with West. A couple of days later, he saw his friend and asked about the Klan material.

"Shitfire, Tom, I don't have that stuff anymore," West said. "I gave it to Cliff Wilson and Cliff's in jail."

When Landrum passed on the message, Lee had yet another idea. "Ask Vic if he could get them robes from Wilson's wife."

Landrum thought Norman Lee had become more trouble than the bad boys he had to deal with in Youth Court. He dropped his pursuit of the Klan robes, even though Lee insisted that they were needed for a Klan renaissance.

"The Klan ain't dead," Lee said. "Dubie and me got to be inactive because of this Masonite stuff, but the Klan's still got life."

Landrum regularly turned in reports to the FBI about his conversations with the Lee brothers. A few days after Norman Lee gave up on efforts to get the ceremonial robes, Landrum had a brief talk with his brother. Dubie Lee assured him of his innocence in the Masonite killing and claimed to be confining his activity to "farming and minding my own business."

"You been to any Klan meetings lately?" Landrum asked.

"Hell, no," Dubie said. "I'm too busy keeping out of trouble."

≈

HEARTENED BY Sessum's conviction, within a month the state put Henry deBoxtel on trial for murder in the same Hattiesburg courtroom. During the jury-selection process, deBoxtel's lawyers, Arrington and Percy Quinn, rejected one potential juror on the grounds that he belonged to the NAACP. They accepted another Black man, however. During a recess, Bowers offered an interesting observation that was picked up by reporters covering the trial. "We liked his looks because he had a round African head. He's a real cute little nigger."

After Pitts's appearance—the centerpiece of the state's case—deBoxtel's attorneys argued that Pitts's testimony failed to describe any murderous activity by deBoxtel during the raid. They contended that Pitts traveled in the car with Sessum that night; though he said deBoxtel's car had been deployed to attack the store, he could not claim to have seen deBoxtel destroy anything.

After conferring for less than two hours, the jury reported it was "hopelessly deadlocked." Judge Stanton Hall, who had presided over the Sessum case, sent the panel to dinner with instructions to continue deliberations. They came back to the courtroom later that night, still split "six to six" over guilt or acquittal. The judge declared a mistrial, and the operator of the Chow House in Ellisville—one of Bowers's closest associates—escaped conviction.

Afterward, the Forrest County sheriff, Gene Walters, concluded that the state "never put deBoxtel at the Dahmer house. Pitts put him at the store, but not down at the house where Dahmer was killed. I think that was the difference in the two cases."

≈

UNDETERRED BY THE hung jury in the deBoxtel case, the prosecutors moved ahead with the series of trials they planned against other Klansmen. At the same time, the Justice Department turned up the pressure by obtaining from a federal grand jury new indictments for conspiracy in the Dahmer firebombing against sixteen members of the White Knights.

Next up in state court would be the imperial wizard himself. He had allegedly ordered the hit but had not gone on the raid; as a result, Bowers would be charged with arson, but not murder. The trial would take place in May, and the star witness would again be Pitts.

In setting the scene earlier for the extensive use of Pitts by the prosecution, the *Laurel Leader-Call* had also speculated about his safety. "The state is painfully aware of the fact that a bullet through the head or heart of its prized package could change in an instant the complexion of the series of trials scheduled here in connection with the nationally-publicized Vernon Dahmer case. The roosting place of the key witness between court appearances has remained as closely guarded as the man himself. Every precaution is being taken to discourage potential sharpshooters and snipers."

Actually, Bowers's defense team, led by Arrington, knew exactly where Pitts's "roosting place" was located. It had been at the Alamo Plaza Motor Courts Motel on a major highway in Jackson. In the 1950s, when motor inns were a fad, the Alamo Plaza reigned as a desirable destination, but it had lost much of its allure by the end of the next decade. Deeming the place a satisfactory and inexpensive site, U.S. marshals installed Pitts in a room in the motel and looked the other way when his girlfriend came to visit. With Pitts's guard down, Arrington hired a photographer to capture pictures of Pitts and his friend, wearing a two-piece bathing suit, frolicking in the motel pool.

Once Pitts had told the court of hearing Bowers call for Dahmer's elimination at a Klan meeting outside Laurel a month before the fatal attack, he was subjected to a cross-examination by Arrington. The attorney began by suggesting, "So you've become the maharajah of the Alamo?"

"The what?" Pitts wondered.

"The maharajah of the Alamo," Arrington repeated.

"You mean in Texas?"

"I mean in Jackson, Mississippi."

"No sir. I don't believe so," Pitts sputtered.

Pitts's credibility was further undermined by a medical officer at a state hospital in Laurel who said he had once treated the witness for "pituitary giantism." He explained that Pitts had an abnormal head, which resulted in a "massively enlarged jaw which has increased progressively in size and interfered with the alignment of his teeth." Bowers's defense team figured the strategy would play well in the region, where a term like "pituitary giantism" sounded to unlettered listeners like some sort of perversion. Southern politics had a history of candidates being tarred by opponents for having daughters who "matriculated" in college and went on to become "thespians" in New York.

While Pitts was portrayed as a sybarite with an outsize head, Bowers cultivated a courtroom image of a mild-mannered Christian gentlemen. He sat quietly at the defense table, dressed in a suit, gently nodding in satisfaction as character witnesses testified to his good works, which included teaching Sunday school at the Hillcrest Baptist Church.

Before the case went to the jury, Forrest County district attorney Jim Finch tried to redeem Pitts's testimony by pointing out that there was no deal between Pitts and the prosecutors that would enable him to escape imprisonment. During redirect questioning, Finch asked Pitts, "You know where you're going when you get out of Federal custody, don't you?"

"Yes sir."

"And that's to Parchman prison?"

"Yes sir." Pitts had already pleaded guilty to state charges of murder in the Dahmer case and for kidnapping Jack Watkins as well.

Finch paused dramatically, then asked, "You know the Klan's rule for handling anyone who gives the kind of testimony you've given here?"

"Yes, I do."

"What's the penalty?"

"Death," Pitts said. Although he had an active role in Dahmer's murder and had taken part in other Klan crimes, Pitts testified he had become a state witness because "I couldn't go along with the things being planned in Jones County—the killing and murdering and things."

The jury deliberated for twenty-two hours. Eleven members of the panel voted to convict Bowers, but they were thwarted by one juror who held out for acquittal. A mistrial was declared on May 18. Despite their disappointment, the Forrest County prosecutors resolved to stick to their schedule of trials into the summer.

The imperial wizard remained free, but it was obvious that the

White Knights units in Jones County had been decimated by the defections of Billy Roy Pitts and others, constant dissension in the ranks, the conviction of Sessum, and the prospect of new trials.

Rather than making an attempt to rebuild his forces in his hometown, Bowers shifted his attention some fifty miles to the north, to the area around Meridian where four years earlier the White Knights first won infamy with the triple murder in Neshoba County. As in that 1964 operation, originally designed to eliminate the bearded Jewish outsider Michael Schwerner, Bowers's next target for terror would be Mississippi Jews.

CHAPTER 24

To Bowers and his followers, Jews represented another "Other." Along with African Americans and Catholics, they were anathema to the Klan's ideals of an Anglo-Saxon civilization and inimical to their brand of Christianity. There was more than a speck of the Third Reich in the White Knights' doctrine, and Bowers sometimes accentuated their attitude with Nazi salutes.

After the White Knights left behind a trail of evidence in the assault on the Dahmer home that led to the string of prosecutions, many members of the Jones County Klan lost their thirst for violence. Seeing his organization demoralized and disintegrating, the imperial wizard looked for new targets to strike in order to reinvigorate his forces. Synagogues and the homes of prominent Jews seemed to him to be logical objectives.

Actually, the White Knights' most infamous offensive had been triggered by animosity toward the civil rights volunteers. It rankled the Klan that so many of the college students involved in Freedom Summer were Jewish. When Schwerner, Goodman, and Chaney were put to death in Neshoba County it demonstrated the depth of the Klan's anti-Semitism and racism.

Three years later, a new disciple for Bowers appeared at the imperial wizard's door. Thomas Tarrants was a twenty-year-old with a hatred of Jews. He already had a record for harassing Blacks and Jews in his home state of Alabama after dropping out of high school to work for a group known as the Christian Military Defense League, a gang of racists in Mobile influenced by older associates of J. B. Stoner's anti-Semitic National States' Rights Party. The group perceived a Jewish threat to the South, a belief reinforced by a kernel of intelligence they learned at their meetings: Karl Marx had been a Jew.

As Tarrants would write, "I believed America was being undermined by Communists, socialists, liberals, and civil rights leaders who were influenced by a secret Jewish conspiracy intent on gaining control of the world."

Having escaped with probation for a federal charge in Alabama for possession of an illegal weapon, Tarrants moved to Laurel in 1967 to apply for a job at Masonite. Conveniently, Bowers's living quarters in his Sambo Amusement Company lay next door. Tarrants sought out the imperial wizard and told him of his willingness to attack Jews. Gladdened to find this enthusiastic acolyte, Bowers deputized him to serve as a one-man terror unit who would operate outside of Jones County because relatively few Jews lived in the Piney Woods region.

＝

DESPITE MISSISSIPPI'S REPUTATION as a haven for Protestant peckerwoods dedicated to the preservation of segregation, there were strong Jewish outposts in the state's larger cities of Jackson and Meridian as well as in communities along the Mississippi River, where immigrant Jewish peddlers from Europe had settled in the nineteenth century. In many cases, their descendants grew into prosperous merchants. Several synagogues in the state nurtured large congregations, and Jews lived comfortably as neighbors beside Baptists, Methodists, and Episcopalians.

Most of these residents accepted identification as Jews but were troubled to be thought of as aliens. There was a strong desire among

Mississippi Jews to assimilate into the general population, to share conventional views about politics and social issues. In the 1960s, the civil rights movement created a dichotomy for them. Given the history of discrimination that afflicted the Jewish people, there was a natural tendency to sympathize with anyone who suffered from prejudice. At the same time, the arrival in Mississippi of Jewish students determined to beat down the walls of segregation linked the Mississippi Jews with an unpopular cause in the state. There were awkward moments when liberal rabbis spoke out against Mississippi's racial mores to a congregation with conservative members embarrassed by the presence of the civil rights workers.

In the South during that period, bigotry was not practiced exclusively against Blacks. In the years immediately following the *Brown v. Board of Education* decision, dozens of bombs were planted not only in Black churches but at synagogues and Jewish community centers. Dynamite was discovered before it exploded at temples in Charlotte and Gastonia, North Carolina, but bombers later damaged the Nashville Jewish Center and a synagogue in Miami on the same day. Then, in 1958, the Temple in Atlanta, the spiritual center for the city's redoubtable Jewish population, was struck by fifty sticks of dynamite. Jews across the South realized that they, too, were vulnerable.

Tarrants chose Jackson's Temple Beth Israel for his first attack three months after meeting Bowers. He had a lone accomplice, his girlfriend, Kathy Ainsworth. The attractive elementary-school teacher was an anomaly in Klan circles, a woman belonging to an organization dominated by men. She was married to a health-club manager in Jackson but had become secretly paired with Tarrants because of their mutual loathing of Blacks and Jews. Her husband and her friends knew little of her extremist beliefs. And none of them knew of her double life: a popular instructor of fifth-grade children by day, a terrorist by night.

Under the cover of darkness, on the night of September 18, 1967, the couple left a load of dynamite attached to a burning fuse at the synagogue and sped away before it exploded. The blast shook houses

blocks away and collapsed a wall of the building. Windows were shattered, a water pipe was blown out, and several rooms were ruined by
the man-made storm.

Temple Beth Israel was selected because of its prominence in
the state capital. Its rabbi, Perry Nussbaum, a native Canadian, was
known to hold views that clashed with the racial sentiments of much
of white Jackson as well as some of his own synagogue's members.
During the wave of church burnings around Mississippi in 1964,
Nussbaum had helped found a Committee of Concern, a biracial
group composed of people from different faiths working to rebuild
the burned-out houses of worship.

The bombing of Temple Beth Israel caused greater public outrage than the destruction of scores of Black churches around the
state. It also presented a fresh challenge to the FBI. Within days of
the attack, Al Binder, a member of the congregation, met with Roy
K. Moore to discuss the case. Moore explained that many of the
FBI breakthroughs in the battle against the Klan had come through
paid informants. For some of the information, the payments were
handsome. Without making a direct appeal for contributions,
Moore told his visitor the FBI funds were limited. The implication
was clear. He felt wealthy members of the congregation should be
willing to help.

The conversation served as the origin for another extralegal
effort by the FBI. Although it was not widely known at the time, FBI
agents had already been charged with the authority to go beyond
conventional means in their investigations through the domestic-
intelligence program code-named COINTELPRO. Just as the
bureau had felt justified in calling in the Mafia hit man Gregory
Scarpa to beat information out of Lawrence Byrd, the FBI was now
prepared to work with Jewish leaders to establish a slush fund to
pay for questionable activities that had the potential to eradicate
the bombers as so many disagreeable insects. Eventually, an informal call for contributions went out to prominent Jews around the
state from a network of people who supported B'nai B'rith's Anti-
Defamation League. Top secrecy surrounded the endeavor.

≈

TARRANTS BRANCHED OUT from his campaign against the Jews to plant a bomb at the home of a white dean at Tougaloo College, a predominantly Black institution outside Jackson that hosted civil rights workshops. No one was injured, but the attack sent new ripples of fear through the capital city. A month later, violence returned to the Piney Woods. With Bowers as his guide, Tarrants went on a reconnaissance mission with the imperial wizard to case the home of an NAACP activist, the Reverend Allen Johnson. The next night, Tarrants left a bomb in the carport of the minister's home. When it detonated, it destroyed the carport, an automobile, and part of the house. Rev. Johnson and his family, sleeping in their bedrooms, escaped injury and lived to welcome Dr. Martin Luther King Jr. to their renovated house the next year.

Kathy Ainsworth accompanied her boyfriend on the next raid, in Jackson. They singled out a Methodist layman identified as an integrationist because of his association with the Committee of Concern. His name was Bob Kochtitzky—it sounded Jewish. The bomb destroyed part of the two-story house but failed to hurt its inhabitants.

Rabbi Nussbaum was the next target. Tarrants and Ainsworth delivered dynamite to his house two nights before Thanksgiving, then drove slowly and inconspicuously away from the nicely groomed neighborhood before their package exploded. Nussbaum and his wife survived, but were shaken by the experience. Indignant, the rabbi demanded that the FBI put a stop to the terror. In response, the agents moved the Nussbaums to a motel under a fictitious name.

The next day, about fifty members of Jackson's Jewish community met at a popular downtown motel to determine a course of action. There were calls to form a vigilante group in order to kill Klan suspects. One man had a more modest proposal: hire a Mafia mobster to come to Jackson and "break some arms and legs." The group decided on a more sophisticated approach. They pledged to raise $25,000 anonymously to augment reward money already put up by the city of Jackson.

≈

THE OPERATION AGAINST the Jews almost came to an abrupt halt five days before Christmas, when a night marshal in the little Mississippi town of Collins grew suspicious about a car with Alabama license plates and with two men inside, parked at a closed service station. Tarrants and his patron, the imperial wizard, had come to Collins to rake with bullets the home of a Black minister. Before Tarrants and Bowers could complete their mission the marshal stopped to inspect the car and discovered the visitors had a .45-caliber machine gun. The men were arrested and Tarrants charged with illegal possession of a dangerous weapon. However, the pair was released on bond before authorities made a connection between Tarrants and the bombing campaign.

The action moved to Meridian, once the state's second-largest municipality, a hub for highways and railroads ninety miles east of Jackson. The city had always had a substantial Jewish population, made up of wealthy businessmen descended from German Jews who arrived in Meridian a century earlier. The Threefoot Building, a seventeen-story structure that towered over downtown, took its name from the American translation of Dreifus, a family of German Jews. Meridian Jews had also built an opera house and another "skyscraper," the eleven-story Lamar Hotel. They worshipped at a synagogue with the same name as the one in Jackson, Temple Beth Israel.

Although some of the team that executed the three civil rights volunteers in nearby Neshoba County were from Meridian—including the assassin Alton Wayne Roberts and renegade members of the Meridian police force—there was not a great deal of apprehension among members of the synagogue's congregation when Stoner, the leader of the National States' Rights Party, came to town to whip up his own flock in a series of rallies brimming with anti-Semitic remarks. However, the local rabbi, Milton Schlager, was concerned. He had befriended Schwerner, who used Meridian for the base of his Freedom Summer activities and he believed danger for Jews still lurked in the area.

In May 1968, Al Binder, the Jacksonian who had met with the FBI chief following the temple attack there, was invited to speak at a B'nai B'rith meeting in Meridian. He warned the group, "Listen to your rabbi. Take him seriously. He knows what he's talking about. I know from my experiences in Jackson."

Less than four weeks later, Klansmen struck at the Meridian temple, a modern complex that housed a sanctuary, a religious-education building, and a recreational facility, in a neighborhood lush with woods. The bomb blew through the education building's roof, knocked down a wall, and left a large carpet of broken glass. That night Tarrants had a new partner, Danny Joe Hawkins, a White Knight from Jackson with a well-deserved reputation for violence. Though Tarrants was not yet known to investigators, both the FBI and Jackson police considered Hawkins a suspect in the latest attack. When officers had attempted to question him earlier, he had cursed and threatened to kill them. Bowers liked his style and added Hawkins to his tiny cadre of self-styled sappers-at-large in Jackson and Meridian.

To confront the threat, Meridian Jews turned to law enforcement for help. At one time, it was thought that as many as half of the eighty-five members of the Meridian police force were either Klansmen or sympathizers of the Invisible Empire. But the police chief, Roy Gunn, upset over the unrest the Klan was causing, had turned from segregationist to stern moralist, and had purged his department of troublemakers and won the trust of Jewish citizens. He also adopted FBI extralegal tactics. Gunn ordered a squad of policemen he called "blackshirts" to intimidate local Klansmen by blowing up low-level bombs near their homes or shooting into their windows at night.

Meanwhile, the FBI beefed up its presence in Meridian. When a Jewish delegation met with agents they asked what was needed to break the Klan. They heard the same answer Moore had given in Jackson: money to buy information. The agents were assured that concerned Jews would provide the funds.

═══

THE ARRANGEMENT AMONG the FBI, Meridian police, and worried Jews led to unusual negotiations with the Roberts brothers, two of the most menacing Klan figures in the Meridian area. Alton Wayne Roberts had already been tried and found guilty in the Neshoba case; he was free on bond while his conviction was appealed. Raymond Roberts did not have his brother's criminal record, but authorities believed he was also involved in night-riding exercises.

Jewish leaders involved in raising the funds were convinced that local toughs were responsible for the synagogue bombing in Meridian. In a meeting with Chief Gunn and Mayor Al Green, members of the Jewish delegation were asked if they would be willing to buy "bodies" rather than information. It was suggested that a professional assassin from a northern state could be imported to have the brothers "liquidated." According to a memo written about the meeting, A. I. "Bee" Botnick of New Orleans, the regional director of the Anti-Defamation League, had a better idea. Why not use the money to turn the Robertses into informers? Botnick "told the mayor and the chief to take the two Roberts brothers out on a dark road at night and beat the hell out of them to within an inch of their lives," the memo reported. "He said that if they would do this and then offer money, the Roberts brothers would talk."

By this time, Tarrants had become a suspect in the synagogue bombings, after news of his arrest with Bowers in Collins trickled up the FBI vine of intelligence. He fled to North Carolina, a fugitive.

To expedite discussions with the Roberts brothers, the FBI approached their attorney, Tom Hendricks, a retired FBI agent himself. The lawyer concluded that persuading the brothers to talk might be a way for him to clear his clients of suspicion in the synagogue case and make some money at the same time. The Roberts brothers and Hendricks agreed to attend a "prayer meeting" at the home of Meridian FBI agent Frank Watts. The language was not what would have normally been heard at church. Watts addressed the brothers as "sons of bitches" and warned they would be dogged relentlessly by investigators unless they cooperated. After three hours of back-and-forth threats and talk, the Roberts brothers indicated they might be willing to give information privately but would never testify publicly. The price of their cooperation would be steep. Negotiations would continue in a few days.

To soften up the brothers, the FBI picked up Alton Wayne and wordlessly drove him to a spot in Neshoba County where they knew he had murdered the civil rights workers. Meridian police took the harassment a step further. A patrolman shot out a picture window in Raymond Roberts's house.

Through their attorney, the brothers offered to give the names of the two men who had bombed the Meridian synagogue and now planned to kill a Jewish businessman in the city. In exchange, they expected tens of thousands of dollars in cash. Hendricks counted on collecting $10,000 himself. Nearly two weeks after the Temple Beth Israel bombing in Meridian, the brothers, their lawyer, and the authorities began a series of clandestine meetings in a trailer at the dead end of a gravel road well outside of town. These were tense sessions. After the officers disarmed both brothers of the guns they were carrying, they often argued and bargained for hours. The Robertses confirmed that Tarrants and Hawkins had bombed the temple and they agreed to help set a trap when the two men came again to Meridian to kill.

Hours after one critical encounter with the Roberts brothers in the trailer, FBI agents Watts and Jack Rucker, his partner, along with a trusted police detective, Luke Scarbrough, met with I. A. Rosenbaum, the president of Meridian's Temple Beth Israel congregation. Rosenbaum said $25,000 in twenty-dollar bills would be flown immediately from Jackson to Meridian. When the money arrived, most of it was stored in a bank's safe-deposit box. That night the Roberts brothers and their lawyer met again with the FBI agents, and Scarbrough put $1,000 worth of twenty-dollar bills on the table. Gesturing toward the money, Watts told the brothers, "Over here, you've got money coming . . . or you can have your ass shot off one night." Alton Wayne gathered up the money and put it in his pockets. It would serve as a down payment. The rest would come after Tarrants and Hawkins fell into the trap.

Two days later, Raymond Roberts drove to a meeting with an unsuspecting Danny Joe Hawkins at a café between Meridian and Jackson. Raymond told Hawkins that the FBI had put heavy pressure on the two brothers. He appealed to Hawkins to schedule the next hit in Meridian at a time when he and Alton Wayne could arrange to have an airtight alibi.

Within a week, the terrorists targeted Meyer Davidson, a member of the Meridian temple who had been heavily involved in the campaign to raise reward money. Hawkins told Raymond Roberts that he and Tarrants would be coming soon to blow up Davidson's home. They would be driving Hawkins's green Buick Electra. They scheduled the bombing for June 27 to coincide with an appearance in Meridian by "Brother Dave" Gardner, a redneck comedian who specialized in racist jokes. The Klansmen figured that the large crowd Brother Dave usually attracted would require heavy details of police, far from Davidson's home.

Beforehand, the Roberts brothers each demanded $10,000 right away. After the cash was turned over to them, they revealed the plan to strike Davidson's house. On the night of June 27, a team of heavily armed FBI agents and officers from the Meridian police "blackshirts" fanned out quietly through the neighborhood. A demolition team from the Meridian Naval Air Station also waited in hiding near Davidson's house, which had been cleared of occupants. They maintained the vigil for nine hours, but the terrorists never came.

The next day, Raymond Roberts met with Tarrants and Hawkins, who explained they delayed the strike because they needed more time and money. It was rescheduled for Saturday night, June 29. That evening, the FBI and police established another stakeout surrounding Davidson's house. Roughly twenty blackshirts were deployed in drainage ditches and bushes. The FBI's Watts and Rucker commandeered a house across the street from the Davidson home, where they watched from a bedroom window. Other FBI agents and police officers waited in cars hidden around the neighborhood to block any attempts by the occupants of the green Buick to escape.

While the posse waited, the Roberts brothers met Tarrants at a Meridian truck stop and discovered he was accompanied by a pretty young woman—attired in provocative short shorts—instead of Hawkins. They were told that Hawkins had been replaced on the mission because Hawkins feared he was being watched too closely by the FBI. After finishing their business with Tarrants, the brothers went to a local honky-tonk, where they intended to start a fight that would draw enough attention to provide themselves an alibi. Inside the joint, called the Travelers Club, Raymond used a pay phone to call the police and tell them that Tarrants was on his way—with a woman he had never seen before.

At 12:45 a.m., Tom Tarrants and Kathy Ainsworth rode into an ambush.

≈

AFTER PARKING THE CAR near the Davidson home, Tarrants climbed out, clutching a gun in one hand and a package with the bomb in the other. He was met by a volley of gunfire. Staggering back to the car, wounded, he sought desperately to drive away. A wild chase lasted for fifteen blocks. The careening Buick was pierced repeatedly by bullets. Finally, a police car rammed the fleeing auto into a fire hydrant. Tarrants blundered out and tried to climb an electrified chain-link fence, only to be knocked to the ground by a shock and more shotgun blasts. When Watts got to the scene he saw a wounded man as bloody as if he had come from an abattoir. There is no way he will live, Watts thought.

Searching the car, police officers found a submachine gun, two loaded automatic pistols, a hand grenade, a canister of Mace, two hundred rounds of ammunition, fourteen blasting caps, a long length of fuse, a pair of handcuffs—and another grim surprise. Crumpled on the front floorboard lay the body of Kathy Ainsworth with a mortal gunshot wound in the back of her neck.

CHAPTER 25

A COUPLE OF DAYS BEFORE the Fourth of July 1968, Tom Landrum saw an acquaintance from the White Knights while shopping in a store in Ellisville. The man had always seemed reasonably levelheaded to Landrum. Though a Klansman from another county and a hard-core segregationist, he objected to the extreme measures of the White Knights and believed the campaign of murder and arson had proved counterproductive. "I didn't like those people getting shot up at Meridian," he told Landrum. "It was downright foolish going up there under the circumstances."

Landrum agreed that it had been another setback for the White Knights.

"I think the old White Knights are dead," the man declared. "There might always be some sort of underground Klan to try to keep things in place, but the old White Knights are dead."

～

THE KLAN TRIALS in Forrest County resumed later that month with a racially mixed jury, including three Blacks, to hear the case against Bill "Lightning" Smith. As testimony began, Ellie Dahmer described the attack on her home; FBI agents introduced evidence found at the scene; and Klansman T. Webber Rogers testified that Smith had attended meetings where the Dahmer project was planned. For the fifth time that year, Pitts gave a vivid account of the raid and identified Smith as the assailant who shot out the front window of the Dahmer house.

Rather than presenting character witnesses on behalf of their client, Smith's defense attorneys first called on several people to testify about the unattractive background of two of the state's witnesses. A couple from Covington County said they had seen Rogers with "a woman who was not his wife" near the Leaf River. Then two men claimed to have seen Pitts in New Orleans in the company of a woman other than his wife. A minister and two others told the jury about conduct that they felt displayed Pitts's "bad character."

In a departure from previous strategies, Smith's attorney, Carl Berry, called on the defendant to take the stand. Already balding at thirty-two, Smith appeared fretful. He acknowledged that he had joined the Klan at the request of his boss at the prosthetics store, Cliff Wilson, and said he had been inducted by four hooded men in a ceremony in November 1964 at Lawrence Byrd's farm. Though he declared he was bound by a White Knights oath never to disclose the identity of other Klan members, he went on to single out Bowers as the imperial wizard, Nix as the Klan's state investigator, and Sessum as an exalted cyclops. He volunteered the information that he had attended his last klavern meeting "about two months before the Dahmer incident" but insisted he had dropped out of the Klan shortly after the murder.

Recounting his short life in the White Knights, Smith said he had attended Klan meetings at his boss's firm, Laurel Brace and Limb, and admitted that he once enjoyed displaying a .45-caliber automatic army pistol to impress new members about the need to abide by the Klan oath.

He also confirmed that he owned a 12-gauge pump shotgun and used double-aught buckshot as ammunition for the weapon. The prosecutors smiled when they heard this testimony, for this was the gun whose spent shells the Landrum sons collected at the turkey shoot, similar to those found near the ruins of the Dahmer house. It turned out to be helpful evidence.

After spending a night sequestered, the jury returned a guilty verdict on the morning of July 19. Judge Stanton Hall, by now a veteran of the Klan trials, sentenced Smith to life imprisonment at the state penitentiary at Parchman.

≈

IT WAS TIME FOR the prosecutors to confront another formidable defendant, the Laurel Jaycees' "Man of the Year," on charges that he helped murder Vernon Dahmer. To present himself as a country club member rather than Klansman, Cliff Wilson hired a battery of respectable attorneys instead of relying on tired Klan lawyers.

Once Pitts had finished with his predictable testimony in which he starkly put Wilson at the scene of the firebombing, the defense team counterattacked. They did not dare call Wilson as a witness, but they summoned his wife, who swore that he had been sleeping in the bed with her the night the Dahmer house was set ablaze. They also presented eighteen witnesses—with elegant and honorable reputations—to attest to the sterling character of the defendant.

Torn by the conflicting testimony, the jury was unable to agree on either conviction or acquittal. Judge Hall was forced to declare another mistrial. But the judge refused to release Wilson on bond, and the prosecutors promised to hound the prosthesis maker until they could send him to prison. Jim Finch, the district attorney for Forrest County, had made his intentions clear after Bowers's trial ended without a conviction. "They can bring all the wizards and lizards and thugs from Jones County down here, and I still won't back off," he promised.

≈

LAWRENCE BYRD, the most enigmatic of all the Klan defendants, went into his trial bewildered that the FBI and the prosecutors would bring charges against him. Had he not given them a long statement—albeit under duress—that amounted to a crucial description of events surrounding the firebombing of Dahmer's home? Had he not set up Cecil Sessum for his interrogation by the FBI? And had he not shared other tidbits of information with his federal handlers during the period in which he cooperated with the FBI? "Seems like nobody gives a big fiddledy-fuck about me anymore," Byrd moaned to one of his friends. Instead of cutting him slack, the prosecutors were hell-bent on pressing charges against him even though he had never been near the Dahmer property.

To the FBI, Byrd had proved to be an undependable asset. He had disavowed his original statement—the product of his beating by Gregory Scarpa and his accomplices—and his behavior had become too unpredictable to trust.

By the time Byrd's trial began in Hattiesburg early in November, his lone ally in law enforcement, Chet Dillard, the former district attorney in Jones County, had lost in his quest for reelection and could offer no help.

Byrd would not face a murder charge. No one accused him of participating in the raid. But on the face of his own statement, Byrd had acted as a conspirator. He attended a Klan meeting where Bowers decreed death for Dahmer, and within hours of the attack he came to the aid of deBoxtel, who had abandoned Travis Giles's car near the Dahmer property. Byrd was formally charged with arson, and his statement became evidence against him in the trial. His defense in shambles, it took only twelve minutes for the jury to report a guilty verdict. Stunned by the rapidity of the judgment, Byrd was speechless when he heard Judge Hall's sentence: ten years' imprisonment in Parchman.

⁓

TOM LANDRUM'S MISSIVES to the FBI grew scarcer. There seemed to be little to report. In his few conversations with Klansmen, their talk was guarded and there was no mention of any plans to revive terrorist activity.

The last organized effort to have an impact in Laurel took place in the fall of 1968, when many of the Klansmen rallied behind the presidential campaign of Alabama governor George C. Wallace. The segregationist, who had tried to "stand in the schoolhouse door" to prevent integration at the University of Alabama in 1963, inveighed loudly against the federal government. He crooned a siren's song that stoked the anger of southerners upset over the march of desegregation orders. He also won support in the North. In 1968, Wallace ran as an independent candidate for president. But Asa Carter, the aide who had once written angry speeches for the governor that were tailored for southern audiences and who had advised Jimmy Swan in Mississippi the year before, was no longer at Wallace's side. Wallace wanted to be a national figure, not a provincial one.

"It's a sad day in the country when you can't talk about law and order unless they want to call you a racist. I tell you that's not true, and I resent it," Wallace said in his public appearances, his language sometimes garbled by the heat of his message. "They gonna have to pay attention because all people in this country, in the great majority, know the Supreme Court of our country has made it almost impossible to convict a criminal. You walk out of this building and someone knocks you in the head, that person will be out of jail if you don't watch out."

In a country traumatized by the assassinations of Martin Luther King Jr. and Robert Kennedy, widespread outbreaks of urban rioting, and unrest over the war in Vietnam, Wallace became a voice for voters unhappy over the course of modern history. He campaigned on his "law and order" platform and presented himself as the only candidate who appealed to those disgruntled voters.

His rhetoric throbbed with suggestions of violent reactions. "You elect me President," he promised, "and I go to California or I come to Tennessee and if a group of anarchists lay down in front of my automobile, it's gonna be the last one they ever gonna want to lay down in front of." Even as he appealed for support in states outside the South, he became an unofficial spokesman for the remnants of the Ku Klux Klan.

A few days before the election, Landrum dropped by B. F. Hinton's store. His front window was decorated with a large Wallace poster. "That's my man," Hinton told him, "and I'm proud to say my business is the George Wallace headquarters for Jones County." Landrum noticed that on a table Hinton had several books for sale that extolled the virtues of the Alabama governor.

Landrum learned that he had been assigned by Hinton to serve as a poll watcher for the Wallace interests in the Glade community near his home. "What am I supposed to do?" he asked. "I've never done that before."

"You just make sure you keep people 150 feet back from the voting box," Hinton said. "If you see anybody voting for somebody else, try to make sure they're voting for Wallace. Be sure no niggers cause trouble. And if you see any violations, call it to the attention of the person in charge of the box." He had a list of precincts, and Landrum saw that several other Klansmen had been appointed to work as poll watchers.

As an afterthought, Hinton asked if Landrum knew what had happened to his ceremonial Klan robe.

"Last I heard," Landrum said, "all that material was given to Cliff Wilson shortly before he got arrested."

"Aw, hell," Hinton said. "I wanted that robe as a souvenir."

"Well, then, you need to go see Mrs. Wilson."

"I don't want it that bad," Hinton said.

The reign of the White Knights might have been expiring, but the 1968 election was a rare, satisfying moment for them. The Alabama insurgent won roughly two-thirds of the votes in Jones County and swept through Mississippi like a torrent in a thunderstorm, winning 63 percent of the statewide vote. In the end, Wallace carried four other hard-core southern states: Alabama, Arkansas, Louisiana, and South Carolina.

≈

BEFORE THE CLOSE of the year, Frank Lyons, accused of being one of the eight night riders, was also put on trial and the pattern of testimony was repeated. Pitts told his story, which put Lyons in the car driven by deBoxtel that targeted the Dahmer store. Pitts was then subjected to another withering cross-examination that picked apart his trustworthiness. Lyons's jury split, six to six, resulting in yet another mistrial.

By this time, Pitts had begun to unravel. After pleading guilty to taking part in the Dahmer raid he had been sentenced in state court to life in prison for murder as well as ten years' imprisonment on an arson charge; he also faced five years in prison on a federal charge of conspiracy. It was his hope that his cooperation would mitigate the severity of his sentences. However, his role as the chief government witness in the Dahmer trials had led to a life in purgatory. As a witness, he had been tested repeatedly by fierce cross-examinations. He heard the honesty of his testimony questioned. Admittedly, he had been a scoundrel for much of his life, but after months of torment after the Dahmer attack and the Watkins kidnapping, he believed he had reached a constructive turning point when he decided to cooperate with the FBI. Now his commitment was being shredded in every courtroom appearance. He felt he was being taunted for his lack of education. Even the size of his head had been ridiculed.

Once he was moved from the Alamo Plaza Motor Courts by the U.S. marshals, Pitts found himself shuttled among drab motel rooms in New Orleans and out-of-the-way towns in Texas. He had little freedom of movement, and he felt cut off from his mistress, Laura Welborn, as well as members of his family. When he was able to talk with Laura or his wife, Bunnie, by phone, the women battered him with complaints about his absence or his inability to provide financial support.

Even the marshals, who had been lenient while he was holed up in Jackson, turned on him. One of them told Pitts he was nothing more than "a 75 dollar a week pimp for the FBI." In telephone calls with his mistress, he complained repeatedly that one marshal named Tully Reynolds was drinking heavily and had become especially abusive, threatening to move him from the relative comfort of a motel room into a jail. Pitts's depression descended at the worst time of year— Christmas. He felt abandoned, alone, and unappreciated for all of the testimony he had given and the risks he had taken. On Christmas Eve, Laura Welborn made three frantic telephone calls to one of the FBI agents working on the case. She said Pitts had been crying during their phone conversations and had begged her to ask the FBI to intervene; otherwise, he feared "something might happen" at the travel lodge where he was staying that night.

Earlier in the month, when the marshals relaxed their guard, Pitts had somehow managed to buy a .32-caliber revolver from a store in Longview, Texas. Three nights before the end of the year, he was sequestered at the tawdry Dixie Motel in Tyler, Texas, when his guardians heard a shot in his room. Hurrying inside, they found the government's star witness lying facedown on the floor in a puddle of his own blood. He had left a sealed envelope containing a note on his bed. It was a sad and ungrammatical message, filled with misspellings, addressed to Bob Lee and another agent of the FBI:

> Give This to My Mother & dad and for The F.B.I. ever thing that I told in cort is True. Some one over here or over there is lie-ing To Me. I can't go on like This. Mr. Tully Reynolds Took My Money and wont Let Me see Laura. I love her so much I love My Two Boy's Travis Ray and Rickey I love My Mother and dad. I sent a true statement of What Went on over here. I cant live without Laura and My two Boy's I love Bunnie to so you see what one hafe of My trouble is The other is Tully But I for Give him for it. I am praying that God will for Give Me. May God be With you all . . .

Apparently, he had wanted to end his life with a bullet fired into his heart. But as with so many projects he had undertaken in his life, he failed again. The shot left a gaping wound—though authorities later described it as "superficial"—in his chest but missed the mark. Rushed by ambulance to a local hospital, Pitts recovered. He would survive and testify again, and again, and again.

≈

SAM BOWERS WAS becoming equally experienced in the courtroom. In January 1969, the prosecutors in Hattiesburg made another effort to convict the imperial wizard. Throughout the trial Bowers sat quietly, wearing a confident expression even though he faced two Blacks on the jury. After a fractious afternoon of deliberation, the jurors were sequestered.

While they slept, Laurel was rocked by an accident as apocalyptic as a scene from a grade B movie. A Southern Railway freight train conveying sixteen tank cars, each filled with twenty-three thousand gallons of liquid petroleum, derailed at 4 a.m. in a Black neighborhood, setting off a succession of explosions. Concussions rattled windows and doors across the town, and flames leaped heavenward with such intensity that the firelight could be seen in Jackson, eighty-five miles away. Along the tracks, the inferno quickly consumed the houses and stores constructed with cheap wood and corrugated tin, and the conflagration spread for blocks. Before it could be brought under control, hundreds of homes, five churches, six schools, and many stores were damaged or destroyed.

By morning, there was speculation that the firestorm had been symbolic, a biblical curse visited on Laurel to make the city pay for the Klan violence and the strife at Masonite. That afternoon, two members of Bowers's jury held out for acquittal, resulting in another mistrial.

≈

JUDGE HALL CONVENED the second trial of Cliff Wilson a few days later. Though Pitts would be tagged a "confessed liar" because of his earlier denials of involvement in the raid, his testimony nevertheless proved devastating. He identified Wilson as an officer in the White Knights who held the title of "county investigator." But the real drama of Pitts's testimony came in a long colloquy between the witness and a young Forrest County prosecuting attorney, James Dukes, who was pinch-hitting for the seasoned Jim Finch. The district attorney had collapsed from exhaustion after opening arguments on the first day.

Following up on Dukes's short, skillful questions, Pitts's simple answers had the effect of a jackhammer when he described the actions of the raiding party.

Q. After you got your instructions, then what happened?
A. We went to the Vernon Dahmer home in Cliff Wilson's car, and Henry deBoxtel followed in the Ford car with his men. As we turned into the driveway of the Vernon Dahmer house I looked back and saw that the Ford car turned in toward the store. It was close by the house.

Q. All right?
A. Then we all jumped out of the car real quick, out of the Cliff Wilson car and Bill Smith started shooting the picture window out of the house, out of the Vernon Dahmer home. Cecil Sessum took the jugs of gasoline and I ran with him to the front of the house. As I was running toward the front of the house Cliff Wilson was running toward the carport of the house.

Q. What did he have?
A. He had two jugs of gasoline, a shotgun and a pistol.

Q. All right, and he was to take care of the [Dahmer] cars?
A. Yes sir.

Q. Then what happened there in front of the house?
A. Bill Smith had shot the window out in front of the house. Cecil Sessum uncapped the jugs of gasoline and took a pocket knife from his

pocket and jabbed holes in the top of some of the jugs and he threw the jugs into the living room of the house, or in what I believed was the living room of the house.

Q. Did he throw them where this window had been?

A. Yes sir, and I had crouched down in front of the house next to the house while he was throwing the jugs of gasoline into the house. He had a gasoline-soaked rag wrapped around a forked stick that he took and lit—this torch that he had made—and throwed it into the house and ignited the gasoline.

Q. What happened when he threw that torch in there after the gasoline?

A. Huge flames of fire began roaring through the house.

Q. And then what happened?

A. Then we ran back to the car and there was continuous shooting going on.

Q. Was the defendant, Cliff Wilson, there?

A. He was.

Q. Did it happen in his presence?

A. It did.

In his defense, Wilson again called on some of the same character witnesses who appeared at his first trial to vouch for his good name, an elite group that included a physician, a school principal, a minister, a banker, and the state president of the Jaycees. Wilson's wife repeated her testimony that the defendant had been sleeping in the bed with her when the night riders struck the Dahmer home.

This time, however, the word of Pitts—a ruffian, an unfaithful husband, a low-level employee at a local shop—was given more credibility than the testimony of witnesses from Laurel's grander social circles. The jury deliberated six hours before returning a guilty verdict, and the judge gave Wilson a life sentence.

≈

THE PROSECUTIONS and convictions brought the White Knights to a standstill. Landrum had no meetings to attend and little information to impart to the FBI. His confidential reports tailed off in early 1969 to a few short paragraphs dealing with random contacts with members of his old klavern.

His last memo to the FBI contained accounts of a few conversations. Dubie Lee was still muttering about the Masonite situation and said he had participated in a "Scab City" parade in Laurel but never mentioned the Klan.

Landrum wrote that he saw one fellow who asked if there had been any Klan activity going on. "I said if there had, I hadn't heard of it. He said he heard they might start some meetings when the weather got better. . . . I saw Norman Lee. He said something might break and asked would I be interested. I told him to let me know, that my being interested would depend on what broke."

Landrum's final entry involved a chance encounter at an out-of-town store with a Klansman from another county whose name he didn't know. "He asked were things quiet in Jones County. I said yes. He said they were in Perry County, too."

Landrum eventually had a talk with Bob Lee at his office at the courthouse, where there was nothing suspicious about the FBI agent checking in with the Youth Court counselor. "Not much to tell you these days," Landrum said.

"I know that, Tom. No need to stay in regular contact anymore. But if anything comes up, we want you to be in touch."

Landrum felt relieved. Sitting at home with his wife that evening, he said, "Sweetheart, it looks like we've been put out of business."

"That's a good thing," Anne said. "I didn't mind the work, but I never could get the worry out of my mind. You know I worried that they might find you out. But at the same time, I was proud of what you did. You didn't have to do it. You didn't have to put yourself at risk, but you did, and as a result, I'd like to think our community is a better place. I like the thought of some of those men behind bars, even though I know more ought to be."

≈

WHILE STATE PROSECUTORS in Hattiesburg pursued the White Knights in their series of trials, the Justice Department delivered its own body blow to the organization in the spring of 1969 when a federal grand jury indicted sixteen members of the Jones County White Knights in connection with the Dahmer case. Pitts had pleaded guilty by this time, but the other seven men in the Dahmer raiding party faced new charges, along with Klan leaders Bowers and Nix and others, including the hapless Byrd. After preliminary motions, the government dropped charges against several of the defendants who had no direct role in the attack. U.S. district judge Dan Russell moved the trial upstate to Meridian, but relied on a jury pool from Hattiesburg. Eventually, twelve white jurors were chosen.

Before the trial began in April, Judge Russell got an anonymous threat; rather than being intimidated, he ordered U.S. marshals to protect the witnesses and the jurors. He also instructed the marshals to shackle the eleven remaining defendants in chains when they were transferred from their cells to the courtroom each day.

The trial followed a predictable path. Pitts named names and offered his firsthand recollection of the night riders' assault. His credibility was attacked by the defense. The defendants also relied on character witnesses and the testimony of wives and others who provided alibis.

The jury considered the case for eleven hours before reaching a muddled verdict on May 10. Travis Giles, Frank Lyons, and Lester Thornton were acquitted. The jury was unable to agree on a decision for Bowers, Nix, Sessum, deBoxtel, Wilson, Lightning Smith, or Charles Noble, resulting in a mistrial for them. The judge granted Byrd a mistrial because hearsay evidence had been presented against him.

Byrd, Sessum, Wilson, and Smith, who were already serving

prison sentences, were kept in custody and returned to Parchman. The others were released. But Bowers, Nix, deBoxtel, and Noble could not relax yet. Each man knew that he could be tried again.

In July, the imperial wizard was put on trial in Hattiesburg for the third time, charged again with the murder of Vernon Dahmer. Another integrated jury—eight whites and four Blacks—heard testimony from Pitts and others but became snarled when they tried to agree on a verdict. Eight voted to convict; four to acquit. Bowers escaped with his fourth mistrial in the Dahmer case—three in state courts and one in federal court.

Nevertheless, Bowers still had his federal conviction in the Neshoba County case hanging over him. His last appeal was exhausted in February 1970, when the U.S. Supreme Court declined to hear his case. That spring, Bowers turned himself in to federal authorities and was sent to McNeil Island penitentiary in Washington State to begin serving his ten-year sentence.

The White Knights of the Mississippi Ku Klux Klan essentially faded into oblivion. But a few of its most memorable figures would emerge, nearly thirty years later, in an eerie afterlife.

Epilogue

MOST OF THE CASES involving members of the White Knights ran their course over the next few years.

Somehow, Thomas Tarrants survived his wounds. He insisted that he had never belonged to the Klan, resisted offers of money and preferential treatment by the FBI if he would supply information on his criminal cohorts, and relied on a claim of insanity for his defense. In the fall of 1969 he was convicted of "the capital offense of attempting to place a bomb near a residence" and sentenced to serve thirty years at Parchman. He escaped from prison the next year, but was quickly captured. He began to read the Bible as a convict and by 1976 he had convinced authorities that his life had taken a "dramatic change" for the better. He was released into a program that allowed him to attend the University of Mississippi, where religious groups embraced him. Tarrants became a minister and wrote two books about his experiences. The second one, published in 2019, was called *Consumed by Hate, Redeemed by Love*.

Travis Buckley had his conviction in the kidnapping of Jack Watkins reversed by the state supreme court in 1969. With his ability to practice law restored, Buckley would continue to be retained by Klansmen.

Lawrence Byrd had his ten-year sentence commuted to five years by Governor John Bell Williams in September 1970. Shortly afterward, officials in Jones County supported his release and he won parole. He served less than two years altogether in prison and lived to work on charity projects in Jones County with another volunteer, retired FBI agent Bob Lee.

Jesse White, identified as an informant, escaped retaliation by the White Knights but wound up with a five-year prison sentence in 1970 for his role in the shooting of T. Webber Rogers. Billy Carr, who fired the shots that wounded Rogers, had received a similar sentence in 1968 in state court after being convicted of attempted murder as well as assault and battery.

Billy Roy Pitts, who was serving a five-year state sentence for accompanying Buckley on the mission to intimidate Watkins, was quietly paroled in September 1971. As part of a deal to reward him for acting as the chief prosecution witness in a number of White Knights cases, Pitts was freed from a life sentence for murder on the condition that he leave Mississippi. He disappeared into Louisiana, where he would live without notice until a sudden turn of events twenty-seven years later.

Cliff Wilson got out of prison just before Christmas in 1972. In a move that caused controversy, the new governor, Bill Waller, released him into a program allowing the former "Man of the Year" to work by day at a charity hospital that served Laurel and to go home at night. The governor explained that the artificial arms and legs Wilson made were desperately needed there. Before Waller was elected, he had been one of the lawyers representing Wilson on his appeal. Wilson, meanwhile, demonstrated his return to the good graces of his hometown by becoming "born-again" during a service at a Baptist church in Laurel, where he walked down the aisle and accepted Jesus Christ as his Savior.

Cecil Sessum and "Lightning" Smith were both paroled in 1978. They had spent more time in Parchman, the state penitentiary in the Mississippi Delta, than any of the other Klansmen who went on the raid at the Dahmer home. Sessum and Smith had each been given life sentences but served less than ten years.

≈

IN THE END, all four men who rode in Wilson's car and attacked the Dahmer home served time. None of the other four—charged with burning down the adjacent grocery and terrorizing Dahmer's elderly aunt—was convicted. As the Forrest County sheriff observed when Henry deBoxtel's trial ended in a deadlock, it seemed that the juries reserved guilty verdicts solely for those who firebombed Dahmer's house and caused his death.

For two decades there was no movement in Mississippi for further prosecution of the Klansmen who had brought carnage and terror to the state in the 1960s. Then in 1990 a cry arose from Black neighborhoods in Jackson to put Byron De La Beckwith back on trial for the murder of Medgar Evers. Two mistrials had taken place in 1964, but there was no statute of limitations to prevent another attempt to try him. After a Jackson newspaper reported that a state segregationist agency, the Mississippi Sovereignty Commission, had spent public money to screen an earlier jury on behalf of Beckwith's defense at the same time that a district attorney was prosecuting him, reopening the case was deemed justified.

Despite the widespread belief that Beckwith had gotten away with murder, the suspect never tried to skulk into the background. He appeared as a guest speaker at Klan rallies around the state and ran for lieutenant governor, and his freedom served as an irritant to forces for racial reconciliation. He won a bit of notoriety in 1973 when he was arrested with a time bomb in his car, on his way to the New Orleans home of A. I. Botnick, the regional director of the Anti-Defamation League. For that caper Beckwith served three years in a Louisiana prison.

After a series of legal skirmishes, Beckwith faced a third trial in 1994 for the murder of Evers. This time he found himself, at the age of seventy-three, confronted with an unsympathetic public. Many people in Mississippi were eager to try to redeem their state for its history of racist violence. In a dramatic trial in Jackson that relived some of the most memorable and murderous moments of the civil rights campaign, Beckwith was convicted. He spent the last seven years of his life in prison.

Encouraged by the outcome of Beckwith's trial, prosecutors pursued other well-known suspects in cold cases from the same era. They were old men by now, but their records as Klansmen were chilling. One of the targets was Edgar "Preacher" Killen, the hatchet-faced sawmill operator and part-time minister who was thought to have rounded up the White Knights gang that executed the trio of civil rights activists in Neshoba County in 1964. Killen was hounded by investigations for years and finally brought to trial when he was eighty. On his way into the courtroom in a wheelchair, he lashed out angrily at photographers and reporters with his fists and snarls. On the forty-first anniversary of the murders, on June 21, 2005, he was convicted of manslaughter. Killen spent the remainder of his life in Parchman, dying there thirteen years later.

〜

PERHAPS THE MOST audacious step in the search for justice came in 1998 when authorities in Forrest County, with the assistance of the state attorney general's office, made a decision to again go after the imperial wizard.

After serving six years in federal prison for his conviction in the Neshoba case, Sam Bowers had returned to Laurel, his Invisible Empire destroyed and his livelihood reduced to hustling pinball and vending machines. Nevertheless, he retained recognition across the state, remembered as the man who once led the most violent cells of the Klan. In fact, Bowers himself yearned for a place in history. In 1983, he submitted to a remarkable series of interviews with the Mississippi Department of Archives and History that were to be sealed for fifty years. The lengthy document became public prematurely after it was subpoenaed. In one passage Bowers appeared to

be saying that he had been willing to go to prison to protect the freedom of another key conspirator in the Neshoba case. The implication was clear: he was speaking of Preacher Killen.

With Beckwith doomed to die behind bars (his death would
come in 2001) and investigators nibbling at Killen, members of
Vernon Dahmer's family started a campaign to seek justice for his
murder. Vernon Dahmer Jr. appeared on television, appealing to
Mississippi citizens to come forward with information on the case.
Though the Dahmers' effort had the support of Mississippi attorney
general Mike Moore, the revival of the case proceeded slowly, in fits
and starts, through the late 1990s, by the local prosecutor's office.

Then there were two significant developments. Jerry Mitchell,
an investigative reporter for the *Clarion-Ledger* in Jackson who had
devoted his career to breaking news stories that helped solve civil
rights cold cases, discovered that a vital witness in the Dahmer
case—Billy Roy Pitts—was living in a small south Louisiana town;
unaccountably, he had been freed from his prison term for kidnapping and never served a minute of his life sentence for murder.
Pitts was brought back to Mississippi by authorities to reprise in the
courtroom his tale of Bowers's death sentence for Dahmer and the
subsequent raid that took his life.

An important new witness appeared, almost out of nowhere: Bob
Stringer, who had worked for Bowers as a teenager and heard the
order for a Code Four. As an act of repentance, Stringer was ready to
tell of his experience at John's Restaurant in the winter of 1966. Three
decades later, Stringer suffered from a gambling addiction and had
enrolled in a recovery program calling on him to make amends to
someone he had wronged. Stringer concluded that he had wronged
the Dahmer family by failing to implicate Bowers for his role in
Dahmer's death. After a number of agonizing telephone calls and
private meetings between Stringer—accompanied by friends—and
two of Dahmer's sons, Stringer agreed to testify.

In May 1998, a Forrest County grand jury indicted Bowers and
Charles Noble for murder and arson and Deavours Nix for arson. By

this time, Henry deBoxtel, who figured in the deadly conversation Stringer overheard and drove one of the cars filled with night riders, was dead.

Judge Richard McKenzie ordered Bowers and Noble held on $200,000 bond but released Nix on his own recognizance. Nix had appeared in the courtroom in a wheelchair equipped with an oxygen tank. He said he had cancer and his lungs had been burned by radiation treatments. Not long afterward, Mitchell, the industrious reporter, got a tip that Nix was playing golf. He quickly dispatched a photographer to the golf course to capture a picture of Nix in full swing. Judge McKenzie had Nix hauled back to court and ordered him to post a $50,000 bond.

In the late summer of 1998, just after his seventy-fourth birthday, Bowers was brought to trial in Hattiesburg. Dressed in a frayed cord suit and wearing two Mickey Mouse pins in his lapels, the imperial wizard listened as his former associates told of his insistence that Dahmer be killed. Once again, Bowers was represented by Travis Buckley, whose ineffectiveness reached comic proportions. After Buckley demanded that one witness identify participants at a White Knights meeting, he was startled by the answer: "Well, you were there, Mr. Buckley."

At another point, Buckley summoned Nix to testify on behalf of the defendant, a decision that backfired badly. Nix called Bowers "a real, real nice man" and described the Klan as a "benevolent" club that handed out fruit baskets at Christmas. The courtroom audience as well as the jury laughed.

On cross-examination, prosecutor Robert Helfrich asked Nix the color of his robe. "I didn't have no robe," he responded.

Helfrich handed Nix a copy of a photograph seized at his home during a search by authorities. "What does this person have on?"

"Looks like it might be a robe."

"With a hood?"

"Mmm-hmm."

"Holding a gun?"

"Yes sir."

When Nix protested that the robed figure in the photo was not him, Helfrich reminded him that Nix's exasperated wife had told him after the search of their house, "They found that crazy, silly picture of you with the pointed hood on."

At the end of the week, Bowers seemed resigned to his fate. As the jury filed into the courtroom to deliver its verdict, the imperial wizard began emptying his pockets of personal items and transferring them into an attaché case. After he was pronounced guilty, three Black deputy sheriffs led him from the courtroom.

Nix would have been the next to face trial. During his testimony in the Bowers case, he sat in a wheelchair with oxygen tubes in his nostrils. His hands trembled, he said, from an adverse reaction to medicine. Most spectators believed Nix to be staging a scene of pity. But within a few weeks, the onetime state director of investigations for the White Knights was dead at the age of seventy-two.

The final defendant, Noble, held a responsible job at Sanderson Farms, a giant poultry producer with headquarters in Laurel that rivaled Masonite for local importance. He was fifty-five when he stood trial thirty-three years after the attack on Dahmer. Tom Landrum still remembered him as the boy he had coached in football. Noble's trial wound up, as so many of the White Knights' days in court had ended, indecisively. In 2002, prosecutors asked Judge McKenzie to dismiss the indictment against Noble. They told the court that their key witness, Billy Roy Pitts, was gravely ill with cancer. Pitts died at his home in Denham Springs, Louisiana, in 2005. He was sixty-one.

Noble died in 2017. His obituary said, "He will be remembered as a loving father and grandfather and as having a passion for bass fishing." It made no mention of the wintry night in 1966 that led to him being charged with murder.

Sam Bowers, the imperial wizard of the White Knights of the Mississippi Ku Klux Klan, died in a prison hospital in Parchman following a heart attack in 2006. He was eighty-six.

Bowers's loyal mouthpiece, Travis Buckley, would die before the end of the decade.

Bob Stringer, tortured by his youthful activities in the Klan and an addiction he could never quite overcome, committed suicide.

≈

WHILE THE WHITE KNIGHTS were effectively destroyed within five years of the organization's inception, the demons of racism and anti-Semitism that they worshipped were still alive a half century later. Some places in the South continued to harbor ancient ideas about white supremacy, but the ugliness was on full display in other regions of the country as well. In 2019, nearly one thousand hate groups were being tracked across the nation—from the West Coast, across the upper Midwest, to urban settings on the East Coast—by the Southern Poverty Law Center, an organization that closely monitors the Klan and its kindred spirits.

Racist rabble-rousers found new ways to recruit followers, first through incendiary radio talk shows, then with websites and message boards promoting on the internet the same old values held by Sam Bowers. It led to a modern slaughter of innocents by zealots intruding on houses of worship.

Dylann Roof, a young white man, killed nine members of a Bible-study group at a Black church in downtown Charleston, South Carolina, in 2015 for no other apparent reason than his objection to the color of their skin. Before he was captured he left a trail of internet posts of himself clutching a gun and the Confederate battle flag, two symbols cherished by the Ku Klux Klan.

The same sort of horror visited the North three years later when eleven Jews were murdered during Shabbat services in a Pittsburgh synagogue. Robert Bowers (unrelated to the imperial wizard), charged with the crime, was found to traffic in racist and anti-Semitic rants on the internet.

Violence also erupted on the streets of Charlottesville, Virginia, the home of Thomas Jefferson and a great university, when an army of disgruntled neo-Confederates and neo-Nazis, in crude battle gear and bearing guns, clashed with a counterdemonstration by civil rights partisans.

Meanwhile, the White House was occupied by a Twitter-obsessed leader whose remarks and frenzied rallies often resembled the language and political fire of George Wallace.

Yet in the Piney Woods region of southeastern Mississippi, as a testament to the work of Vernon Dahmer, Black men were elected in the twenty-first century as mayors in both Laurel and Hattiesburg. More than a decade after Bowers's death, Johnny Magee, the mayor of Laurel, still remembered when the imperial wizard terrorized his community by leading Klansmen on drives through Black neighborhoods, flying Confederate battle flags from their cars' radio aerials. "It was always intimidating because we felt subservient," Magee recalled. Today a peace that seemed unimaginable in the 1960s prevails. Prominent citizens—Black and white—who dared challenge the racist institutions had a hand in the progress. But little-known people like Tom Landrum, who acted in secret, had helped. He had been one of the rare good men ready to confront evil.

Two decades after Bowers's final trial, Landrum labored to stitch together the pieces of the past, recognizing that the principal characters in the Bowers case were all dead, while most of the other prominent members of the White Knights were also represented by headstones.

In the summer of 2018, Landrum sat with his wife in their comfortable home out from Laurel—the same house, plus some additions, where they had lived for half a century. He was reminiscing with a visitor about his time in the White Knights. He had worked undercover for the FBI for nearly four risky years, without pay, and he had only one regret. He was concerned that his membership in the Klan might become an unwelcome legacy. Landrum had been identified, along with many others, as a Klansman by Lawrence Byrd in his strange statement to the FBI in 1966, and the old district attorney, Chet Dillard, had made that information public in a book he self-published many years later.

Not many people read about it. If they had, it really didn't register adversely; many in Jones County had enrolled in the Klan during that tumultuous period. The White Knights' ranks included a lot of men who did nothing more than attend meetings in the hope that a strong organization might frighten off segregation with its impressive numbers. Many of them quit, soured by the violence, escaping the stigma that the Klan left on others. But Landrum was troubled that there might be whispers in his community that he had been a White Knight.

He preferred to be known simply as the patriarch of Landrum's Homestead and Village, a unique attraction—characterized in one newspaper as "a walk back in time"—built on the land surrounding his home. It featured log cabins cut out of the forest, a faux blacksmith shop and smokehouse, a mystery house with deceptive mirrors, a hive of other primitive buildings, a steam engine, an ancient tractor, and sundry farm implements. Tourists and schoolchildren on field trips wandered the grounds each day.

For one of the site's latest additions, Landrum bought the sign that once adorned John's Restaurant and moved it to the homestead as another relic from Jones County's past. It was the one mischievous move he would make to acknowledge a link with the White Knights.

He and Anne had never told their children. But as he aged, the secret began to leak within their family, along with the assurance that he had joined the Klan out of a duty to undermine the organization. As he explained to his children, "I felt it was important for somebody to do something." Pressed to tell more about his experience, he and Anne revealed that they had preserved a regular journal of his reports to the FBI. At first, the papers had been kept in a lockbox in Jackson by Anne's mother; eventually they passed into the Landrums' hands. Much later, the thick volumes were shared with the rest of the family. But hardly anyone else in Jones County knew Tom Landrum had been a White Knight, and no one outside his tight circle of confidants ever knew he had been working with the FBI.

"I'd like to think I helped a little," he said, but he didn't want to aggrandize his role.

Tom Landrum was then in his late eighties. When he stood, his height was still imposing, though his gait had become unsteady; sometimes when he talked about those days his mind drifted just a bit. But he had reached one firm decision: he wanted to set his own record straight.

He had his collection of reports to the FBI, and he had his memories to draw on. In a string of conversations that went on periodically for more than a year, he and his wife elaborated on that time with their visitor. They remembered their fear. "To this day," he said, "I never go to our kitchen sink to wash my hands without thinking somebody's going to shoot me in the back."

Landrum recalled Sam Bowers as a shadowy figure who kept his distance and never actually threatened him. He thought some of the White Knights officers were dangerous, others were braggarts and two-faced no-accounts. Then there were men he considered merely misled and harmless. But real menace had existed in the Jones County group. Deavours Nix radiated evil, Landrum said. "There were times when I felt like he wanted to slit my throat." He was uncomfortable around the dour Henry deBoxtel, too. And he figured Dubie Lee would have been the one to bushwhack him if Landrum's mission had ever been discovered.

Lawrence Byrd was a puzzle. "We were friends with his family, but he always seemed shifty." It saddened Landrum to think about the "boys"—young men back then—whom he had thought of as "good boys" and who turned out to be night riders. Men like Charles Noble, whom he had coached, and others he had counseled, such as his friend Speed Lightsey, who owned a farm and two service stations and had no business belonging to the Klan. Landrum barely knew Billy Roy Pitts, but it was clear the fellow had consigned himself to a lifetime of mental torture and repentance for his youthful folly.

The Landrums' sons Bruce and Mike sometimes joined their

father for these talks, and they all smiled remembering the turkey shoot, the day they collected Lightning Smith's spent shotgun shells.

Cecil Sessum remained the great enigma to Landrum. It was as though he had been possessed by inner goblins. It was still hard to think of this mild-mannered man as a terrorist. Landrum saw Sessum a couple of times outside prison. Once Sessum had been granted leave to visit his ailing father, and he dropped by to say hello. While Sessum was temporarily free, Nix hosted a "homecoming" party for Sessum at his house, but Landrum had not been invited. After he was released years later, Sessum arranged another visit with Landrum and complained that his parole restricted his movements and prevented him from owning a gun for hunting.

Landrum thought it odd that Sessum served more time in prison than any other White Knight. While at Parchman, he completed several vocational programs and became skilled at making leather accessories. Never knowing that Landrum had reported on his activities as the exalted cyclops of Unit Four, Sessum gave him a leather watchband he had specially tooled.

Landrum lost track of Sessum. He vanished from Jones County. The last Landrum heard, he was living down near the Gulf Coast.

Cecil Sessum died in coastal Jackson County. Word of his death reached Jones County on December 9, 2019, but Landrum never learned the news. That same day the old coach and youth counselor, weakened by illness, had been discharged from a hospital and into the hands of hospice workers at his home. Three days later, Tom Landrum died. He was eighty-seven.

In recognition of his good reputation in Jones County, hundreds of people stood in long lines to pay their respects at a funeral home visitation on a Sunday afternoon just before Christmas. Among the mourners was his friend Charles Pickering and his wife. Other than Pickering, who had gone on to become a federal judge, and members of the Landrum family, no one else there was aware of the secret chapter of Tom Landrum's life.

Acknowledgments

This book was inspired by the journals kept by Tom Landrum during the four years he secretly reported to the FBI on the activities of the White Knights of the Mississippi Ku Klux Klan during their campaign of terror in the 1960s. Landrum, a white Mississippian, was asked by the FBI to join the racist group and serve as an unpaid informant. Before his death in 2019, Landrum made hundreds of pages of his reports available to me. In addition, Tom and his wife, Anne, welcomed me into their home near Laurel for extensive interviews concerning the troubled time when they risked their lives to work quietly in the effort to break the Klan's grip on many places in Mississippi. I am very grateful for the Landrums' gracious assistance. Their son Mike and his wife, Amy, also went out of their way to be helpful and hospitable on my visits to Laurel and Hattiesburg. I deeply appreciate their support as well as the cooperation of all the other Landrum children: daughters Deborah Upton and Susan Landrum and sons David and Bruce.

While Landrum's often-daily messages to the FBI formed the backbone for my research and vividly conveyed the racial hatred, suspicion, absurdity, and personality conflicts alive within the Klan at the time, the papers of Robert B. Helfrich at the McCain Library and Archives at the University of Southern Mississippi enabled me to expand on Landrum's account. Helfrich, now a state judge, led the successful prosecution of Sam Bowers in 1998 when Helfrich was an assistant district attorney. To prepare for the case, Helfrich gathered thousands of FBI documents and other material used in the long struggle to bring Bowers and other members of the White Knights to justice. The collection represents a veritable gold mine for anyone interested in this violent period in American history. The USM library has many other valuable papers and oral histories relevant to the civil rights movement in Mississippi, and I'm thankful for the guidance provided by curators Jennifer Brannock and Carla Carlson.

The Mississippi Department of Archives and History and its director, Katie Blount, and the J. D. Williams Library at the University of Mississippi, where Jennifer Ford is in charge of Special Collections, again proved to be good and reliable sources of information for me.

I found useful material in a number of publications that are identified in the endnotes, but I'd like to give special attribution for two books written by late friends of mine that were instrumental in filling out chapters 4, 7, and 24 in my own book. *Count Them One by One* by Gordon Martin contains a rich recollection of Vernon Dahmer's voter-registration campaign in Forrest County at a time when Martin was a young Justice Department lawyer investigating cases where local officials defied the law and denied Blacks the right to vote. *Terror in the Night* by Jack Nelson remains the groundbreaking and authoritative account of the White Knights' assault on Jews in Mississippi and the formation of an alliance between the FBI and Jewish fundraisers that led to an illicit slush fund and a fatal ambush in Meridian in 1968.

I have drawn on my own experiences as a journalist. Born in Mississippi, I've written about the state, off and on, since the early days of the civil rights movement in the 1960s. I knew a few of the characters in this book, including John Doar and Jim Ingram. Years ago, I interviewed Roy K. Moore. All of these men were on the side of the angels during the struggle against the Klan. I also covered the raucous politics of that era and knew plenty of Mississippians sympathetic to the Klan. Virtually all of these people are dead now.

In recent years, Charles Pickering—the former Jones County prosecuting attorney who fought the Klan and eventually served as a prominent federal judge—has become a friend and was a sounding board for me during this project. He corroborated many of the events Landrum mentioned in his journals. (I should add that Judge Pickering has no recollection of one incident Landrum reported that I describe in the book: a bizarre meeting between a prosecutorial team, including Pickering, and several shadowy criminals.)

I covered the final trial of Sam Bowers for the *Boston Globe*, where I was a reporter for more than a quarter century. For an article I wrote in 1998—weeks before Bob Stringer would become a surprise witness—Stringer confirmed to me that as a boy he had heard Bowers invoke the Klan's "Code Four" to authorize Dahmer's death. For the same long pretrial story I interviewed Ellie Dahmer at her home, which had been rebuilt on the site of the destruction the White Knights left behind the night of their murderous raid. Vernon Dahmer Jr. cooperated with me at length.

On the first day of the trial, Judge Dickie McKenzie invited reporters into his chamber to follow the voir dire proceedings—the selection of jurors. With a small group arrayed around a long table, I found myself sitting next to the imperial wizard himself. Bowers was wearing two Mickey Mouse pins on his coat lapels. During one recess, in an attempt to strike up a conversation, I asked Bowers about the Mickey Mouse display. He looked at me silently, put an index finger to his closed lips, and shook his head slowly. He kept that quiet demeanor throughout the trial and refused to testify. But we heard from, among others, Billy Roy Pitts, T. Webber Rogers, and Bob Stringer for the prosecution and Deavours Nix for the defense. During the course of the trial I was able to talk with the Klan lawyer, Travis Buckley, once he learned that the reporter from the *Globe* was a native Mississippian. All of these characters had prominent roles in this book.

Twenty years after the trial that sent Bowers to prison for the remainder of his life I was asked if I would be interested in seeing Landrum's documents. I need to thank Mike Frascogna and John

Evans for helping to lead the Landrum family to me when they were searching for someone to be given Tom's secret journals.

During the three years in which this book was researched and written, I was a fellow at the Overby Center for Southern Journalism and Politics and a member of the faculty at the School of Journalism and New Media at the University of Mississippi. My good friend Charles Overby provided me with a spacious campus office that I kept cluttered. He called it "more of a museum than an office." Thank you, Charles, and thanks, too, to Chi Kalu, the center's computer whiz, and to Jack Lawton, the journalism school's resident IT specialist. As a child of the hot-press and typewriter age, I needed all the help I could get. I'd also like to acknowledge my friends on the faculty and staff at the journalism school as well as the Sally McDonnell Barksdale Honors College.

For my sixth book, it was good to be back in the very capable hands of my editor, John Glusman, who has a wealth of knowledge and an expert eye. I'm also grateful for the help of Helen Thomaides, the assistant editor, who was vigilant in walking me through many details.

Very special thanks to my agent, Deborah Grosvenor, who has become a valued friend since she began faithfully representing me in 1997.

Finally, I owe much gratitude to my children, Carter and Leighton, their respective spouses, Allison and Campbell, and my six grandchildren, Cameron, Davis, Morgan, Merrick, Wyatt, and Brynn, for their love and loyal support.

Notes

Abbreviations:

AITL   Author interview with Tom Landrum
TLJ   Tom Landrum journals
RBH   Robert B. Helfrich papers, McCain Library and
           Archives, University of Southern Mississippi

Prologue

1 **May 8, 1951:** AITL; Larry Rohter, "The Echoes of an Execution Reverberate Loud and Clear," *New York Times*, May 5, 2010.
2 **With the climax:** NPR, "Willie McGee and the Traveling Electric Chair," *Radio Diaries*, 2010; John Herbers and Anne Farris Rosen, *Deep South Dispatch: Memoir of a Civil Rights Journalist* (Jackson: University Press of Mississippi, 2018).
3 **Tom Landrum, a high school:** AITL.

Chapter 1

7 **The Ku Klux Klan first emerged:** Richard Aubry McLemore and Nannie Pitts McLemore, *Mississippi through Four Centuries* (River Forest, IL: Laidlaw Brothers, 1949).
8 **It led to the resurrection:** Sam Bowers, interviews by Debra Spencer, 1983–84, Mississippi Department of Archives and History.

8   the birth of the White Knights: Taylor Branch, *Pillar of Fire: America in the King Years 1963–65* (New York: Simon & Schuster, 1998).
11   Tom Landrum, the youthful: AITL.
11   Local historian Ed Payne: Ed Payne, "Landrums in Gray & Blue: Conflicting Loyalties in Piney Woods Mississippi," *Renegade South* (blog), October 24, 2017.
13   By the time Tom Landrum: AITL.
17   But for Leonard Caves: AITL; TLJ, July 26, 1965.
17   Landrum was a frequent: Leonard Caves obituary, *Laurel Leader-Call*, August 8, 2014; AITL.
19   In the middle of July 1965: AITL.
21   When he left his office: AITL; author interview with Anne Landrum.
22   The next evening: AITL.
23   Landrum's next step: Ibid.
24   When Landrum joined: TLJ, August 12, 1965; AITL.
24   After a few miles: TLJ, August 12, 1965.

Chapter 2

26   The next day: TLJ, August 13, 1965; AITL.
26   Sessum dabbled in religion: RBH, Cecil Sessum files.
27   Sessum followed a gospel: Rev. Bob Jones Sr., "Is Segregation Scriptural?," radio address, aired April 17, 1960, on WMUU.
27   "You're doing the right thing": AITL.
28   John's Restaurant had another purpose: RBH, Deavours Nix files.
28   Tom Landrum knew Nix slightly: Ibid.; AITL.
29   They went upstairs: AITL.
30   Landrum had a low opinion: TLJ, August 13, 1965.
30   Anne scribbled down: Anne Landrum, interview by author; AITL.
31   Once Landrum paid: AITL.
32   Although the Klan movement: Southern Poverty Law Center website, www.splcenter.org.
32   But first, Landrum would see: AITL.
33   Before he joined the White Knights: Jay P. Pederson, "Masonite International Corporation," *International Directory of Company Histories* (Detroit, MI: St. James Press, 2004), vol. 63.
34   But Landrum's original perception: AITL.
35   "I can see this is a group": TLJ, August 13, 1965.
35   Landrum got a better sense: TLJ, August 24, 1965.
36   Landrum heard Lawrence Byrd: TLJ, August 31, 1965.
37   One involved the young man: Ibid.
37   A few nights later: TLJ, September 15, 1965.

39   Not all of the Klan's targets: TLJ, August 31, 1965.

39   The imperial wizard: Robert A. Slayton, *Empire Statesman: The Rise and Redemption of Al Smith* (New York: Free Press, 2001).

Chapter 3

41   In the weeks: TLJ, August 26, 1965.

42   Landrum, already uneasy: AITL.

42   Some members felt: TLJ, September 15, 1965.

43   To Landrum, the meetings: TLJ, October 11, 1965.

43   Bowers reappeared: TLJ, October 19, 1965.

44   Bowers talked little: Charles Marsh, *God's Long Summer: Stories of Faith and Civil Rights* (Princeton, NJ: Princeton University Press, 1997).

44   In private conversations: RBH, Sam Bowers files.

45   Bowers's pedigree: Sam Bowers, interviews by Debra Spencer, 1983–84, Mississippi Department of Archives and History.

48   The last bit of conformity: RBH, Bowers files.

48   By the time: Ibid.; Bowers, interviews.

49   "I had become": Bowers, interviews.

49   It was an attitude: Curtis Wilkie, "God Says Kill Them," *Boston Globe*, January 16, 1994.

50   Though Bowers: Bowers, interviews; Marsh, *God's Long Summer*; RBH, Bowers files.

50   He found biblical: Marsh.

51   Bowers espoused the doctrine: Bowers, interviews.

52   In February 1964: RBH, Bowers files.

52   The first leader: Eleanor B. Lang, "The Ku Klux Klan in Jones County" (student research paper, 1976), McCain Library and Archives, University of Southern Mississippi; RBH, Bowers files.

53   Two weeks before: RBH, Bowers files.

54   Bowers spurned: Ibid.; Bowers, interviews.

55   A copy of the letter: RBH, Bowers files.

Chapter 4

59   Despite his relative: Gordon A. Martin Jr., *Count Them One by One: Black Mississippians Fighting for the Right to Vote* (Jackson: University Press of Mississippi, 2010).

60   Dahmer needed few incentives: Taylor Branch, *Pillar of Fire: America in the King Years 1963–65* (New York: Simon & Schuster, 1998).

62   Some of the White Knights: Ellie Dahmer, interview by author, 1998.

63 **Dahmer was a product:** Natasha Trethewey, "Southern Gothic," in *Monument: Poems New and Selected* (Boston: Houghton Mifflin Harcourt, 2018); Branch, *Pillar of Fire*.

64 **Vernon and Ellie Dahmer:** Hollis Watkins, oral history, McCain Library and Archives, University of Southern Mississippi.

64 **Dahmer's lifelong relationship:** Branch, *Pillar of Fire*; John Dittmer, *Local People: The Struggle for Civil Rights in Mississippi* (Urbana: University of Illinois Press, 1994).

65 **Meanwhile, the freedom struggle:** Dittmer, *Local People*.

66 **While he was:** Watkins, oral history.

66 **When another youthful activist:** Branch, *Pillar of Fire*.

67 **At a COFO meeting:** Minutes of COFO meeting, January 18, 1964.

68 **The Civil Rights Act:** Branch, *Pillar of Fire*.

Chapter 5

69 **Tom Landrum got a mysterious:** AITL.

70 **"From Magee, Mississippi":** TLJ, October 31, 1965.

70 **When Anne came home:** AITL; Anne Landrum, interview by author.

71 **Landrum arrived at the service station:** TLJ, October 31, 1965; AITL.

72 **For the first time:** TLJ, October 31, 1965; RBH, Bowers files.

73 **He was interrupted:** TLJ, October 31, 1965; AITL.

74 **"This was one":** TLJ, October 31, 1965.

74 **The FBI failed:** RBH, Bowers files.

75 **As he sensed himself:** AITL; Charles Pickering, interview by author.

76 **In those years:** Charles Pickering, *A Price Too High: The Judiciary in Jeopardy* (Macon, GA: Stroud & Hall, 2007); Pickering, interview.

76 **From the time:** Pickering, interview.

77 **However, once it became apparent:** W. O. "Chet" Dillard, *Clearburning: Civil Rights, Civil Wrongs* (Jackson, MS: Lawyer's Publishing Press, 1992).

77 **One night Pickering:** Pickering, interview; Dillard, *Clearburning*.

78 **In fact, Landrum:** AITL; Pickering, interview.

80 **Motivated by a sense:** AITL.

Chapter 6

82 **Anger over the strides:** AITL.

83 **The victim was:** Stanley Nelson, *Devils Walking: Klan Murders along the Mississippi in the 1960s* (Baton Rouge: Louisiana State University Press, 2016).

84 **The dilemma of the White Knights:** TLJ, August 31, 1965.

86 On top of the successful prosecution: Curtis Wilkie, *Dixie: A Personal Odyssey through Events That Shaped the Modern South* (New York: Scribner, 2001).
86 Inside the other circles: TLJ, September 18, 1965.
87 Caves was not the only one: TLJ, September 27, 1965.
88 Within a week: TLJ, October 4, 1965.
88 "Caldwell stated": TLJ, October 26, 1965.
89 Despite frequent descriptions: TLJ, August 26, October 11, 1965.
90 Landrum's own fears: TLJ, October 15, 1965.
91 At one meeting: TLJ, October 28, 1965.
92 The next meeting: TLJ, November 9, 1965.
92 For several months: AITL.
92 The ceremony took place: TLJ, December 2, 1965.
93 "The White Knights is": Bylaws, White Knights of the Mississippi Ku Klux Klan.
94 Landrum made his own: TLJ, December 11, 1965.

Chapter 7

97 The federal legislation of 1965: Gordon A. Martin Jr., *Count Them One by One: Black Mississippians Fighting for the Right to Vote* (Jackson: University Press of Mississippi, 2010).
97 The most impressive: Ibid.; Taylor Branch, *Pillar of Fire: America in the King Years 1963–65* (New York: Simon & Schuster, 1998).
99 For the consumption: Martin, *Count Them One by One*.
100 Like many functionaries: Charles W. Eagles, *The Price of Defiance: James Meredith and the Integration of Ole Miss* (Chapel Hill: University of North Carolina Press, 2009).
100 Renowned for his rudeness: Martin, *Count Them One by One*.
101 The situation in Forrest County: Ibid.
104 Dahmer drew energy: Lawrence Guyot, oral history, University of Southern Mississippi Center for Oral History & Cultural Heritage.

Chapter 8

105 It was also apparent: TLJ, December 21, December 23, 1965.
106 Landrum was hardly: AITL.
107 During the long course: Ellie Dahmer, interview by author, 1998; Ellie Dahmer, testimony, *State of Mississippi v. Samuel Bowers*, Forrest County Circuit Court, 1998.
108 The subject of the "job down south": RBH, T. Webber Rogers files; T. Webber

Rogers, testimony, *State of Mississippi v. Samuel Bowers*, Forrest County Circuit Court, 1998.

109 **Thirty members of the White Knights:** RBH, Deavours Nix files; RBH, Henry deBoxtel files.

109 **A few days later:** RBH, Lawrence Byrd files; RBH, Sessum files.

110 **T. Webber Rogers:** RBH, Rogers files.

111 **The night was unseasonably cold:** RBH, Billy Roy Pitts files.

112 **The focus of Bowers's mission:** RBH, Rogers files.

113 **For an organization:** RBH, George Boutwell files.

114 **Boutwell's Buick:** RBH, Billy Moss files.

114 **A few nights later:** RBH, Nix files.

115 **In early January:** RBH, Bowers files.

Chapter 9

117 **Dahmer's initiative:** Bob Stringer, interview by author, 1998.

118 **"Now listen, you COMMUNIST":** *Klan-Ledger*, 1965, author's collection.

118 **Bob Stringer moved freely:** Stringer, interview.

119 **The next day was Sunday:** Gordon A. Martin Jr., *Count Them One by One: Black Mississippians Fighting for the Right to Vote* (Jackson: University Press of Mississippi, 2010).

120 **Late that night:** Billy Roy Pitts, testimony, *State of Mississippi v. Samuel Bowers*, Forrest County Circuit Court, 1998.

121 **Billy Roy Pitts:** Ibid.

122 **After nearly an hour:** Ibid.

124 **The four men:** Ibid.

124 **Ellie Dahmer awakened:** Ellie Dahmer, interview by author, 1998; Ellie Dahmer, testimony, *State of Mississippi v. Samuel Bowers*, Forrest County Circuit Court, 1998; Ellie Dahmer, oral history, University of Southern Mississippi Center for Oral History & Cultural Heritage; Bettie Dahmer, testimony, *State of Mississippi v. Samuel Bowers*, Forrest County Circuit Court, 1998.

125 **Meanwhile, twelve-year-old:** Dennis Dahmer, testimony, *State of Mississippi v. Samuel Bowers*, Forrest County Circuit Court, 1998.

126 **Exposed by the light:** Ellie Dahmer, interview; Ellie Dahmer, testimony; Bettie Dahmer, testimony.

126 **While the Dahmer family:** Pitts, testimony.

127 **After the gang:** Ibid.

128 **When the Dahmers reached:** Ellie Dahmer, testimony.

129 **Dahmer was able to talk:** *Hattiesburg American*, January 14, 1966.

129 **Later in the long morning:** Ellie Dahmer, testimony.

130 **The death certificate:** RBH, Mississippi State death certificate, January 11, 1966.

130 **More than three hundred Blacks:** Martin, *Count Them One by One*; Patricia

Michelle Boyett, *Right to Revolt: The Crusade for Racial Justice in Mississippi's Central Piney Woods* (Jackson: University Press of Mississippi, 2015).

130 **Not lost on the public:** Boyett, *Right to Revolt*.
130 **Another move took place:** Ibid.

Chapter 10

132 **Lawrence Byrd:** RBH, Lawrence Byrd files.
134 **That the dimensions:** Billy Roy Pitts, testimony, *State of Mississippi v. Samuel Bowers*, Forrest County Circuit Court, 1998.
135 **That evening, Sessum:** RBH, Byrd files.
137 **That same night:** RBH, Delmar Dennis files.
137 **The next night:** TLJ, January 11, 1966.
138 **"The Dahmer killing":** Ibid.
139 **One of the first pieces:** L. C. Brooks, testimony, *State of Mississippi v. Samuel Bowers*, Forrest County Circuit Court, 1998.
140 **Within twenty-four hours:** AITL.
140 **The same day that Landrum:** TLJ, January 12, 1966.
142 **He talked about:** AITL; Anne Landrum, interview by author.
143 **Sessum himself:** RBH, Byrd files.

Chapter 11

146 **The FBI's confidence:** Final report of the U.S. Senate's Select Committee to Study Governmental Operations with Respect to Intelligence Operations, Book III (1976).
147 **Through its network:** Jim Ingram and James L. Dickerson, *The Hero among Us* (Brandon, MS: Sartoris Literary Group, 2013).
147 **At the outset:** W. O. "Chet" Dillard, *Clearburning: Civil Rights, Civil Wrongs* (Jackson, MS: Lawyer's Publishing Press, 1992).
148 **Less than two weeks:** FBI memorandum from Jackson FBI office to New York FBI office, January 21, 1966.
149 **The informant:** Fredric Dannon, "The G-Man and the Hit Man," *New Yorker*, December 16, 1996.
149 **Byrd was not:** RBH, Lawrence Byrd files.
150 **First, he would have to recover:** Dillard, *Clearburning*.
150 **Like most stories:** Ibid.
151 **For the record:** *Laurel Leader-Call*, January 27, 1966.
151 **For the purpose:** RBH, Byrd files.
151 **Two days later:** TLJ, January 27, 1966.
152 **A week later:** TLJ, February 4, 1966.

153 **In his report:** Ibid.
153 **After his latest eruption:** Dillard, *Clearburning.*
154 **Byrd's condition:** Ibid.; RBH, Byrd files.
154 **Suspicions that other members:** TLJ, February 11, 1966.
154 **Landrum was one:** Ibid.; TLJ, February 12, 1966.
155 **Landrum had some:** AITL.
156 **One night Landrum:** Ibid.
157 **Around the same time:** RBH, Byrd files.
157 **Gerald Martin:** TLJ, February 12, 1966.
158 **In the midst of:** TLJ, February 11, 1966.

Chapter 12

159 **The congressional investigation:** Walter Goodman, *The Committee* (New York: Farrar, Straus and Giroux, 1968).
162 **Though five years younger:** "Robert Shelton, 73, Leader of Big Klan Faction," *New York Times*, March 20, 2003.
163 **Bowers and Nix:** Travis Purser, testimony, transcript of hearings into "Activities of Ku Klux Klan Organizations in the United States" by House Committee on Un-American Activities [HUAC], February 1966.
163 **After Purser was dismissed:** Deavours Nix, testimony, HUAC.
164 **However, the appearance:** *Washington Post*, February 2, 1966.
164 **When Bowers refused:** Samuel H. Bowers, testimony, HUAC.
165 **Bowers may have produced:** *Klan-Ledger*, 1965, author's collection.
165 **(Bucklew was often):** W. O. "Chet" Dillard, *Clearburning: Civil Rights, Civil Wrongs* (Jackson, MS: Lawyer's Publishing Press, 1992).
166 **One paper:** Bowers, testimony, HUAC.
167 **The next day:** J. E. Thornhill, testimony, HUAC.
170 **Neither Bowers nor Nix:** TLJ, February 4, 1966.

Chapter 13

171 **Nix's complaint against the FBI:** Deavours Nix, affidavit, February 14, 1966.
173 **In Jim Ingram's own account:** Jim Ingram and James L. Dickerson, *The Hero among Us* (Brandon, MS: Sartoris Literary Group, 2013).
173 **After Nix was told:** RBH, Deavours Nix files.
173 **Two police cars:** Ingram and Dickerson, *The Hero among Us*; RBH, Daburn files.
173 **Like many publicly elected officials:** W. O. "Chet" Dillard, *Clearburning: Civil Rights, Civil Wrongs* (Jackson, MS: Lawyer's Publishing Press, 1992).

175 **Privately, Dillard went so far:** Dillard, *Clearburning*; RBH, Melvin "Pete" Martin files.
176 **Martin acknowledged his role:** RBH, Martin files.
176 **Agent Jim Ingram:** Ingram and Dickerson, *The Hero among Us.*
178 **Ingram had a parallel assignment:** Jim Ingram, interview by author, 1994.
179 **Suspicions about who:** RBH, Charles Lamar Lowe files.
179 **More misadventures:** Ibid.
179 **In fact, many members:** RBH, Billy Roy Pitts files.
180 **In a February 23 report:** TLJ, February 23, 1966.
180 **The next afternoon:** RBH, Lawrence Byrd files.

Chapter 14

183 **Tom Landrum:** TLJ, March 7, 1966.
184 **The latest document:** Cecil Sessum, affidavit, March 7, 1966.
184 **According to Byrd:** RBH, Lawrence Byrd files; Lawrence Byrd, statement to FBI, March 2, 1966.
185 **"I told Sessum":** Byrd, statement to FBI.
185 **Sessum said personal animosities:** Ibid.
186 **Following the last dry run:** Ibid.
186 **Sessum's tale:** RBH, Daburn files.
187 **On the night of February 27:** Byrd, statement to FBI.
189 **At the end:** Ibid.
191 **For intrigue, Sessum's account:** Sessum, affidavit.
192 **Born in 1914:** Society of Former Special Agents of the FBI, undated tribute to Roy K. Moore; *Concordia Sentinel*, October 16, 2008.
193 **Sessum claimed Moore:** Sessum, affidavit.
194 **There was a pause:** Ibid.
195 **Sessum insisted he was reporting:** Ibid.
196 **According to the FBI's version:** RBH, Sessum files.
197 **Sessum was asked:** Ibid.

Chapter 15

199 **In the weeks:** Jim Ingram, testimony, *State of Mississippi v. Samuel Bowers*, Forrest County Circuit Court, 1998; author interview with confidential law enforcement source, 2019.
200 **By March 7:** RBH, Daburn files; FBI memo, March 7, 1966.
200 **While the FBI:** RBH, Lawrence Byrd files; Lawrence Byrd, statement to FBI, March 8, 1966.

201 **Later the same day:** TLJ, March 7, 1966.

201 **The next night:** TLJ, March 8, 1966.

202 **Tension between Bowers and Byrd:** RBH, Daburn files; Byrd, statement to FBI, March 10, 1966.

203 **In search of credible information:** TLJ, March 9, 1966.

205 **The conversation caused:** AITL.

206 **V. L. Lee:** TLJ, March 1, 1966.

206 **A few days after:** RBH, Daburn files; Speed Lightsey, statement to FBI, March 13, 1966.

207 **Unknown to any other:** RBH, Daburn files; Henry deBoxtel, statement to FBI, March 7, 1966.

208 **Meanwhile, Byrd reported:** RBH, Daburn files; Byrd, statement to FBI, March 21, 1966.

209 **Sessum's sense of dread:** RBH, Cecil Sessum files.

Chapter 16

211 **Thirty-year-old Cecil Sessum:** RBH, Daburn files.

213 **The FBI dragnet:** Ibid.

213 **However, the principal target:** RBH, Sam Bowers files.

213 **Within hours of the arrests:** *Laurel Leader-Call*, March 28, 1966.

214 **The same day:** RBH, Bowers files.

214 **Three days after:** Ibid.

215 **Before long, Bowers:** *Laurel Leader-Call*, April 11, 1966.

Chapter 17

216 **Three weeks elapsed:** TLJ, April 19, 1966.

217 **When he returned:** AITL; Anne Landrum, interview by author.

218 **A week later:** TLJ, April 26, 1966.

218 **In his report the next day:** TLJ, April 27, 1966.

219 **Landrum found more dissension:** TLJ, May 3, 1966.

220 **A sparsely attended meeting:** TLJ, May 10, 1966.

221 **A couple of days later:** TLJ, May 12, 1966.

221 **The man replied:** TLJ, May 15, 1966.

222 **Lightsey eventually forced:** TLJ, May 17, 1966.

222 **After the meeting:** TLJ, May 18, 1966.

223 **Six days later:** TLJ, May 24, 1966.

223 **Since he had become secretary:** Ibid.

223 **The problems between Lee and Lightsey:** TLJ, June 21, 1966.

224 **Out of curiosity:** Ibid.
224 **Dispirited by the rise:** TLJ, June 24, 1966.
225 **Four nights later:** TLJ, June 28, 1966.
225 **In his report:** Ibid.

Chapter 18

226 **According to Byrd, he received:** RBH, Lawrence Byrd files.
227 **Three nights later:** RBH, Daburn files.
228 **The same week:** RBH, Byrd files.
229 **Actually, Byrd had good reasons:** RBH, Henry deBoxtel files.
229 **The hostility was amplified:** TLJ, May 31, 1966; RBH, Daburn files.
229 **Landrum had known:** AITL.
230 **In June Landrum:** TLJ, June 25, 1966; RBH, Daburn files.
230 **On October 10:** RBH, Daburn files.
231 **The notoriety earned Beckwith:** Curtis Wilkie, "God Says Kill Them," *Boston Globe*, January 16, 1994.
231 **During the same week:** RBH, Cecil Sessum files.
232 **The FBI also learned:** RBH, Byrd files.
232 **Despite all the promises:** RBH, Daburn files.

Chapter 19

234 **Since Norman Lee's:** TLJ, July 4, 1966.
236 **Tommy Thornton:** TLJ, July 8, 1966.
236 **Spec Stewart:** TLJ, July 12, 1966.
236 **A few days later:** TLJ, July 27, 1966.
237 **Near the end of July:** TLJ, July 29, 1966.
238 **Landrum attended another:** TLJ, August 2, 1966.
239 **At the next meeting:** TLJ, August 9, 1966.
239 **Although some men:** Ibid.; TLJ, August 7, 1966.
240 **Of all the ringleaders:** AITL.
240 **Pressing Landrum for membership:** TLJ, August 7, 1966.
240 **Days before the new school year:** TLJ, August 9, 1966.
242 **Two weeks later:** TLJ, August 16, 1966.
243 **When Landrum telephoned Lightsey:** TLJ, August 17, 1966.
243 **Norman Lee wanted:** TLJ, September 6, 1966.
244 **Increasingly, the Klan:** TLJ, October 8, 1966.
245 **Landrum discovered:** TLJ, November 15, 1966.
246 **Meanwhile, Lightsey:** TLJ, October 19, 1966.

246 **Making his rounds:** TLJ, November 8, 1966.
247 **Just before Thanksgiving:** TLJ, November 17, 1966.
249 **Bowers made one other effort:** RBH, Sam Bowers files.

Chapter 20

251 **Tom Landrum learned:** TLJ, March 21, 1967; AITL; Charles Pickering, interview by author.
252 **The tale seemed dizzying:** TLJ, March 21, 1967.
252 **Almost from the beginning:** W. O. "Chet" Dillard, *Clearburning: Civil Rights, Civil Wrongs* (Jackson, MS: Lawyer's Publishing Press, 1992).
252 **Pickering told Landrum:** TLJ, March 21, 1967.
254 **To further complicate:** *Citizen-Patriot*, undated, Landrum collection.
256 **According to prosecutors:** *Buckley v. State*, 223 So. 2d 524 (1969)—Mississippi Supreme Court order reversing Travis Buckley conviction, June 2, 1969.
257 **Tom Landrum got a further:** TLJ, May 24, 1967.
258 **Dillard, who vacillated:** Dillard, *Clearburning*.
259 **On the same day:** Patricia Michelle Boyett, *Right to Revolt: The Crusade for Racial Justice in Mississippi's Central Piney Woods* (Jackson: University Press of Mississippi, 2015).
259 **In an address:** TLJ, July 27, 1967.
260 **Three months into:** TLJ, August 18, 1967.
261 **Dillard and Pickering:** Boyett, *Right to Revolt*; Pickering, interview.
261 **Landrum had never doubted:** AITL.

Chapter 21

262 **The issue had come up:** TLJ, January 19, 1967.
263 **Maddox earned national prominence:** Richard Severo, "Lester Maddox, Whites-Only Restaurateur and Georgia Governor, Dies at 87," *New York Times*, June 25, 2003.
263 **Though it all sounded outlandish:** TLJ, January 19, 1967; Curtis Wilkie, *Dixie: A Personal Odyssey through Events That Shaped the Modern South* (New York: Scribner, 2001).
264 **According to one tale:** TLJ, February 1, 1967.
264 **Meanwhile, the Jones County Klan:** TLJ, February 8, 1967.
265 **A week later:** TLJ, February 10, 1967.
266 **The White Knights:** "Jimmy Swan, Honky-Tonkin' in Mississippi," *Bopping* (blog), November 23, 2009.
267 **A thin, wiry man:** Mississippi Department of Archives and History, Jimmy Swan files.

267 **Although he appeared:** Curtis Wilkie, "Peppery Politics at the Fair," *Clarksdale Press Register*, August 3, 1967.

267 **For his 1967 campaign:** Mississippi Department of Archives and History, Jimmy Swan files.

268 **As his campaign:** Ibid.

268 **Barnett, the erstwhile:** Ibid.

269 **Despite his language:** RBH, Daburn files.

272 **If Swan had never:** Ibid.

273 **Bowers and Swan:** RBH, Sam Bowers files.

273 **Before long:** Bill Minor, *Eyes on Mississippi: A Fifty-Year Chronicle of Change* (Jackson, MS: Prichard Morris Books, 2001).

274 **Bowers plunged:** TLJ, February 15, 1967.

274 **Bowers found:** TLJ, March 10, 1967.

274 **In a roundup:** Minor, *Eyes on Mississippi*.

274 **Members of the White Knights:** TLJ, March 30, April 7, 1967

Chapter 22

277 **The disarray caused:** TLJ, February 2, 1967.

278 **Landrum then elaborated:** AITL.

278 **The federal government:** Douglas O. Linder, "Mississippi Burning Trial (1967)," Famous Trials, https://famous-trials.com/mississippi-burningtrial.

280 **Those convicted:** TLJ, October 2, 1967.

280 **Landrum invited Leonard Caves:** TLJ, October 19, 1967.

280 **Landrum went alone:** TLJ, October 2, 1967.

281 **Two weeks later:** TLJ, October 19, 1967.

282 **Another member of the White Knights:** Billy Roy Pitts, statement to the FBI, September 30, 1967.

283 **Keenly aware that Pitts's:** TLJ, November 10, 1967.

283 **November 11:** TLJ, November 11, 1967; Tom, Bruce, and Mike Landrum, interview by author.

285 **A White Knights meeting:** TLJ, November 13, 1967.

285 **The Klan meetings:** TLJ, October 16, November 3, 1967.

286 **For the White Knights:** TLJ, December 4, 1967; AITL.

286 **Though his mood:** AITL.

289 **On December 29:** RBH, Sam Bowers files.

Chapter 23

290 **Even as investigators:** Charles Marsh, *The Last Days* (New York: Basic Books, 2001).

291   **An exemplary citizen:** TLJ, January 27, 1968.
291   **After learning that the banquet:** Charles Pickering, interview by author.
291   **The elaborate dinner:** Marsh, *The Last Days*.
293   **In his testimony:** *Buckley v. State*, 223 So. 2d 524 (1969).
293   **During the trial:** UPI article in *New Orleans States-Item*, February 5, 1968.
293   **Tom Landrum:** AITL; Anne Landrum, interview by author.
294   **The White Knights:** *Hattiesburg American*, March 16, 1968.
295   **By an extraordinary coincidence:** Patricia Michelle Boyett, *Right to Revolt: The Crusade for Racial Justice in Mississippi's Central Piney Woods* (Jackson: University Press of Mississippi, 2015).
297   **Norman Lee:** TLJ, March 2, April 10, April 29, June 8, 1968.
298   **Heartened by Sessum's conviction:** *Meridian Star*, March 20, March 22, 1968.
299   **Undeterred by the hung jury:** *Meridian Star*, March 27, 1968.
299   **In setting the scene:** *Laurel Leader-Call*, March 14, 1968.
300   **Once Pitts had told:** Marsh, *The Last Days*.
301   **Before the case:** *Laurel Leader-Call*, May 16, 1968.

Chapter 24

303   **Three years later:** Jack Nelson, *Terror in the Night* (New York: Simon & Schuster, 1993); Thomas A. Tarrants, *Consumed by Hate, Redeemed by Love* (Nashville, TN: Nelson Books, 2019).
304   **As Tarrants would write:** Tarrants, *Consumed by Hate*.
304   **Despite Mississippi's reputation:** Leo E. Turitz and Evelyn Turitz, *Jews in Early Mississippi* (Jackson: University Press of Mississippi, 1995).
305   **In the South:** Melissa Fay Greene, *The Temple Bombing* (New York: Addison-Wesley, 1996).
305   **Tarrants chose:** Nelson, *Terror in the Night*.
306   **The conversation:** Author interview with confidential source.
307   **Tarrants branched out:** Nelson, *Terror in the Night*.
308   **The operation:** Tarrants, *Consumed by Hate*.
309   **In May 1968:** Nelson, *Terror in the Night*.
309   **To confront the threat:** Ibid.
310   **The arrangement among:** Ibid.
310   **Jewish leaders:** Ibid.
310   **To expedite:** Ibid.
311   **Hours after:** Ibid.
312   **Two days later:** Ibid.
313   **While the posse:** Ibid.
313   **After parking:** Tarrants, *Consumed by Hate*; Nelson, *Terror in the Night*.

Chapter 25

315 **A couple of days:** TLJ, July 2, 1968.
315 **The Klan trials in Forrest County resumed:** RBH, Daburn files.
317 **It was time:** Charles Marsh, *The Last Days* (New York: Basic Books, 2001).
318 **Byrd would not face:** *Byrd v. State*, 228 So. 2d 874 (1969)—Supreme Court of Mississippi order confirming the judgment, November 24, 1969.
319 **"It's a sad day":** Jody Carlson, *George C. Wallace and the Politics of Powerlessness* (New Brunswick, NJ: Transaction Books, 1981).
319 **His rhetoric throbbed:** Ibid.
320 **A few days before:** TLJ, October 31, 1968.
321 **Before the close:** Patricia Michelle Boyett, *Right to Revolt: The Crusade for Racial Justice in Mississippi's Central Piney Woods* (Jackson: University Press of Mississippi, 2015).
321 **Even the marshals:** "Shooting Incident of Billy Roy Pitts," FBI report, December 30, 1968; RBH, Billy Roy Pitts file.
323 **While they slept:** Marsh, *The Last Days*.
323 **Judge Hall convened:** *Wilson v. State*, 234 So. 2d 303 (1970)—Supreme Court of Mississippi order confirming Cliff Wilson conviction, April 20, 1970.
326 **His last memo:** TLJ, January 14–15, 1969.
326 **Landrum eventually:** AITL; Anne Landrum, interview by author.
327 **While state prosecutors:** Boyett, *Right to Revolt*.

Epilogue

329 **Somehow, Thomas Tarrants:** Thomas A. Tarrants, *Consumed by Hate, Redeemed by Love* (Nashville, TN: Nelson Books, 2019).
329 **Travis Buckley:** *Buckley v. State*, 223 So. 2d 524 (1969).
329 **Lawrence Byrd:** Patricia Michelle Boyett, *Right to Revolt: The Crusade for Racial Justice in Mississippi's Central Piney Woods* (Jackson: University Press of Mississippi, 2015).
330 **Jesse White:** Ibid.
330 **Billy Roy Pitts:** Ibid.
330 **Cliff Wilson:** Roy Reed, "Release of Klansman, Jailed for Killing Black Leader, Is Decried in Mississippi," *New York Times*, December 24, 1972.
330 **Cecil Sessum:** Boyett, *Right to Revolt*.
331 **For two decades:** Curtis Wilkie, "God Says Kill Them," *Boston Globe*, January 16, 1994.
332 **Encouraged by:** Richard Goldstein, "Edgar Ray Killen, Convicted in '64 Killings of Rights Workers, Dies at 92," *New York Times*, January 12, 2010.
333 **Then there were two:** Jerry Mitchell, *Race against Time* (New York: Simon & Schuster, 2020).

333 **An important new witness:** Curtis Wilkie, "Your Day of Judgment Soon Will Be Nigh," *Boston Globe*, July 10, 1998.

334 **Judge Richard McKenzie:** Mitchell, *Race against Time*.

334 **In the late summer:** Curtis Wilkie, "Ex-Member Casts Klan Activities as Benevolent," *Boston Globe*, August 21, 1998.

335 **The final defendant:** "Judge Dismisses Indictment in Dahmer Case," Associated Press, January 17, 2002.

335 **Noble died:** Funeralinnovations.com, September 25, 2017.

335 **Sam Bowers:** Jennifer Lee, "Samuel Bowers, 82, Klan Leader Convicted in Fatal Bombing, Dies," *New York Times*, November 6, 2006.

337 **Two decades after:** Tom and Anne Landrum, interviews by author, 2018 and 2019.

Index